AIMING FOR LIBERTY

AIMING FOR LIBERTY

THE PAST, PRESENT, AND FUTURE OF FREEDOM AND SELF-DEFENSE

DAVID B. KOPEL

Merril Press
Bellevue, Washington

Merril Press, P.O. Box 1682, Bellevue, WA 98009

www.merrilpress.com

Phone: 425-454-7008

Distributed to the book trade by

Midpoint Trade Books,

27 W. 20th Street, New York, N.Y. 10011

www.midpointtradebooks.com

Phone: 212-727-0190

Library of Congress Cataloging-in-Publication Data

Kopel, David B.

  Aiming for liberty : the past, present and future of freedom and self-defense / David B. Kopel.

    p. cm.

  ISBN 978-0-936783-58-1

  1. Gun control--United States. 2. Firearms ownership--United States. 3. Firearms--Law and legislation--United States. 4. Arms control. I. Title.

  HV7436.K67 2009

  323.4'30973--dc22

                          2009034765

Printed in the United States of America

"Reflect that her glory has been built up by men who knew their duty and had the courage to do it. Make them your examples and learn from them that the secret of Happiness is Freedom, and the secret of Freedom, Courage."

Thucydides, History of the Peloponnesian War, book 2, chapter 6 (translation by Alfred Zimmern, The Greek Commonwealth).

Dedicated to Paul Gallant & Joanne D. Eisen, my colleagues at the Independence Institute, and my frequent co-authors. They love liberty and truth, and they always aim to vindicate the rights of the oppressed.

TABLE OF CONTENTS

The Heller Case   1

The origins of the DC handgun ban. The flimsy arguments of the anti-gun forces. The Stevens dissent and the Brady Campaign. Chemerinsky's questionable history. No more slippery slope?

Gun Control and Discrimination   15

The Klan's Favorite Law: Gun control in the postwar South. Brothers In Arms: How civil rights flowed from a rifle barrel. Selective Disarmament: No Guns For The Poor.

The Anti-Gun Agenda   27

Bait-'n'-Switch: Gun-prohibition lobbyists are after much more than AK-47s. Defenseless on the bayou: New Orleans gun confiscation. A world without guns.

Some Deceptions and Errors Used to Promote Anti-Gun Laws   39

The legislative legend: "cop-killer" bullets. Misfiring at Harlon Carter. The fallacy of "43 to 1." What if the government had to obey gun-control laws? The hidden agenda behind gun storage Laws.

Religious Perspectives on Freedom from the Ancient World   54

To your tents, O Israel. Armed Jews Week. Perpetua and Felicity.

Religious Perspectives on Freedom from the West   69

John of Salisbury. The Virgin of Guadalupe. Nicholas Owen: God's carpenter. Jonathan Mayhew, and the Catechism of the American Revolution.

Schools and Children   89

"Zero tolerance" is a thought-control program. The Resistance: Teaching common-sense school protection. Follow the Leader: Israel and Thailand set an example by arming teachers.

International Freedom   101

How the United Nations helps mass murderers. Global gun prohibition lobby: Ban arms sales to Israel. Off target: Canada's gun registry was created to stop massacres, but failed again. Gun bans & African genocide: The disarming facts. Genocide in Ethiopia. Uganda government uses UN gun control mandate to terrorize Ugandans. UNRWA and Palestinian Suffering. The UN needs another member.

Law Enforcement Abuses and Solutions   133

Officer Politics: Police department scandals are a result of increased federal involvement and racial hiring practices. Smash-up policing: When law enforcement goes military. Restore flexibility to US sentences. Jurors' rights to vote their conscience.

Culture   143

Tune out, light up: In terms of destroying years of life, television is far worse than tobacco. The Founders' reading of Roman history. Uncertain Uncertainty: Postmodernism unravels.

American Heroes   162

Thomas Jefferson. Andrew Jackson and the Battle of New Orleans. Don't mess with (armed) Texans: The real lesson of the Alamo. The Hero of Gettysburg: Winfield Scott Hancock shot straight. Her own bodyguard: Gun-packing First Lady.

In 1974, after President Gerald Ford took the Oath of Office, he spoke to the American people: "My fellow Americans, our long national nightmare is over. Our Constitution works; our great Republic is a government of laws and not of men. Here the people rule."

His words are apt today. The 32-year nightmare of the law-abiding citizens of Washington, DC, is over. They can legally use firearms in defense of their homes against violent predators.

For nearly seven decades the US Supreme Court stood idle while lower federal courts nullified the Second Amendment. Independence Day celebrations were especially joyful in the week after the Supreme Court finally vindicated America's first freedom.

It was wonderful to have the opportunity to play a part in one of the most important Supreme Court cases in American history. On the morning of June 26, I felt like Sam Gamgee, in *The Lord of the Rings* when he finally saw the evil ring falling to its destruction in the volcano at Mount Doom.

There is still much to be done to restore Second Amendment rights in the United States. Nor will those rights will be truly secure as long as the United Nations continues its relentless attacks. Those attacks will stop when enough governments in other nations change their policies because the people of those nations demand that they stop. So over the long term, American human rights advocates must help their friends in other countries begin to change the political culture in those countries, as we have changed the political culture in the United States. Justice Scalia's opinion reminds us the right to arms and the right of self-defense are not granted to Americans by the Second Amendment. They are inherent natural rights which belong to everyone.

A new chapter has opened in the story of mankind's struggle for freedom. Working with groups like the Second Amendment Foundation, the Independence Institute, and the National Rifle Association, together we can seize the historic opportunity in the early 21st century to protect and to advance in our nation and in our world the eternal truths of the Declaration of Independence.

This book lays out some of the present threats to the Second Amendment and other civil liberties, and remembers the inspiring men and women whose devotion to freedom has made our present liberty possible.

One of the great joys of two decades of writing on public issues has been the opportunity to collaborate with a wonderful group of co-authors. Several of the essays in this book were originally co-authored pieces with Paul Gallant, Joanne D. Eisen, Mike Krause, Robert Racansky, and the late Senator Paul Simon.

THE HELLER CASE

CHAPTER 1

THE ORIGINS OF THE DC HANDGUN BAN

The DC bans on handguns and armed self-defense were the products of extremism and bigotry that have been harming the good citizens of the District of Columbia for decades.

Why were the District's gun laws the most severe of any city in the United States? There are two key reasons: first, the city of DC is not part of a state, and second, the amazing corruption and incompetence of the DC city government.

Anti-Second Amendment politicians can be found in many American cities; but in most states, their prejudices may be tempered by working with legislators from suburban or rural areas. An urban legislator may, at least, get to know a rural colleague who can explain the constructive parts of the hunting culture.

One of the best aspects of American state legislatures is that they bring together public servants with tremendous diversity in their backgrounds. The DC city council, however, often displays an obvious lack of experience with intellectual and social diversity. In such a homogeneous and intellectually sterile atmosphere, anti-gun-owner prejudice thrives.

Most states have pre-emption laws that restrain the local zealots who may destroy civil rights, property rights, contract rights and other rights. Unfortunately for the citizens of the District of Columbia, there is no state legislature to protect them from anti-freedom local politicians.

The Constitution (Article I, § 8) grants Congress total authority over DC, so theoretically, Congress could have passed legislation to protect the constitutional rights of DC residents. Yet the District's lobbyists successfully prevented the passage of reform legislation. For example, in 2007 and 2009, Congress considered legislation that would have given DC's US House delegate (gun prohibitionist Eleanor Holmes Norton) full voting rights in the House. During the debate, the legislators voted to attach an amendment to restore Second Amendment rights for DC residents. Incredibly, the DC government lobbyists then asked for the entire bill to be halted.

In other words, the DC government is so prejudiced against gun owners that the government would sacrifice voting rights for DC citizens rather than permit those citizens to exercise Second Amendment rights.

The DC government is good at lobbying, but at almost nothing else. DC's city government is perhaps the most dysfunctional of any large American city. Unlike former Mayor (and current DC Councilman) Marion Barry, current Mayor Adrian Fenty does not appear to be personally corrupt, but the DC city government suffers from endemic corruption and waste.

Among the prime victims are the children of Washington, DC. The DC school system spends almost $13,000 per pupil—more than any state except New York and New Jersey—yet much of the "per pupil" spending is consumed by administrative waste and fraud. Many school buildings are falling apart due to years of maintenance neglect. From time to time the government "discovers" deficits of several tens of millions of dollars in the schools budget.

In the Winter 2003 issue of *City Journal* magazine, an idealistic young teacher named Joshua Kaplowitz detailed how he became a DC teacher in order to help inner-city children achieve the American dream, but was thwarted at every turn by an administrative bureaucracy which is content with out-of-control classrooms, incompetent teachers and worthless principals—so long as the tax money keeps rolling in.

The District's police department is often not much better. Tucker Carlson, in two articles in *Policy Review* in 1993, reported that many DC officers are so illiterate that they cannot fill out a simple police report, and so apathetic that they skip court appearances.

Have things improved since then? Consider the following report from a DC resident, written on July 8, 2007: "Yesterday, two men tried to break into my friend's home while she was inside. One man attempted to pry the door open and the other tried to get in the window. She called the police and, because the men were still milling around in a nearby alley, she was able to identify the perpetrators. One of them had just been released that morning; he had been either charged or convicted (not sure on details) for robbery.

"The police told her that 'DC doesn't have an attempted burglary statute' and so they could not arrest the men. They let them go, although now they know who my friend is, where she lives and that she fingered them to the cops." (bamber.blogspot.com)

Actually, DC does have an attempted burglary statute, so the police officers were either incompetent or making up an excuse for their inaction.

The District government refuses to assume any responsibility for compensating crime victims who suffer because of the District's incompetence.

The leading case (but hardly the only one) is *Warren* v. *District of Columbia.* [444 A.2d 1 (1982).]

In *Warren*, three women lived together in a house. Two of the women were upstairs when they heard their roommate downstairs being attacked by men who had broken in. The women called the police. After half an hour, the woman downstairs stopped screaming. So the two upstairs women, believing that the police had finally arrived, went downstairs. In fact, police never did come.

The downstairs woman had been beaten into silence. The intruders then grabbed the two women who had just come downstairs. As the court later wrote: "For the next fourteen hours the women were held captive, raped, robbed, beaten, forced to commit sexual acts...."

The DC Court of Appeals ruled that the rape and assault victims could not even recover their medical expenses from the DC city government, because the government has no legal obligation to protect anyone.

Even if the women had owned a rifle or shotgun, it would have been illegal for them to use it against the predators. According to DC Code § 7-2507.02, every rifle and shotgun had to be "unloaded and disassembled or bound by a trigger lock or similar device unless such firearm is kept at his place of business, or while being used for lawful recreational purposes within the District of Columbia."

In other words, the DC "safe storage" law requiring that guns be locked and unusable at all times had no exception for defensive gun use in the home against a violent attacker.

In a political sense, gun prohibition made a lot of sense for the DC city government. Unable or unwilling to provide effective police protection, and determined not to compensate crime victims who suffer because of the government's own failures, DC politicians need a scapegoat for the city's crime disaster. Rather than crack down on criminals, the DC government cracked down on law-abiding gun owners.

The viciousness of the crackdown—particularly the prohibition of the use of any firearm for self-defense—may have the same root as Great Britain's *de facto* ban on armed self-defense. To acknowledge the legitimacy of armed defense is to admit that the government cannot protect everyone all the time. The admission is considered insulting by some governments, and thus armed self-defense must be forbidden.

The corollary of the DC government's legal position that it has no obligation to pay compensation to crime victims—regardless of how much its police are at fault—is that firearm manufacturers must pay crime victims and also pay the DC city government itself, regardless of fault. DC was among the cities that participated in the Brady Center's junk lawsuits against firearm manufacturers.

Even though no firearm manufacturer even sold guns in the District, and even though all the companies had complied with the vast body of laws which make firearms the most heavily-regulated consumer product in the United States. (No other consumer product requires the buyer to get advance permission from the FBI or the state police for every retail purchase.)

A 1991 DC law made gun manufacturers absolutely liable for every injury inflicted with any semi-automatic firearm that holds 12 or more rounds. For example, a woman who lives in Arizona buys a Remington Model 552 Speedmaster there. Years later, the woman and her family move to DC. One night, a gang breaks into the family's home and begins attacking the children.

The woman uses her .22 to shoot the intruders, correctly believing that employing the firearm is the only way to stop her children from being murdered.

Under the DC absolute-liability law, the criminals had a right to sue Remington for compensation for the injuries they received during the shooting. It was irrelevant under the DC statute that the gun was lawfully sold in another state, that Remington does not sell guns in the District or that the "victims" were violent predators.

Remington would likewise be liable if the gun were stolen in Arizona and, years later, sold to a DC criminal who shot another DC criminal.

In 1992, the Senate, using its explicit constitutional authority over the District of Columbia, voted to repeal the DC liability statute. The repeal, though, was removed in backroom maneuvering by then-Sen. Fritz Hollings (D-S.C.) acting at the behest of the tort lawyers lobby.

Finally, in 2005 the federal Protection of Lawful Commerce in Arms Act preempted almost all abusive anti-gun lawsuits, including those promoted by the DC city government. The application of the PLCAA to the DC tort liability statute was upheld by the DC Court of Appeals in January 2008.

Yet before the *Heller* decision, the mother in the above scenario would still have been a criminal under DC law, because the DC gun lock law included no exception for emergency self-defense and because DC outlawed her rifle as a "machine gun."

The destruction of the right to self-defense was no accident. As city councilman Dave Clarke (a longtime anti-gun advocate) explained when he was pushing the handgun and self-defense ban, "I don't intend to run the government around the moment of survival."

Clarke's law put all DC citizens in the same position as the slaves who lived in DC before the Civil War. Then, DC's gun laws were based on the slave codes of Maryland and Virginia, both of which had donated the land for the District. Those laws forbade slaves from owning or carrying firearms without their master's consent. Our nation's capital should be a shining example of freedom, but bigots turned the city into a miserable example of the dangers of prohibition.

In the 1995 *George Mason University Civil Rights Law Journal* article "Second-Class Citizenship and the Second Amendment in the District of Columbia," Stephen Halbrook examined the history of the DC gun laws. He showed that when Congress abolished slavery in the District in 1862, and re-pealed the District's slave codes, Congress intended, among other things, to protect the Second Amendment right of the freedmen to keep and bear arms.

In the 20th century, public swimming pools and most other places in Washington, DC, were racially segregated. The segregation laws disgraced not only DC itself, but the entire nation.

The National Rifle Association stood firm against the racists as the NRA's shooting range at its DC headquarters was always open to everyone equally, regardless of race.

Beginning with the 1976 handgun and home defense ban, our nation's capital—and therefore our entire nation—was again disgraced by bigotry in the District.

The gun prohibition laws were also an insult to the memory of the great man for whom the city is named, George Washington—who was an avid gun collector with more than 50 handguns, muskets and other firearms. As Secretary of State Thomas Jefferson wrote to President Washington in 1796, "One loves to possess arms, though they hope never to have occasion for them."

Today, extremists in the DC government despise the possession of arms and disdain the right of survival. In the 1954 case of *Bolling* v. *Sharpe*, the US Supreme Court invalidated the District's laws segregating the public schools. In 2008, the Supreme Court acted against another bigoted DC law that violated the Constitution.

THE FLIMSY ARGUMENTS OF THE ANTI-GUN FORCES

What are the best arguments of the most dedicated enemies of Second Amendment rights? Let's look at the briefs filed in *District of Columbia v. Heller*. In January 2008, 20 *amicus curiae* briefs were filed in support of District of Columbia Mayor Adrian Fenty's efforts to preserve the DC bans.

Several of the briefs came from gun ban organizations. The Violence Policy Center's (VPC) brief claimed that handguns today are even more dan-gerous than when the DC City Council enacted the ban in 1976. These days, sales of self-loading pistols outpace those of revolvers. Technological advances have made pistols more compact, or higher in ammunition capacity, or more effective for self-defense than in 1976. These improvements are obviously the result of manufacturers trying to cater to consumer preferences, although the VPC blamed everything on the wickedness of gun manufacturers.

VPC claimed that high-powered revolvers such as the .50-caliber S&W model 500 (very useful for carrying in areas where a bear attack is possible, I might add) are actually "vest-busters," made for killing police officers.

5

The final section of the brief warned that handguns are inappropriate for self-defense because panicked handgun users' (the brief makes sure not to call them "crime victims") hands will be trembling so much as to "easily result in the killing of an innocent bystander." The VPC did not provide any data about how often this actually happens (in truth, hardly ever, as detailed in Gary Kleck's in-depth research on defensive gun use), but instead offered a citation to one of its own monographs.

Like the VPC, the Coalition to Stop Gun Violence (CSGV) explicitly favors a handgun ban. The brief filed by the CSGV's legal arm, the Educational Fund to Stop Gun Violence, argued that the Constitution provides the death penalty for treason and authorizes Congress to use the militia to "suppress insurrection." Accordingly, the brief concluded that the Second Amendment could not have been intended to allow the people to use firearms to resist or overthrow a tyrannical government.

The claim is contradicted by the writing of James Madison himself, and by many others, including Hubert H. Humphrey, who explained:

> "Certainly one of the chief guarantees of freedom under any government, no matter how popular and respected, is the right of citizens to keep and bear arms. This is not to say that firearms should not be very carefully used and that definite safety rules of precaution should not be taught and enforced. But the right of citizens to bear arms is just one more guarantee against arbitrary government, one more safeguard against a tyranny which now appears remote in America, but which historically has proved to be always possible." ["Know Your Lawmakers," *Guns*, Feb. 1960, p. 4.]

The brief for the Brady Center—the legal arm of the Brady Campaign—was joined by the International Association of Chiefs of Police, Major Cities Chiefs and some smaller police groups, mostly of command officers.

The main problem for the Brady lawyers' reasoning is that, although they assembled collections of quotes and arguments that would seem persuasive if you only read their brief, most of what they wrote is readily contradicted once you look at the entire record.

For example, they insisted that the only purpose of the Second Amendment was federalism—to limit federal interference with state militias.

But one only has to look at the DC government's official Constitution for the proposed state of "New Columbia" (what DC would be called if it were granted statehood). The "New Columbia" Constitution parallels the federal Bill of Rights, including a word-for-word copy of the Second Amendment. Nothing in a state constitution could limit federal power. Thus, the DC government's own actions disprove the *Heller* argument of the Brady Center (and of the DC government itself) that the Second Amendment is only about federalism.

Not to be outdone, Janet Reno returned, along with a collection of other officials from the Reno/Clinton Department of Justice, in a brief arguing that the official position of the Department of Justice since the 1930s has been that there is no individual right to arms, and that the Second Amendment is only a "collective right" of state governments.

One of the brief's biggest problems with this argument was dealing with the testimony of President Roosevelt's attorney general, Homer Cummings, before Congress during the passage of the National Firearms Act (NFA) of 1934. The NFA imposed a tax and registration requirement on machine guns, short shotguns and short rifles.

Cummings was asked about whether Congress could instead enact an outright ban, and Cummings replied that there might be constitutional problems.

Reno and her ex-staffers claimed that Cummings was not talking about the Second Amendment; he was saying that the congressional tax power (which is the basis for the NFA) might not extend to banning things, rather than taxing them (and registering them in order to enforce the tax).

However, what Reno omitted is the context of what Attorney General Cummings said. In the hearing before the House Ways & Means Committee, Representative David J. Lewis of Maryland said, "I have never quite understood how the laws of the various States [restricting concealed firearms] have been reconciled with the provision in our Constitution denying the privilege to the legislature to take away the right to carry arms." He continued, regarding the proposed machine gun bill: "I was curious to know how we escaped that provision in the Constitution."

Attorney General Cummings explained: "If we made a statute absolutely forbidding any human being to have a machine gun, you might say there is some constitutional question involved. But when you say, 'we will tax the machine gun' and when you say that 'the absence of a license showing payment of the tax has been made indicates that a crime has been perpetrated,' you are easily within the law."

Rep. Lewis followed up: "In other words, it does not amount to prohibition, but allows of regulation."

Attorney General Cummings replied: "That is the idea. We have studied that very carefully." (Hearings Before the House Committee on Ways and Means on H.R. 9066, 73rd Congress, 2d Sess., 1934, pp. 18-19.)

The social science evidence was covered in a high-strung brief from the American Academy of Pediatrics and a more sober one from the American Public Health Association. These two briefs had to twist themselves into knots to claim that DC's law is needed to solve the problem of gun accidents.

Fatal gun accidents have declined by 86 percent since 1948, while the per capita firearms supply has risen by 158 percent. Fatal gun accidents involving children have declined even more steeply, so that the odds of a child under 10 being killed by an accident in a swimming pool are about a hundred times greater than the risk of a child being killed in a gun-related accident.

Eighteen members of the US House of Representatives filed a brief arguing that, "Interpretation of the Second Amendment to resolve this case should be informed by Congress' legislative activities and role as a constitutional interpreter." The brief listed various gun control laws enacted by Congress.

Although the brief did not say so, five different congressional enactments have declared that the Second Amendment is an important individual right.

Another gun-ban organization, the Legal Community Against Violence (LCAV), filed a brief on behalf of Baltimore, Cleveland, Los Angeles, Milwaukee, New York City, Oakland, Philadelphia, Sacramento, San Francisco, Seattle and Trenton. The brief was joined by the US Conference of Mayors, an association of big-city mayors.

The most absurd part of the LCAV was crediting the tremendous drop in New York City crime under Mayor Giuliani, who was elected in November 1993, to the ban on so-called "assault weapons" adopted during the crime-ridden reign of Mayor David Dinkins in 1991. Of course, that's impossible, since so-called "assault weapons" constituted far less than 1 percent of the guns used in New York City's crime. For example, in 1988, of 12,138 guns seized by New York City police, only 80 were "assault-type" firearms. ("Handguns, not Assault Rifles, are NYC Weapon of Choice," White Plains *Reporter-Dispatch,* March 27, 1989.)

The LCAV also credited a 1998 New York City law requiring handguns be sold with a locking device and a 2000 law requiring the same for long guns. Yet New York City's law-abiding gun owners were never part of the crime problem to begin with. And making them spend a few extra dollars to buy a trigger lock would not have made a difference.

Many of the amicus briefs reached into American history to find precedent for DC's extreme law. The best they could find was an 1837 Georgia law, which they described as a ban on concealable "weapons." More precisely, it banned the sale or carrying of all handguns except horsemen's pistols.

These briefs were obviously reliant on the scholarship of Ohio State's Saul Cornell. Like Cornell, the briefs omitted the rest of the story. In the 1846 case of *Nunn v. State*, the Georgia Supreme Court declared the handgun ban to be an unconstitutional violation of the Second Amendment.

THE STEVENS DISSENT AND ITS DEFENDERS

Justice Stevens's dissent does as well as possible with the materials available in support of his position. But the Stevens denial of the Standard Model of the Second Amendment founders on the word "the."

If you read the Scalia majority and the Stevens dissent in parallel, Justice Stevens keeps a serious intellectual contest going for a while. The majority and dissent argue about the rules of construction for preambles: to what extent, if any, does a preamble (in this case, about the importance of the militia) limit the operative clause (the right of the people)? Both the majority and the dissent cite various authorities on statutory construction from around the Founding Era.

The two sides argue about the meaning of "bear arms." Each side can cite many examples of the term being used in its preferred way—to mean *only* bearing arms in military service (Stevens) or to mean bearing arms in a variety of ways, including personal defense and hunting (Scalia). Even if the reader believes, as I do, that Scalia wins the argument on points, the fight is hardly a knock-out.

But for the neutral reader, the fight over original meaning has to come to an end when the opinions analyze "the" right to keep and bear arms. The DC Circuit opinion pointed out that the phrasing indisputably shows that the right was a pre-existing one. That is, the right to keep and bear arms already existed before the Second Amendment was written. The Second Amendment merely imposed a legal requirement that the right not be infringed by the federal government. The 1875 Supreme Court decision in *Cruikshank* said the same thing, as both the majority and dissent agree.

So what was "the" right that pre-existed the Constitution? The majority opinion provides an obvious answer. It was the right of having arms for personal defense, as guaranteed by the 1689 English Declaration of Right, and as expounded by Blackstone: "the natural right of resistance and self-preservation," which was effectuated by "the right of having and using arms for self-preservation and defence."

If the majority is right on this point, then the Stevens dissent is plainly wrong; the Second Amendment *was* intended to protect a personal right to arms for self-defense. So Stevens spends a good deal of effort claiming that the 1689 English Declaration of Right and the 1789 Bill of Rights were intended to address different problems. His main support for the argument is that the state ratification debates were replete with anti-Federalist objections about the potential for abuse of the militia powers which are granted to Congress in Article I.

But Stevens's theory requires that we ignore an obvious source of original meaning: James Madison himself. Madison's notes for his speech introducing the Bill of Rights into the US House of Representatives indicate that his arms rights amendment was based on the English arms right, and that it was intended to remedy two key defects in the English right. The first was that the English right applied only to Protestants (who constituted about 98 % of the population). Second, because any act of Parliament can be negated by a later Parliament, the 1689 Parliament's adoption of the Declaration of Right would constrain the monarch, but not effectively constrain future Parliaments. According to Madison, "They [the proposed Bill of Rights] relate 1st. to private rights — . . . fallacy on both sides — espec[iall]y as to English Decln. of Rts — 1. mere act of parl[iamen]t. 2. no freedom of press — Conscience . . . attainders — arms to Protest[an]ts." [James Madison, "Notes for Speech in Congress Supporting Amendments", June 8, 1789, in 12 *The Papers of James Madison* 193-94 (Charles F. Hobson & Robert Rutland eds., 1979).]

Suppose that Madison's notes had been destroyed, and we had no knowledge of them. Would Stevens's theory still be plausible?

Not really. If the pre-existing right is *not* the traditional Anglo-American right to have arms for personal defense, then what is "the" pre-existing right? Stevens claims that the pre-existing right was a right to serve in the militia while armed. Yet, as the majority points out, Stevens cannot cite a shred of evidence in support of his assertion of a pre-existing militia right.

Alone among the twenty amicus briefs filed in support of the handgun ban, Dennis Henigan's brief for the Brady Center recognized the critical importance of "the." The brief addressed the problem by pointing out that the state militia system long predated the Constitution. Indeed, according to Henigan, it could be traced all the way back to King Henry II's 1181 Assize of Arms. (The Assize required all free men to have particular types of weapons, depending on their social rank.) The brief should have followed the militia roots even further, back to King Alfred the Great's (871-901) system of the Saxon fyrd. (Jefferson and other American Founders lauded the rough liberty of the Saxons, and disdained the rigid aristocracy imposed by the Normans.)

But whether one is talking about Massachusetts militia laws from 1775, or their English ancestors, those militia laws never speak of a "right" of serving armed in the militia. Militia service, like paying taxes, was always recognized as a duty. In the Whig tradition, it was an especially honorable one, but a duty nonetheless.

So there was no pre-constitutional militia right. There being none, the only possible antecedent for "the" right to keep and bear arms is the explicit English right to personal arms for self-defense, and its antecedent in natural law. That issue settled, Stevens's claim that Second Amendment was originally intended to be a militia-only right collapses.

In a Cato Institute on-line debate after *Heller,* Henigan did what he should have done in his brief, and cited two state constitutions which he said show that there was a pre-existing militia right. However, neither of his new claims were plausible.

Henigan pointed to the 1776 North Carolina Declaration of Rights "That the people have a right to bear arms, for the defence of the State...", and the 1780 Massachusetts Constitution: "The people have a right to keep and bear arms for the common defence..."

To state the obvious, both of these provisions refer to "a" right to arms. You can't tell from the text alone whether these provisions refer to a pre-existing right.

More fundamentally, Henigan was wrong that these provisions are only about the militia. For example, in 1844, the North Carolina Supreme Court held that the state constitutional provision protects the right to arms for personal defense, but does not protect gun ownership by free blacks, because free blacks were (supposedly) not part of the social compact. [*State v. Newsom*, 27 N.C. 250.]

Likewise, it is hardly clear that the Massachusetts right was militia-only. In *Commonwealth v. Blanding* (1825) Massachusetts Chief Justice Parker wrote, "The liberty of the press was to be unrestrained, but he who used it was to be responsible in case of its abuse; like the right to keep fire arms, which does not protect him who uses them for annoyance or destruction."

The explanation only makes sense if individuals have a general right to firearms for all purposes, rather than the right to have firearms solely for militia service. Just as there is a general right of freedom of the press for all purposes (but not to abuse that right by libeling someone) so there is a general right to arms for all purposes (but not to abuse that right by using guns for annoyance or destruction).

In the 1896 case of *Commonwealth v. Murphy*, the Massachusetts Supreme Judicial Court upheld a ban on unlicensed mass armed parades in public; the defendant claimed that the ban violated the state's right to arms.

The court disagreed, and explained that "The protection of a similar constitutional provision has often been sought by persons charged with carrying concealed weapons, and it has been almost universally held that the legislature may regulate and limit the mode of carrying arms." The Court then supplied a string cite to cases from Tennessee, Texas, Alabama, Arkansas, Indiana, and Missouri (plus one contrary case from Kentucky). The "similar constitutional provision" in every one of these cases was a state right to arms clause which indisputably protected the right of everyone (not just militiamen) to have firearms in their home for self-defense and other purposes.

In 1976, the Massachusetts court rejected a criminal's challenge to the state law restricting the possession of sawed-off shotguns. The court declared that the state constitutional arms right was only for militiamen, and that it no longer existed for any practical purpose, since the National Guard now had its own guns. The decision did acknowledge the earlier view might have been different: "there is nothing to suggest that, even in early times, due regulation of possession or carrying of firearms, short of some sweeping prohibition, would

11

have been thought to be an improper curtailment of individual liberty or to undercut the militia system."

Similarly, Justice Breyer's dissenting opinion in *Heller* recognized that the original view of the Massachusetts Constitution appears to have been a general (not militia-only) right to arms:

> "Samuel Adams, who lived in Boston, advocated a constitutional amendment that would have precluded the Constitution from ever being 'construed' to 'prevent the people of the United States, who are peaceable citizens, from keeping their own arms.' 6 Documentary History of the Ratification of the Constitution 1453 (J. Kaminski & G. Saladino eds. 2000). Samuel Adams doubtless knew that the Massachusetts Constitution contained somewhat similar protection."

Language nearly identical to the Massachusetts provision ("common defence," with no explicit mention of any other purpose) appears in the state constitutions of Arkansas, Florida, South Carolina, and Tennessee—and has been interpreted in all those states to include the right of individuals who are not in the militia to have guns in their home for personal defense. (A contrary 1986 decision in Maine was quickly overturned by the people with a 1987 constitutional amendment.)

One justification for recognizing individual home protection as guaranteed by the "common defense" language is that families which protect themselves by thwarting or deterring violent criminals *are* contributing to the common defense of society. That's just what the people of New Orleans did when the police force deserted the city after Hurricane Katrina.

Henigan may argue that the 1976 Massachusetts court and the 1986 Maine court got it right, and all the other courts were wrong. But the very fact that so many courts—and especially the courts closest in time to ratification of the state constitutions—disagree with Henigan's interpretation shows the error of his claim that the Massachusetts right, and therefore the Second Amendment, have a clear context which proves that they were never intended to protect the right to possess arms for home defense.

CHEMERINSKY'S QUESTIONABLE HISTORY

Erwin Chemerinsky, Dean of the University of California at Irvine law school, claims: "From 1791, when the Bill of Rights was adopted, until June 26, 2008, not one law—federal, state, or local—was found to violate the Second Amendment."

Not true. As the *Heller* majority opinion points out, Georgia's handgun ban was declared an unconstitutional violation of the Second Amendment by the Georgia Supreme Court in 1846, in *Nunn v. State*. Also, the 1902 Idaho case of *In re Brickey* relied on the Second Amendment and the state constitution in voiding a law which banned gun carrying.

Besides, even if Chemerinsky were right, someone could have written in 1930, "Not one law has been declared unconstitutional on the basis of the Free Exercise clause." The same point could have been made in 1930 about most of the other freedoms in the First Amendment, and about many other constitutional freedoms. It was not until 1965 that the Supreme Court declared a law unconstitutional under the First Amendment's free speech/press clauses. (In *Lamont v. Postmaster General,* the Court held that requiring a person to go to the post office to pick up "communist political propaganda", rather than have the Post Office deliver the propaganda to his home, was too great a burden on freedom of the press. It might be noted that many gun registration or licensing laws impose far more severe burdens than the burden which *Lamont* found to be unconstitutional.)

A long period of judicial failure to enforce a right does not create a rule that future judges should fail to do their duty to protect an enumerated right.

Like other advocates of nullifying the Second Amendment by interpreting its main clause so as to have no practical meaning, Chemerinsky contends that the *Heller* majority did not respect the introductory clause of the Second Amendment: "The only way to give meaning to both clauses is to conclude that the Second Amendment protects a right to have firearms only for purposes of militia service."

To the contrary, Alaska, Hawaii, and South Carolina have language identical to the Second Amendment in their state constitutions. The right is treated as a standard (not militia-only) individual right in Alaska and South Carolina, while Hawaii courts have thus far been agnostic. Many other state constitutions have other language which would seem (at least for some modern readers) to be militia-only, such as a right to arms for which "the common defense" is the only stated purpose. But the vast majority of state constitutional cases have interpreted these arms rights as encompassing a right to arms for a variety of lawful purposes, including self-defense in the home. For details, see my 2002 article "What State Constitutions Teach About the Second Amendment" in the *Northern Kentucky Law Review*.

Chemerinsky's militia-only reading of the Second Amendment is contrary to a long tradition in American law. The only counter-tradition is the Supreme Court's failure to act against lower federal courts' aggressive, politically-minded misreading of *United States v. Miller*. Fortunately, the period of Supreme Court indifference to the Second Amendment has ended, as the period of Supreme Court indifference to the First Amendment ended several decades ago.

No more slippery slope?

When the *Heller* decision was announced, the Brady Campaign began claiming that the case would pave the way for new gun controls, since gun owners would no longer be afraid that registering all guns, licensing all gun owners, and banning some guns would push gun ownership down the slippery slope towards total prohibition of all guns.

Gun owners who do what the Brady Campaign wants, by withdrawing from political involvement to protect their rights, would be making a terrible mistake.

First of all, *Heller* was a 5-4 decision. Even if a Supreme Court a few years from now did not formally over-rule *Heller*, the Court could constrict *Heller* so tightly that it could be the last case which meaningfully applied the Second Amendment. A future Court could also greatly reduce *Heller*'s scope by refusing to make it enforceable against state and local governments.

Second, nothing in *Heller* stops the United Nations' current global campaign against firearms ownership. The international gun prohibition lobby IANSA (International Action Network on Small Arms) brags that it is the "the organization officially designated by the UN Department of Disarmament Affairs (DDA) to coordinate civil society involvement to the UN small arms process." The UN's official representative of civil society favors handgun prohibition, prohibition of any rifle that can shoot 100 meters (i.e., almost all rifles), prohibiting gun ownership for self-defense, and drastic reductions in levels of gun ownership.

IANSA and the UN are currently working on an Arms Trade Treaty to eliminate gun sales to countries which violate human rights—which by the UN and IANSA definition means the United States; the UN and IANSA have already declared that laws like those in the US, which allow a woman to shoot a rapist, are a violation of the human rights of the rapist. The Brady Campaign, incidentally, is a member organization of IANSA.

We know that there are often four Justices—and sometimes five—who will use unratified treaties (like CEDAW, the Convention on the Elimination of all forms of Discrimination Against Women), or treaties which are not even applicable to the United States (like the African Convention on the Rights of the Child), as guidance in interpreting the US Constitution. In a few years, there could be several more such Justices.

Did *Heller* reduce the immediate risk of the slippery slope? Yes. Will that protection survive an presidency in which the US delegation at the United Nations (as in the Clinton years) enthusiastically supports the global prohibition campaign? A new Supreme Court with just one more Justice who is hostile to the Second Amendment, and who believes in using international "norms" to constrict American rights? Constitutional rights advocates who think that the slippery slope problem has been resolved once and for all would be naïve.

Gun Control and Discrimination

THE KLAN'S FAVORITE LAW: GUN CONTROL IN THE POSTWAR SOUTH

If you believe everything that Michael Moore says in *Bowling for Columbine* and his books, then you would think that pro-gun Americans are white racists, and that gun control would be a wonderful way to help minorities. But a look at America's past reveals what historian Clayton Cramer has accurately called "The Racist Roots of Gun Control."

After the Civil War, the defeated Southern states aimed to preserve slavery in fact if not in law. The states enacted Black Codes which barred the black freedmen from exercising basic civil rights, including the right to bear arms. Mississippi's provision was typical: No freedman "shall keep or carry fire-arms of any kind, or any ammunition."

Under the Mississippi law, a person informing the government about illegal arms possession by a freedman was entitled to receive the forfeited firearm. Whites were forbidden to give or lend freedman firearms or knives.

The Special Report of the Anti-Slavery Conference of 1867 complained that freedmen were "forbidden to own or bear firearms and thus rendered defenseless against assaults" by whites. As a letter printed in the Jan. 13, 1866, edition of *Harper's Weekly* observed: "The militia of this county have seized every gun found in the hands of so-called freedmen in this section of the county. They claim that the Statute Laws of Mississippi do not recognize the Negro as having any right to carry arms."

Congress's "Report of the Joint Committee on Reconstruction" set forth the factual case for the need for a 14th Amendment to protect the liberties enumerated in the federal Bill of Rights. At the Committee's hearings, General Rufus Saxon testified that all over the South, whites were "seizing all fire-arms found in the hands of the freedmen. Such conduct is in clear and direct viola-

15

tion of their personal rights as guaranteed by the Constitution of the United States, which declares that 'the right of the people to keep and bear arms shall not be infringed.'"

Despite the Black Codes, and at the suggestion of Reconstruction governors and other leaders, blacks often created militias to resist white terrorism. For example, in June 1867 in Greensboro, Alabama, the police let the murderer of a black voting registrar escape; in response, a freedman who would later serve in the Alabama State Legislature urged his fellow freedmen to create a permanent militia. "Union League" militias were formed all over central Alabama.

The freedmen slipped from white control. One planter protested that his workers were "turbulent and disorderly," coming and going when they wished, as if they had a choice whether or not to work. The Union League, protested another ex-master, was advising freedmen "to ignore the Southern white man as much as possible...to set up for themselves."

The next spring, the Ku Klux Klan came to central Alabama. The Klansmen, unlike the freedmen, had horses, and thus the tactical advantages of mobility. In a few months, the Klan triumph was complete. One freedman recalled that the night riders, after reasserting white control, "took the weapons from might near all the colored people in the neighborhood."

Sometimes militias consisting of freedmen or Unionists were able to resist the Klan or other white forces. In the South Carolina back-country, where the blacks were a numerical majority, the black militias kept white terrorists at bay for long periods.

While many blacks participated in informal, local militias, most of the reconstruction governors set up official state militias that were racially integrated. Like many other facets of the reconstruction governments (and the racist governments which followed them), the integrated state militias were corrupt. The state militias, which sought to protect the state governments and the election process, were frequently in conflict with informal white militias. Arms shipments from the federal government to arm the state militias were often intercepted and seized by white militias.

Official or unofficial, black militias were the primary target of the white racist resistance. "Pitchfork" Ben Tillman, who would later become one of the US Senate's preeminent white supremacists, joined a "Sweetwater Sabre Club" whose members seized control of South Carolina's Edgefield County from a black militia in 1874-75, and attacked a black militia at Hamburg, South Carolina in 1876.

In areas where the black militias lost and the Klan or other white groups took control, "almost universally the first thing done was to disarm the negroes and leave them defenseless," wrote Albion Tourgée in his 1880 book *The Invisible Empire*. An attorney and civil rights worker from the North, Tourgée would later represent the civil rights plaintiff in *Plessy v. Ferguson*.

The Klan's objective in disarming the blacks was to leave them unable to defend their rights, a Congressional hearing found. Afraid of race war and retribution, whites were terrified at the mere sight of a black with a gun. As legal historian Kermit Hall notes, "From the southern white's point of view, a well-armed Negro militia was precisely what John Brown had sought to achieve at Harpers Ferry in 1859."

The Vicksburg white riot of 1874 typified the problem. According to a Congressional investigation, the whites conducted, "Unauthorized searches by self-constituted authority into private homes, searches for arms converted, as is unusual, into robbery and thieving...." A Congressional report detailed one arms roundup:

> "One poor old man, half crazed, but harmless, sitting quietly in a neighbor's house, is brutally shot to death in the presence of terrified women and shrieking children. He gained his wretched living by hunting and fishing, and had a shot-gun. No one pretended that Tom Bidderman had anything to do with the fight, but he was black, and had a gun in his house, and so they murdered him for amusement as they were going from the city to restore order in the country."

The Radical Republican Congress observed the South with dismay. The Republicans intended to use federal power to force freedom on the South. One of the Radical Republicans' most important tools was the 14th Amendment to the Constitution, which required states to respect basic human rights. While the vague language of the Amendment has produced disagreement about exactly what is covered, the congressional backers seem to have intended, at the least, protecting the core freedoms listed in the national Bill of Rights. Announced Representative Clarke of Kansas: "I find in the Constitution an article which declared 'the right of the people to keep and bear arms shall not be infringed.' For myself, I shall insist that the reconstructed rebels of Mississippi respect the Constitution in their local laws."

The earlier Freedman's Bureau Bill had also been squarely aimed at protecting the right to bear arms. The bill guaranteed federal protection of "the full and equal benefit of all laws and proceedings for the security of person and estate, including the constitutional right of bearing arms."

The Amendment was quickly emasculated by the United States Supreme Court in the *Slaughter-House Cases* and *United States v. Cruikshank*, The Supreme Court understood the social realities of the South. The *Cruikshank* decision gave the green light to the Klan, unofficial white militias, and other racist groups to forcibly disarm the freedmen and impose white supremacy.

One state at a time, white racists took control of government by using armed violence and the threat of violence to control balloting on election day.

Freedmen and their white allies also resorted to arms. But white Republican governors were usually afraid that fully employing the black militias would set off an even broader race war.

The white South, defeated on the battlefield in 1865, had continued armed resistance to Northern control for over a decade. When the North, an occupying power, grew weary of the struggle and abandoned its black and Republican allies in the South, the white South was again the master of its destiny.

In deference to the Fourteenth Amendment, some states did cloak their laws in neutral, non-racial terms. For example, the Tennessee legislature barred the sale of any handguns except the "Army and Navy model." The ex-Confederate soldiers already had their high quality "Army and Navy" guns. But cash-poor freedmen could barely afford lower-cost, simpler firearms not of the "Army and Navy" quality. Arkansas enacted a nearly identical law in 1881, and other Southern states followed suit, including Alabama (1893), Texas (1907), and Virginia (1925).

As Jim Crow intensified, Southern states enacted gun registration and handgun permit laws. Registration came to Mississippi (1906), Georgia (1913), and North Carolina (1917). Handgun permits requirements were passed in North Carolina (1917), Missouri (1919), and Arkansas (1923).

As one Florida judge later explained, the licensing laws were "passed for the purpose of disarming the negro laborers... [and] never intended to be applied to the white population." [*Watson v. Stone*, 4 So. 2d 700, 703 (Fla. 1941) (Buford, J., concurring).]

That gun control has a very unsavory past does not, in itself, prove that all modern gun control proposals are a bad idea. But it does offer reasons to be especially cautious about the dangers of disarming people who cannot necessarily count on their local government to protect them.

BROTHERS IN ARMS: HOW CIVIL RIGHTS FLOWED FROM A RIFLE BARREL

Do minorities have a moral right—and even a moral duty—to resist mob violence? The history of black people in America over the past century suggests that doing so may be necessary in order to protect civil rights.

During the Jim Crow era of the late 19th and early 20th century, blacks often offered only minimal resistance to white rioters, who were frequently abetted by law enforcement officials. For example, in the **Wilmington, North Carolina**, riot of 1898, a mob destroyed a black newspaper after taking offense at a newspaper opinion. Armed whites fatally shot 12 blacks. The leader of the mob was elected mayor.

In August 1900 in New York City, police joined an anti-black riot, often behaving more brutally than other rioters. The mayor, the police commissioner, and the courts covered up the officers' crimes.

The criminals in the extremely destructive East St. Louis riot of 1917 were assisted by the police and by the Illinois state militia. As historian Robert Fogelson recounts in his book *Violence as Protest*, the white rioters:

> "burned houses and, with a deliberation which shocked reporters, shot black residents as they fled the flames. They killed them as they begged for mercy and even refused to allow them to brush away flies as they lay dying. The blacks, disarmed by the police and the militia after an earlier riot and defenseless in their wooden shanties, offered little resistance."

Still, the Missouri legislature thought blacks a threat, and enacted a law requiring a permit to obtain a handgun.

In the Washington, DC, riots of 1919, policemen refused to protect blacks from rampaging soldiers and sailors. After the rioters had been allowed several days without restraint, federal troops were finally called in to suppress the riot.

When whites and blacks rioted against each other in Detroit in 1943, the police tried to "reason" with the white rioters (to little effect) and killed 17 black rioters. A NAACP report blamed the riot on the Detroit police's escalation of violence.

A 1947 report by the President's Committee on Civil Rights, assessing the contemporary problem of lynching, found that "Frequently state officials participate in the crime, actively or passively."

Black leaders such as W.E.B. DuBois, editor of the NAACP magazine *Crisis*, insisted that blacks stop behaving like helpless victims. He wrote with disgust about black people in Gainesville, Florida, who had acted "like a set of cowardly sheep":

> "Without resistance they let a white mob whom they outnumbered two to one, torture, harry and murder their women [and] shoot down innocent men...
>
> No people can behave with the absolute cowardice shown by these colored people and hope to have the sympathy or help of civilized folk...
>
> In the last analysis lynching of Negroes is going to stop in the South when the cowardly mob is faced by effective guns in the hands of people determined to sell their souls dearly."

A. Philip Randolph, editor of the socialist black magazine *Messenger*, agreed: "Always regard your own life as more important than the life of the person about to take yours, and if a choice has to be made...choose to preserve your own and destroy that of the lynching mob."

At a protest meeting held at Carnegie Hall after the New York City riot, one of the speakers, "Miss M.R. Lyons of Brooklyn," told the audience:

> "Let every negro get a permit to carry a revolver. You are not supposed to be a walking arsenal, but don't you get caught again. Have your houses made ready to afford protection from the fury of the mob, and remembering that your home is your castle and that no police officer has a right to enter it, unless he complies with the usage of the law; see that he does not."

Sometimes, as in Memphis, the mere presence of armed blacks constrained white police or mob behavior. In other cases, armed blacks were partially successful; during the 1906 Atlanta riots, according to historian John Dittmer's *Black Georgia in the Progressive Era*, although blacks "were unable to offer effective resistance when trapped downtown or caught in white sections of the city, they did fight back successfully when the mobs invaded their neighborhoods."

Other times, resistance produced heavy bloodshed on both sides. In July 1919, a black who had floated into "white" water near a Lake Michigan beach in Chicago was killed. Whites rioted; blacks fought back with rifles, and the police stood aside. Twenty-three blacks and 15 whites were killed in a week of rioting.

Michigan's law requiring a government permit in order to buy a handgun was enacted after Dr. Ossian Sweet, a black man, shot and killed a person in a mob that was attacking his house because he had just moved into an all-white neighborhood. The Detroit police stood nearby, refusing to restrain the angry crowd.

Indicted for first degree murder, Sweet was acquitted after a lengthy trial at which Clarence Darrow served as his attorney. Black newspapers such as the *Amsterdam News* and the *Baltimore Herald* vigorously defended blacks' right to use deadly force in self-defense against a mob.

Darrow summed up for the jury: "eleven of them go into a house, gentlemen, with no police protection, in the face of a mob, and the hatred of a community, and take guns and ammunition and fight for their rights, and for your rights and for mine, and for the rights of every being that lives. They went in and faced a mob seeking to tear them to bits. Call them something besides cowards."

In Tulsa during and after World War I, the police worked closely with the "Knights of Liberty," a group which wore masks and attacked blacks and union organizers. In the 1921 Tulsa riots, armed blacks protected an alleged black rapist from a lynch mob. A small white army, led by the American Legion and with the approval of the police and city government, burned a one-mile square black district to the ground. As many as 200 blacks died, but about 50 whites also lost their lives in the riot.

Historian John Hope Franklin wrote: "The self-confidence of Tulsa's Negroes soared, their businesses prospered, their institutions flourished, and they simply had no fear of whites...After 1921, an altercation between a white person and a black person was not a *racial* incident...It was just an incident."

After the Tulsa Riots, Herbert H. Harrison, the president of the Liberal League of Negro America, told a New York audience that more white riots were possible soon:

> "I advise you to be ready to defend yourselves. I notice the State Government has removed some of its restrictions upon owning firearms, and one form of life insurance for your wives and children might be the possession of some of these handy implements."

In 1936 in Gordonsville, Virginia, an elderly black man named William Wales and his sister, Cora, shot a sheriff who had come to arrest Mr. Wales on false charges of threatening a white woman. The arrest was a pretext to force the Waleses to sell their property to the town, for a cemetery expansion. An enraged crowd of 5,000 gathered outside the Wales's home. Roy Wilkins, a future head of the NAACP, reported what happened next:

> "There was a slight flaw in the set-up, however. The man and woman had arms and they were not afraid to shoot... The leaders of the five thousand...had numbers. They had machine guns. They had sulphur bombs. They had tear gas bombs. But the two in the house had rifles, shotguns, and perhaps a pistol or two. Not so good. Not half as good as one lone Negro with nothing but his bare hands..."

The mob sent a request that the United States Marine Corps send some men from Quantico to take care of the Waleses. The Marines refused.

After night fell, the crowd threw a torch on the house, and shot the Wales as they were silhouetted against the fire. After the fire had cooled, souvenir hunters hacked the Waleses' bodies into tiny pieces. Wilkins defended the Waleses for standing up to the system after a lifetime of humiliating oppression.

In the 1950s and 1960s, a new civil rights movement began in the South. White supremacist tactics were just as violent as they had been during Reconstruction. Over 100 civil rights workers were murdered, and the Department of Justice refused to prosecute the Klan or to protect civil rights workers adequately. Help from the local police was out of the question; Klan dues were sometimes collected at the local station.

Blacks and civil rights workers armed for self-defense. Daisy Bates, the leader of the Arkansas NAACP and publisher of the *Arkansas State Press* during the Little Rock High School desegregation case, recalls that three crosses were burned on her lawn and gunshots fired into her home. Her husband, L. C. Bates, stayed up to guard their house with a .45 semi-automatic pistol. Some of their friends organized a volunteer patrol.

After the Bates's front lawn was bombed, Mrs. Bates telegrammed Attorney General Herbert Brownell in Washington. He replied that there was no federal jurisdiction, and told them to go to the local police. "Of course *that* wasn't going to protect us," Mrs. Bates remembered.

State or federal assistance sometimes did come—not when disorder began, but when blacks reacted by arming themselves. In North Carolina, Governor Terry Sanford (who later served as an anti-gun US Senator) refused to command state police to protect a civil rights march from Klan attacks—until he was warned that if there were no police, the marchers would be armed for self-defense.

Based in local churches, the Deacons for Defense and Justice set up armed patrol car systems in cities such as Bogalusa and Jonesboro, Louisiana, and within their spheres of operations deterred Klan and other attacks on civil rights workers and black residents. Of civil rights workers killed in the South, almost none were armed.

Secretary of State Condoleezza Rice, a self-described "Second Amendment absolutist," grew up in segregated Birmingham, Alabama, where her father, a Presbyterian minister, was a community leader in the civil rights struggles. According to a Nov. 17, 2004, article in the *Montgomery Advertiser*:

> "During the bombings of the summer of 1963, her father and other neighborhood men guarded the streets at night to keep white vigilantes at bay. Rice said her staunch defense of gun rights comes from those days. She has argued that if the guns her father and neighbors carried had been registered, they could have been confiscated by the authorities, leaving the black community defenseless."

Reverend John Wesley Rice never crossed the dividing line between self-defense and aggression. One man who did, though, was Robert Williams, President of the Monroe, North Carolina, NAACP. In the mid-1950s, Williams began leading demonstrations against the city's whites-only policy at the city swimming pool. Ku Klux Klan death threats came by telephone. Thousands of people gathered at Klan rallies to denounce both Williams and Dr. Albert Perry, another Monroe civil rights advocate. Williams responded by chartering an official NRA gun club, and using it to teach black people how to defend themselves.

Civil rights volunteers, in groups of 50-a-night, took turns standing guard at Albert Perry's house. They dug foxholes, piled up sandbags, and kept steel helmets and gas masks handy. They also stockpiled over 600 firearms.

On the night of October 5, 1957, a Klan motorcade approached the Perry house. The civil rights workers opened fire, having been told not to shoot unless necessary. As the writer Julian Mayfield recalled in James Forman's book *The Making of Black Revolutionaries*:

> "The fire was blistering, disciplined and frightening. The motorcade of about eighty cars, which had begun in a spirit of good fellowship, disintegrated into chaos, with panicky, robed men fleeing in every direction. Some had to abandon their automobiles and continue on foot."

Two years later, Williams began to advocate more than mere resistance to white attacks. On the steps of a courthouse, following trials in which two white men were acquitted of allegedly attacking black women, Williams called for black lynching of white criminals: "if it's necessary to stop lynching with lynching, then we must be willing to resort to that method."

Williams was suspended from the NAACP. He appealed to the NAACP's National Convention. The NAACP convention delegates upheld the suspension, and adopted a Resolution observing that Williams "suggested violence as a means of redress of wrongs and not in self-defense or rights of person and property."

The Convention also adopted a Preamble to the Resolutions Committee report, stating: "we do not deny but reaffirm the right of individual and collective self-defense against unlawful assaults. The NAACP has consistently over the years supported this right by defending those who have exercised the right of self defense..."

Daisy Bates, the Little Rock civil rights leader whose family was armed for self-defense with a Colt .45, spoke in favor of the suspension. The resolution suspending Williams and the addition of the Preamble language about self-defense were both adopted unanimously by the Convention. However, the delegates were voting according to the "unit rule," whereby the delegates from a given region would cast their votes in accordance with the preference of the majority of the delegates within that region. Press reports suggested that there had been 17 votes (out of 781) against condemning Williams, although, pursuant to the unit rule, the official tally was unanimous. There was no suggestion that any of the delegates had voted against the self-defense language in the Preamble.

Also speaking in favor of the suspension resolution had been Rev. Martin Luther King, Jr. King predicted that mass non-violent actions—boycotts, marches, sit-ins, and the like—would liberate blacks, and "retaliatory violence" would not. At the same time, King distinguished Williams' call for lynchings from violence "exercised in self-defense." King described the latter type of violence "as moral and legal" in all societies, and noted that not even Gandhi condemned it.

The civil rights movement of the 20th century is rightly celebrated as one of the greatest victories of non-violent protest in history. But not committing aggressive violence is not equivalent to submitting passively to thugs and murderers. As even the most committed civil rights advocates understood, self-defense is an essential human right; the effect, and often the intent, of gun laws was to take that right away from people who had no other protection. Civil Rights triumphed thanks to people who were willing to put themselves in harm's way—and to defend themselves while doing so.

SELECTIVE DISARMAMENT: NO GUNS FOR THE POOR

When wolves hunt, they pick the easiest prey at the fringe of the herd. Gun control proponents also specialize in picking the most vulnerable, those who are least able to fight back politically. In the United States, the strategy of picking on the most vulnerable targets has often resulted in gun control being aimed at the poor, especially minorities.

A case in point is bans on small, inexpensive handguns. Proponents of the ban emphasize that they are not targeting expensive hunting rifles but merely want to outlaw the small guns that they wrongly call "junk guns" or "Saturday Night Specials".

The kind of people who would be disarmed by "junk gun" laws are people like Gina Cushon. A black woman who lived in Colorado Springs, Ms. Cushon used a small, inexpensive Lorcin handgun to defend her family against a large, drunk male neighbor who was breaking down her door and screaming that he would "kick her ass." Although an overzealous prosecutor brought charges against Ms. Cushon, she was acquitted by a jury because her actions were within the scope of Colorado's self-defense laws.

The campaigners against so-called "junk guns" make sanctimonious claims about just wanting guns to be safe and reliable. Yet their proposed bans always contain an exemption allowing the police to possess and carry such guns—as if the police should have unsafe and unreliable firearms. The police exemption shows that the objective of those laws is not getting rid of unreliable guns but rather taking guns away from poor people.

After John Hinckley's assassination attempt, Handgun Control, Inc., instigated a lawsuit against the company that had made Hinckley's small gun. (Had Hinckley used a bigger, more expensive gun, James Brady and President

Reagan would probably both have been killed.) The federal district court in Washington, DC, rejected the suit, and noted that government action against so-called "Saturday Night Specials" or "ghetto guns" requires one to

> "assume that anyone residing in a 'ghetto' is criminal or suspect. The fact is, of course, that while blighted areas may be some of the breeding places of crime, not all residents of are so engaged, and indeed, most persons who live there are lawabiding but have no other choice of location. But they, like their counterparts in other areas of the city, may seek to protect themselves, their families and their property against crime, and indeed, may feel an even greater need to do so since the crime rate in their community may be higher than in other areas of the city. Since one of the reasons they are likely to be living in the 'ghetto' may be due to low income or unemployment, it is highly unlikely that they would have the resources or worth to buy an expensive handgun for self defense." [*Delahanty v. Hinckley*, 686 F. Supp. 920 (D.DC July 1986).]

As a 1985 study by Professors James Wright and Peter Rossi for the National Institute of Justice concluded: "The people most likely to be deterred from acquiring a handgun by exceptionally high prices or by the non-availability of certain kinds of handguns are not felons intent on arming themselves for criminal purposes (who can, if all else fails, steal the handgun they want), but rather poor people who have decided they need a gun to protect themselves against the felons but who find that the cheapest gun on the market costs more than they can afford to pay."

The model set by the white supremacist Tennessee legislature in 1870 (facially neutral gun laws banning less-expensive guns so as to disarm blacks) is still working today. The Gun Control Act of 1968 bars the import of guns not "particularly suitable" for sporting or recreational purposes.

According to the Bureau of Alcohol, Tobacco, Firearms and Explosives, casual target shooting ("plinking") is not a recreational activity, whereas formal target matches are. Thus, inexpensive handguns commonly used for plinking are barred from import. The effect is to allow imports of expensive guns favored by wealthy shooters while barring guns affordable by poor people.

The ban on so-called "assault weapons" (ordinary guns with politically incorrect cosmetics) was driven by a propaganda campaign claiming that the guns were the "weapon of choice" of gangs—in contrast to "sporting" guns.

The subtext was telling white or middle-class hunters who lived in the suburbs that "their" guns were not at risk. The anti-gunners just wanted to take away guns from "gang members" with darker skins, in the inner cities.

The bait-and-switch worked. Not until after the "assault weapons" ban was enacted did many gun owners realize that their high quality, expensive M1A rifles were now "assault weapons—and that they would no longer be able to buy new 13- or 15-round magazines for their pistols.

Until blocked by a federal court in 1994, the police in Chicago would enter public housing apartments without a warrant and conduct room-to-room metal detector sweeps for guns. The searchers rummaged through drawers, refrigerators, cabinets, and personal effects, confiscating even lawfully purchased rifles and shotguns. [*Pratt v. Chicago Housing Authority*, 155 Federal Rules Decisions 177 (N.D. Ill., 1994); 848 F. Supp. 792 (N.D. Ill., 1994).] LeRoy Martin, then the Chicago police chief, declared his admiration for Nazi and Communist Chinese police practices.

President Clinton praised the Chicago searches, and pushed for a complete ban on gun possession in all public housing units, in which residents would have been forced to "consent" to warrantless searches of their homes. After the *Heller* decision, the NRA and the Second Amendment Foundation brought a suit which ended the ban on firearms ownership in public housing in San Francisco.

Every family deserves to be able to protect itself, whether the family is rich, poor, or in-between, and regardless of skin color or ethnic origins. That's what Dr. Ossian Sweet fought for decades ago, and that's what the Second Amendment fight is still about today.

THE ANTI-GUN AGENDA

CHAPTER 3

BAIT-'N'-SWITCH:
GUN-PROHIBITION LOBBYISTS ARE AFTER MUCH MORE THAN AK-47S

The September 13, 2004, expiration of the federal ban on so-called "assault weapons" was a constitutional moment—as significant for the Second Amendment as the March 3, 1801, expiration of the Alien and Sedition Acts was for the First Amendment. These federal laws were not found unconstitutional by any court, but the laws expired in disgrace because our political system, as expressed through congressional elections, determined them to be infringements on the Bill of Rights.

As detailed by Leonard Levy in his book *Origins of the Bill of Rights*, the political defeat of the Alien and Sedition Acts resulted in a much broader, more speech-protective understanding of the First Amendment. The political defeat of gun prohibition had a similar effect.

There is an important difference between the gun ban enacted in 1994 and the speech ban enacted in 1798. The proponents of the Alien and Sedition Acts were aiming to ban particular types of speech—but nothing more. The Acts were not the work of a lobby that wanted to outlaw most speech, and that saw the speech restrictions of 1798 as merely "a good first step." In contrast, the primary significance of the "assault-weapon" ban was, and still is, paving the way for much more extensive firearms prohibition and confiscation.

In an April 5, 1996, column in the *Washington Post*, Charles Krauthammer, who forthrightly supports total gun prohibition, wrote, "Passing a law like the assault weapons ban is a symbolic—purely symbolic—move in that direction. Its only real justification is not to reduce crime but to desensitize the public to the regulation of weapons in preparation for their ultimate confiscation."

Krauthammer was right. The firearms affected by the 1994 ban were not machine guns; those weapons have been strictly regulated ever since the National Firearms Act of 1934. They did not fire faster than other guns, or use more powerful bullets; they were rarely used in crime.

The 1994 ban squeaked through Congress by just a single vote in both the House and the Senate. To pass anything, proponents had to make significant concessions, such as the now-elapsed ten-year sunset, and removing the proposed registration requirement for lawfully-owned guns made before the ban. Likewise, the executive branch was denied any power to ban additional guns. The Clintons exercised such power anyway, by administratively banning the import of hundreds of models of guns during Clinton's second term—a violation of Bill Clinton's promise to wary Congressional Democrats that the 1994 law would be the end of his administration's anti-gun efforts.

The federal ban covered 19 types of guns by name, and about 200 other guns by generic description. Because the ban defined "assault weapons" by cosmetic features—such as whether a gun had a bayonet lug or a particular kind of grip—it was easy for manufacturers to comply with the ban simply by removing the offending cosmetics.

The relatively limited ban was, however, far less than the gun-prohibition lobbies had wanted, and far less than they still demand. By refusing to re-enact the sunsetting 1994 ban, Congress recognized that the real issue at stake is not just the manufacture of some particular firearms, but the fundamental goal of the gun-prohibition lobbies: the creation of administrative authority to ban and confiscate firearms used for self-defense, as contained in the "assault weapon" bills which have been and are being pushed by anti-gun lobbies.

So-called "assault weapons" first became a major national issue on January 17, 1989, when a drifter named Patrick Purdy attacked a crowded school playground in Stockton, California with a semi-automatic rifle and two pistols. After slaughtering five children and wounding many more, Purdy killed himself.

Purdy had a long police record for offenses such as robbery, receiving stolen property, and the sale of illegal weapons. He even vandalized his mother's car when she refused to give him money to buy drugs. But instead of being sent to prison for his crimes, he always slipped through the cracks of the system, avoided a felony conviction, and wound up back on the street.

In addition, Purdy, a mildly retarded alcoholic, had a record of mental disease for which he should have been committed and treated. In April 1987, he was arrested for firing a pistol at trees near Lake Tahoe. He told the sheriff's deputy that he had a duty to "overthrow the suppressor." After a suicide attempt in jail, he was described in a mental-health report as "a danger to himself and others." The California criminal-justice system put him back on the street again and again and again, and once he and his victims were dead, the gun-prohibition movement incited an angry public to crack down on law-abiding gun owners.

Bills introduced in Congress shortly after the Stockton murders set the stage for broad prohibition of firearms. Ohio Senator Howard Metzenbaum introduced an "assault weapon" bill empowering the Treasury Department (which at the time was in charge of the Bureau of Alcohol, Tobacco, and Firearms) to administratively ban any self-loading gun that could accept a magazine of more than ten rounds. A gun cannot tell the difference between an eight-round clip and a twelve-round clip: Thus, many millions of rifles, and the majority of handguns, would have been subject to prohibition.

Washington, DC, had a similar law, which outlawed any self-loading gun which can accept a magazine of 12 or more rounds. As a result, all semi-automatic handguns and rifles were banned in the District, because they were legally defined as "machine guns."

The Metzenbaum bill directly outlawed over 150 rifles (including .22 caliber) by companies including Remington, Mossberg, and Winchester, and also banned about 75 handguns, including the Glock pistols and the Colt 1911. Quite obviously, a .22-caliber Winchester rifle, or a Colt pistol invented in 1911, were not the types of guns the public was thinking about when the gun-prohibitionists were shrieking about AK-47 rifles.

But the Metzenbaum bill, like all of the "assault-weapon" bills, was really a bait-and-switch. The AK-47 is a Soviet military rifle, which can fire automatically. (If you press the trigger, the gun will fire until all the ammunition has been used.) According to the Defense Intelligence Agency, the AK-47 is a true "assault rifle": It is carried on the battlefield, can be fired automatically, and fires an intermediate-sized bullet. There are only a few hundred AK-47 rifles in the US, mostly in military museums and other collections.

None of the "assault-weapon" bills applied to the AK-47, because the AK-47 was already stringently regulated by the National Firearms Act of 1934, which applies to all automatics. The "assault-weapon" bills were about a) guns that looked like the AK-47 or other military rifles, and b) as many other guns as could be banned, depending on the political climate.

The gun-prohibition lobbies recognize that passing gun bans through a legislature is very difficult, so the lobbies have been diligent in attempting to create administrative authority for gun bans by unelected bureaucrats.

In the House of Representatives, California Democrat Fortney "Pete" Stark introduced legislation to prohibit every self-loading gun that was based on a military or police design. The first self-loading gun *not* based on a military design was not even invented until the 1920s. With the exception of some specialized hunting rifles and target guns, most guns are ultimately derivative of police or military design. Low-caliber pistols such as the .22 Ruger or Colt .25 would have been outlawed under legislation that was sold to the public as merely controlling a few unusual "assault rifles."

In 1990, the House Judiciary Committee went even further, passing H.R. 4225 by Rep. William Hughes of New Jersey. The bill banned the possession or sale of *any* rifle that the Treasury Department did not consider "particularly suitable" for sport. This would have meant the prohibition of all rifles used mainly for self-defense, and all rifles mainly used for target shooting; the Treasury Department, in implementing President George H.W. Bush's administrative prohibition on the import of so-called "assault rifles," had declared in 1989 that the only kinds of guns "suitable for sporting purposes" were guns that were commonly used for hunting.

The notion that target shooting is not a "sporting use" of firearms is nonsense, for target shooting is the oldest of the modern Olympic sports. And many "assault rifles" are required for competition in the top target-shooting competitions, such as the National Matches held every year at Camp Perry, Ohio. To acknowledge target-shooting as a sport would have required acknowledging that most guns labeled "assault rifles" are sporting guns.

Politically speaking, passing gun-confiscation statutes is even harder than passing a prohibition on the future sale of guns. But gun-prohibition advocates did their best. After the Stockton murders, Rep. Howard Berman (D-Los Angeles) introduced H.R. 669 to confiscate 125 models of rifles, 33 different 9mm and .45 caliber pistols, and even four shotguns.

In New York City, gun-prohibition advocates were able to pass a confiscation bill, and the police used gun owner-registration lists to go door to door to persecute registered gun owners who had not provided the city with proof that their guns had been surrendered or moved out of the city.

Testifying in favor the New York City law, a representative from Handgun Control, Inc., (which later changed its name to the Brady Campaign) argued that any gun capable of holding more than six rounds should be considered an "assault weapon."

More recently, the Million Mom March (a subsidiary of the Brady Campaign) has urged that all pump-action guns be prohibited. A pump-action gun is, obviously, not a machine gun or a semi-automatic gun. Pump-action shotguns and rifles are pervasive in American hunting.

Since the expiration of the 1994 federal ban, the gun-prohibition lobbies have united around "assault weapon" bills to outlaw guns from companies such as Winchester, Remington, and Springfield, as well the venerable M1 Garand. The bills would ban guns that were specifically declared to be "recreational firearms" by the 1994 federal gun-ban law. The proposals give the Attorney General unilateral authority to ban any semi-automatic rifle or shotgun that he decides is not "particularly suitable" for sporting purposes.

The bills even ban the semi-automatic Remington 11-87 shotgun that presidential candidate John Kerry received as a gift on Labor Day 2004 in Racine, West Virginia. S. 1431, co-sponsored by Senator Kerry, said that an "assault weapon" is any semi-automatic rifle or shotgun with a "pistol grip."

According to the bill, "The term 'pistol grip' means a grip, a thumbhole stock, or any other characteristic that can function as a grip." Kerry's new Remington has a protrusion below the stock, which a person could grip. The protrusion is not a "pistol grip" in the ordinary meaning of the term, but it is a "pistol grip" as defined by S. 1431.

Although Kerry's failure to wear eye and ear protection while shooting set a bad example on gun safety, Kerry has demonstrated that he's a pretty good trap shooter; he obviously recognized the Remington he received as a high-quality trap gun. Kerry has consistently stated that while he favors "assault weapon" prohibition, he strongly opposes banning sporting guns. Thus, John Kerry, like many other Americans, was a victim of the gun-prohibition lobbies' bait-and-switch.

Kerry was right when he says that nobody needs an AK-47 to go hunting. Kerry has been duped, however, into believing that "assault-weapon" laws are about banning the AK-47, rather than about banning as many ordinary guns as possible, including Kerry's shotgun.

DEFENSELESS ON THE BAYOU: NEW ORLEANS GUN CONFISCATION

After Hurricane Katrina, the government of New Orleans devolved from its traditional status as an elective kleptocracy into something far more dangerous: an anarcho-tyranny—that is, a government that refuses to protect the public from criminals and does prevent people from protecting themselves. At the orders of New Orleans Mayor Ray Nagin, the New Orleans Police, the National Guard, the Oklahoma National Guard, and US Marshals began breaking into homes at gunpoint, confiscating lawfully-owned firearms, and evicting the residents. "No one is allowed to be armed. We're going to take all the guns," said P. Edwin Compass, III, the superintendent of police.

In the days after the hurricane, about 15 percent of the police abandoned their posts; some joined the looting spree. For several days, the police who stayed on the job did not act to stop the looting that was going on right in front of them. To the extent that any homes or businesses were saved, the saviors were the many good citizens of New Orleans who defended their families, homes, and businesses with their own firearms.

These citizens were operating within their legal rights. Louisiana law authorizes citizen's arrests for any felony, and in the past (in the 1964 case *McKellar v. Mason*), a Louisiana court held that shooting a property thief in the spine was a legitimate citizen's arrest.

The aftermath of the hurricane featured prominent stories of citizens legitimately defending lives and property. New Orleans lies on the north side of the Mississippi River, and the city of Algiers is on the south. The *Times-Picayune* detailed how dozens of neighbors in one part of Algiers had formed a militia. After a car-jacking and an attack on a home by looters, the neigh-

31

borhood recognized the need for a common defense; the inhabitants shared firearms, took turns on patrol, and guarded the elderly. Although the initial looting resulted in a gun battle, once the patrols began, the militia never had to fire a shot. Likewise, the Garden District of New Orleans, one of the city's top tourist attractions, was protected by armed residents.

The good gun-owning citizens of New Orleans and the surrounding areas ought to have been thanked for helping to save some of their city after Mayor Nagin, incoherent and weeping, had fled to Baton Rouge. Yet instead these citizens were victimized by a new round of home invasions and looting—government-organized, for the purpose of firearms confiscation.

The Mayor and Governor did have the legal authority to mandate evacuation, but failure to comply is a misdemeanor; so the authority to use force to compel evacuation went no further than the power to effect a misdemeanor arrest. The preemptive confiscation of every private firearm in the city far exceeded any reasonable attempt to carry out misdemeanor arrests for persons who disobeyed orders to leave.

Louisiana statutory law allowed some restrictions on firearms during extraordinary conditions. One statute said that after the Governor proclaims a state of emergency (as Governor Blanco had done), "the chief law enforcement officer of the political subdivision affected by the proclamation may...promulgate orders...regulating and controlling the possession, storage, display, sale, transport and use of firearms, other dangerous weapons and ammunition." But the statute did not, and could not, supersede the Louisiana Constitution, which declares that "The right of each citizen to keep and bear arms shall not be abridged, but this provision shall not prevent the passage of laws to prohibit the carrying of weapons concealed on the person."

The power of "regulating and controlling" is not the same as the power of "prohibiting and controlling." The emergency statute actually drew the distinction in its language, which refers to "prohibiting" price-gouging, sale of alcohol, and curfew violations, but only to "regulating and controlling" firearms. Accordingly, the police superintendent's order "prohibiting" firearms possession was beyond his lawful authority. It was an illegal order.

We saw an awful truth in New Orleans: A disaster can bring out predators ready to loot, rampage, and pillage the moment that they have the opportunity. There was another awful truth: There is no shortage of police officers and National Guardsmen who will obey illegal orders to threaten peaceful citizens at gunpoint and confiscate their firearms.

A WORLD WITHOUT GUNS

"Imagine the world without guns" was a bumper sticker that began making the rounds after the murder of ex-Beatle John Lennon on December 18,

1980. Lennon's widow, Yoko Ono, has served as a spokesperson for Handgun Control, Inc.

So let's try hard to imagine what a world without guns would look like. It isn't hard to do. But be forewarned: It's not a pretty picture.

The way to get to a gun-free world, the gun-prohibition groups tell us, is to pass laws banning guns. So we can begin by imagining the enactment of laws which ban all non-government possession of firearms.

It's not likely that local bans will do the job. Take, for example, New York's 1911 Sullivan Law, which imposed a very restrictive handgun-licensing scheme on New York City. In recent decades, administrative abuses have turned the licensing statute into near-prohibition, except for tenacious people who navigate a deliberately obstructive licensing system. Yet New York City has one or two million illegal guns, according to government officials.

Laws affect mainly those willing to obey them. Where there's an unfulfilled need—and money to be made—there's usually a way around the law. Enter the black market, which flourishes all the more vigorously with ever-increasing restrictions and prohibitions.

So let's imagine, instead, a nationwide gun ban, or maybe even a worldwide ban.

Then again, heroin and cocaine have been illegal in the United States, and most of the world, for nearly a century. Huge resources have been devoted to suppressing their production, sale, and use, and many innocent people have been sacrificed in the crossfire of the "drug war." Yet heroin and cocaine are readily available on the streets of American cities.

Perhaps a global prohibition law isn't good enough. Maybe imposing the harshest penalty possible for violation of such a law will give it real teeth: mandatory life in prison for possession of a gun, or for possession of even a single bullet. (We won't imagine the death penalty, since the Ono crowd doesn't like the death penalty.)

On second thought, Jamaica's Gun Court Act of 1974 contained just such a penalty, and even that wasn't sufficient. On August 18, 2001, Jamaican journalist Melville Cooke observed that today, "the only people who do not have an illegal firearm [in this country], are those who do not want one." Violent crime is worse than ever, as gangsters and trigger-happy police commit homicides with impunity, and only the law-abiding are disarmed.

Yet the Jamaican government wants to globalize its failed policy. In July 2001, Burchell Whiteman, Jamaica's Minister of Education, Youth and Culture spoke at the UN gun control conference to demand the "implementation of measures that would limit the production of weapons to levels that meet the needs for defence and national security."

As long as governments are allowed to have guns, there will be gun factories to steal from. Some of these factories might have adequate security measures to prevent theft, including theft by employees. But in a world with 195 nations, many of them governed by kleptocracies, it's preposterous to imagine that some of those "government-only" factories won't become suppliers for the black market. Alternatively, corrupt military and police could supply firearms to the black market.

We'd better revise our strategy. Rather than wishing for laws (which cannot, even imaginably, create a gun-free world), let's be more ambitious, and imagine that all guns vanish. Even guns possessed by government agents. And let's close all the gun factories, too. That ought to put the black market out of business.

Voilà! Instant peace!

Then again.....it's not very difficult to make a workable firearm. As J. David Truby points out in his book *Zips, Pipes, and Pens: Arsenal of Improvised Weapons*, "Today, all of the improvised/modified designs [of firearms] remain well within the accomplishment of the mechanically unskilled citizen who does not have access to firearms through other means."

In the article "Gun-Making as a Cottage Industry," (*Journal on Firearms & Public Policy*, vol. 3) Charles Chandler observed that Americans "have a reputation as ardent hobbyists and do-it-yourselfers, building everything from ship models to home improvements." The one area they have not been very active in is that of firearm construction. And that, Chandler explained, is only because "well-designed and well-made firearms are generally available as items of commerce."

A complete gun ban, or highly restrictive licensing amounting to near-ban, would create a real incentive for gun making to become a "cottage industry."

It is already happening in Great Britain, a consequence of the complete ban on civilian possession of handguns imposed by the Firearms Act of 1997. Not only are the Brits swamped today with illegally imported firearms, but local, makeshift gun factories have sprung up to compete.

British police already know about some of them. Officers from Scotland Yard's Metropolitan Police Serious Crime Group South recovered 12 handgun replicas which were converted to working models. An auto repair shop in London served as the front for the novel illegal gun factory. Police even found some enterprising gun-makers turning screwdrivers into workable firearms, and producing firearms disguised as ordinary key rings.

In short, closing the Winchester Repeating Arms factory—and all the others—will not spell the end of the firearm business.

Just take the case of Bougainville, the largest island in the South Pacific's Solomon Islands chain. Bougainville was the site of a bloody, decade-long secessionist uprising against domination by the government of Papua New Guinea. The conflict was the longest-running confrontation in the Pacific since the end of World War II, and caused the deaths of 15,000 to 20,000 islanders.

During the hostilities, which included a military blockade of the island, one of the goals was to deprive the Bougainville Revolutionary Army (BRA) of its supply of arms. The tactic failed: the BRA simply learned how to make its own guns using materiel and ammunition left over from World WarII.

In fact, at the UN Asia-Pacific Regional Disarmament Conference held in March 2001, it was quietly admitted that the BRA, within ten years of its formation, had managed to manufacture a production copy of the M16 automatic rifle and other machine guns. Given the facts on the ground in Bougainville, there is reason to wonder about the real intent behind the UN's global gun control campaign. If gun bans cannot succeed on a Pacific Island, the prospect for success elsewhere is very slender.

Likewise, the Philippine Islands have long had a thriving cottage industry to manufacture firearms—despite very restrictive gun laws imposed by the Marcos dictatorship and some other regimes.

It looks like we'll need to revisit our fantasy, yet again.

Okay. By imaginary proclamation, not only do all firearms—every last one of them—vanish instantly, there shall be no further manufacturing.

That last part's a bit tricky. Auto repair shops, hobbyists, revolutionaries—everyone with decent machine shop skills—can make a gun from something. So we must go down the same road as drug prohibition: With primary anti-drug laws having proven themselves unenforceable, secondary laws have been added to prohibit possession of items which could be used to manufacture drugs. Even making suspicious purchases at a gardening store can earn you a "dynamic entry" visit from the local SWAT team.

But laws proscribing the possession of gun-manufacturing items would have to be even broader than laws against possession of drug-manufacturing items, because there are so many tools which can be used to make guns, or be made into guns. What we'd really have to do is carefully control every step in the gun-making process. That means the registration of all machine tools, and the federal licensing of plumbers (similar to current federal licensure of pharmacies), auto mechanics, and all those handymen with their screwdrivers. And we'd need to stamp a serial number on pipes (potential gun barrels) in every bathroom and automobile—and everywhere else one finds pipes—and place all the serial numbers in a federal registry.

Today, the antigun lobbies claim they don't want to ban all guns, but the lobbies insist that registration of every single gun and licensing of every gun owner is essential to keep guns from falling into the wrong hands. If so, it's hard to argue that licensing and registration of gun manufacturing items would not be essential to prevent illicit production of guns.

Control of the manufacturing process would be a very expensive, complicated proposition. Even a one percent noncompliance rate with the "Firearms Precursors Control Treaty" would leave an immense supply of materials available for black-market gun making.

35

In order to ensure total conformity with the treaty, it's difficult to imagine leaving most existing constitutional protections in place. The mind boggles at the kinds of search and seizure laws required to make certain that people do not possess unregistered metal pipes or screwdrivers!

For example, just to enforce a ban on actual guns (not gun precursors), the Jamaican government needed to wipe out many common law limits on police searches, and many common law guarantees of fair trials. We'd have to trash the US Constitution and the constitutions in most other free nations in order to prevent a black market in gun precursors. Still, as the gun-prohibition lobby always says, if it saves just one life, it's worth it.

But, what if, despite the extreme measures, the black market still functions—as it almost always does, when there is sufficient demand?

It's time to seriously revisit our strategy for a gun-free world. Maybe there's a shortcut.

Okay. Let's make a truly radical, no-holds-barred proposal this time, take a quantum leap in science, and go where no man has gone before. We hereby imagine that, from this day forth, the laws of chemical combustion are revoked. We hereby imagine that gunpowder—and all similar compounds—no longer have the capacity to burn and to release the gases necessary to propel a bullet.

Finally, for the first time, a gun-free world is truly within our grasp—and it's time to see what man hath wrought. And for that, all we have to do is take a look back at the kind of world our ancestors lived in.

To say that life in the pre-gunpowder world was violent would be an understatement. Land travel, especially over long distances, was fraught with danger from murderers, robbers, and other criminals. Most women couldn't protect themselves from rape, except by granting unlimited sexual access to one male in exchange for protection from other males.

Back then, weapons depended on muscle power. Advances in weaponry primarily magnified the effect of muscle power. The stronger one is, the better one's prospects for fighting up close with an edged weapon like a sword or a knife, or at a distance with a bow or a javelin (both of which require strong arms). The ability of old-fashioned edged weapons to inflict carnage on innocents was graphically demonstrated by the stabbing deaths of eight-second graders on June 8, 2001, by former school clerk Mamoru Takuma in gun-free Osaka, Japan.

When it comes to muscle power, young men usually win over women, children, and the elderly. It was warriors who dominated society in gun-free feudal Europe, and a weak man usually had to resign himself to a life of toil and obedience in exchange for a place within the castle walls when evil was afoot.

And what of the women? Rich, strong men had little besides their consciences to stop them from having their way with women who weren't protected by another wealthy strongman.

There's yet another problem with imagining gunpowder out of existence: We get rid of firearms, but we don't get rid of guns. With the advent of the blow gun some 40,000 years ago, man discovered the efficacy of a tube for concentrating air power and aiming a missile, making the eventual appearance of airguns inevitable. So gunpowder or no gunpowder, all we've been doing, thus far, amounts to quibbling over the means for propelling something out of a tube.

Airguns date back to around the beginning of the 17th century. Not airguns like the puny Daisy Red Ryder BB Gun with a compass in the stock, longed for by Ralphie in Jean Shepard's 1984 classic *A Christmas Story*. ("You'll shoot your eye out!")

How about a non-powder gun that can hurl a 7.4 oz. projectile with a muzzle energy of 1,082 foot-pounds? Compare that to the 500 foot-pounds of muzzle energy from a typical .357 Magnum round. Even greater projectile energies are achievable using gases like nitrogen or helium, which create higher pressures than air does.

Before the advent of cartridges pre-loaded with gunpowder, airguns were serious weapons. In fact, three hundred years ago, air-powered guns were among the most powerful and accurate large-bore rifles. While the biggest disadvantages were cost and intricacy of manufacture, airguns were more dependable and could be fired more rapidly than firearms of the same period. A butt-reservoir .31 airgun was carried by Lewis and Clark on their historic expedition, and used successfully for taking game. [Robert D. Beeman, "Proceeding On to the Lewis & Clark Airgun," *Airgun Revue* 6 (2000): 13-33.] Airguns even saw duty in military engagements more than 200 years ago.

Today, fully automatic M-16-style airguns are a reality. It is only because of greater cost relative to powder guns, and the greater convenience afforded by powder arms, that airgun technology has not been pushed to its lethal limits.

Other non-powder weapon systems have competed for man's attention, as well. The 20th century was the bloodiest century in the history of mankind. By far the greatest number of deliberate killings occurred during the genocides and democides perpetrated by governments against disarmed populations. The instruments of death included Zyklon B gas, machetes, and starvation.

To imagine a world with no guns is to imagine a world in which the strong rule the weak, in which women are dominated by men, and in which minorities are easily abused or mass-murdered by majorities. Practically speaking, a firearm is the only weapon that allows a weaker person to defend herself from a larger, stronger group of attackers, and to do so at a distance. As George Orwell observed, a weapon like a rifle "gives claws to the weak."

The failure of imagination among people who yearn for a gun-free world is the naïve assumption that getting rid of claws will get rid of the desire to dominate and kill. The undeniable fact is that when the weak are deprived of claws (or firearms), the strong will have access to other weapons, including sheer muscle power. A gun-free world would be much more dangerous for women, and much safer for brutes and tyrants.

The one society in history that successfully gave up firearms was Japan in the 17th century, as detailed in Noel Perrin's book *Giving Up the Gun: Japan's Reversion to the Sword 1543-1879*. An isolated island with a totalitarian dictatorship, Japan was able to get rid of the guns. Historian Stephen Turnbull summarized the result:

> "The growing social mobility of peasants was thus flung suddenly into reverse. The *ikki*, the warrior-monks, became figures of the past...Hidéyoshi had deprived the peasants of their weapons....If a peasant offended a samurai he might be cut down on the spot by the samurai's sword." [*The Samurai: A Military History* (New York: Macmillan, 1977).]

The inferior status of the peasantry having been affirmed by civil disarmament, the Samurai enjoyed *kiri-sute gomen*, permission to kill and depart. Any disrespectful member of the lower class could be executed by a Samurai's sword.

The Japanese disarmament laws helped mold the culture of submission to authority which facilitated Japan's domination by an imperialist military dictatorship in the 1930s, which led the nation into a disastrous world war.

In short, the one country that created a truly gun-free society created a society of harsh class oppression, in which the strongmen of the upper class could kill the lower classes with impunity. When a racist, militarist, imperialist government took power, there was no effective means of resistance. The gun-free world of Japan turned into just the opposite of the gentle, egalitarian utopia of John Lennon's song "Imagine."

Instead of imagining a world without a particular technology, what about imagining a world in which the human heart grows gentler, and people treat each other decently? This is part of the vision of many of the world's great religions. Although we have a long way to go, there is no denying that hundreds of millions of lives have changed for the better because people came to believe what these religions teach.

If a truly peaceful world is attainable—or, even if unattainable, worth striving for—there is nothing to be gained from the futile attempt to eliminate all guns. A more worthwhile result can flow from the changing of human hearts, one soul at a time.

Some Deceptions and Errors Used to Promote Anti-Gun Laws

CHAPTER 4

The Legislative Legend: "Cop-killer" bullets

There never has been a "cop-killer" bullet. The issue is a fiction, invented for purposes of politics, not public safety. In any case, since 1986, federal law has prohibited the rare types of handgun ammunition that have unusual abilities to penetrate body armor.

The Bureau of Alcohol, Tobacco, Firearms and Explosives reports that current ammunition laws are fully sufficient to protect the police, and that attempts to change these laws could lead to increased police fatalities. Notwithstanding the strong warning, some lobbyists and politicians continue to play on public misunderstanding, by using the so-called "cop-killer" issue to demand the power to ban standard rifle ammunition used for hunting.

The story of the nonexistent "cop-killer" bullet begins in 1976 in Massachusetts, when a handgun-confiscation initiative was defeated in a landslide. Then, in 1982 in California, a handgun "freeze" initiative also lost overwhelmingly. The gun-prohibition lobbies began to realize that they would have to work more incrementally, rather than pushing for prohibition outright.

The prohibition lobbies also realized that the police were one of their worst problems. While a few police chiefs or sheriffs could always be found to support prohibition, the vast majority of police—both commanders and line officers—were extremely skeptical of gun control. Something had to be done to turn the police (or at least their Washington lobbyists) against the National Rifle Association.

The something, ironically, was an obscure type of ammunition invented by police officers two decades before. These bullets were known as KTW bullets, after the initials of the three persons who invented them: Dr. Paul Kopsch, and police officers Daniel Turcus and Don Ward.

While ordinary bullets have a lead core, the KTW bullets use brass or iron. The KTW bullet has a conical shape, and was especially designed for shooting through glass or a car door. Of course neither the KTW bullet nor any other bullet was invented for the purpose of killing police officers.

KTW bullets have not been available for sale to the general public since the 1960s.

"Cop-killer" bullets are sometimes called "Teflon bullets," but this name reflects a serious misunderstanding. For example, in the movie *Lethal Weapon 3*, a so-called "Teflon bullet" from a medium-power handgun was supposedly able to penetrate several inches of hardened steel on a bulldozer blade. In the real world, no bullet could perform such a stunt.

Actually, a Teflon coating is applied to the outside of a wide variety of ordinary ammunition. Teflon reduces the lead abrasion caused by the bullet's movement down the barrel of the gun. Thus, the barrel is kept cleaner, and is protected from excessive wear. Also, reduced abrasion means that fewer tiny lead particles are produced, so the air is cleaner—an especially important consideration at indoor shooting ranges.

In addition, a Teflon coating on a bullet also makes the bullet safer to use for self-defense. The Teflon helps the bullet "grab" a hard surface such as glass or metal, and thus significantly reduces the risk of a dangerous ricochet. Similarly, canes or walking sticks are often coated with Teflon, so that they will not slip on hard, smooth surfaces.

So in order to reduce ricochets, KTW bullets as well as many ordinary types of defensive ammunition use Teflon or similar substances.

As police officers know, the vests that they wear are "bullet-resistant," not "bullet-proof." The Bureau of Alcohol, Tobacco, Firearms and Explosives explains that "armor protection is rated in accordance with a specific threat. There is no such thing as 'bullet-proof' armor."

Manufactured from Kevlar (a synthetic fiber that is five times stronger than steel), body armor comes in a variety of grades. The higher the grade, the bulkier and less comfortable the armor is to wear, but the more ammunition it can stop. The highest grades of armor are often called "tactical armor" or "hard armor," and may contain steel or titanium.

At the top of the scale is Threat Level IV armor, which can block even a high-powered rifle bullet. It takes a very strong vest to stop a big-game hunting-rifle bullet: The bullet travels at a high velocity, due to the long length of the rifle barrel; and the bullet has a large mass, because a hunting-rifle bullet must be large enough to bring down a moose, elk, or other large mammal.

Almost the only people who wear hard armor are SWAT team members on high-risk missions. Far more common for ordinary police use is "soft" body armor, made from Kevlar, and rated at Threat Levels IIA through IIIA. Level IIA armor can stop most handgun ammunition, while Level IIIA can stop almost any handgun bullet. Handgun ammunition is much easier to stop than rifle ammunition, since the handgun barrel is much shorter (less velocity) and handgun bullets are smaller (less mass).

Even before the 1986 federal law restricting "armor-piercing ammunition," there had never been a case of a police officer killed with such ammunition penetrating a vest. The BATFE studied every police officer shooting in the years 1985-94 and reported: "No law enforcement officer in the United States has died as a result of a round of armor piercing ammunition, as defined, having been fired from a handgun, subsequently penetrating an officer's protective body armor causing lethal injuries."

Indeed, the BATFE concluded that in the period studied, there had not been *any* instances of officers being killed by *any* type of handgun ammunition penetrating body armor.

Yet in 1995 President Clinton announced his support for a massive new ban on many ordinary types of ammunition. In the speech, President Clinton spoke emotionally about a Chicago police officer who had been fatally shot because a "cop-killer" bullet penetrated his vest. There was only one problem with the story: It wasn't true. The officer was shot by a criminal who used ordinary ammunition. One shot hit the officer in the head. Another shot went through *an opening* in the vest. No shot penetrated the vest.

Although the "cop-killer"-bullet issue had no factual substance, it was politically potent. As with so many other terms invented by gun-prohibition lobbyists, the very name biased the debate in favor of prohibition. The national-al media showed little interest in reporting facts such as the origin of the KTW bullet, or that the KTW was not for sale to the public, or that no police officer had ever been shot at or killed with such a bullet, or that Teflon didn't make bullets more powerful.

Once the bait was set, the switch was made. After the sensational, inaccurate January 1982 broadcast on a NBC report on "cop-killer bullets," New York Democratic Rep. Mario Biaggi (who would later leave Congress due to felony convictions involving extensive personal corruption) introduced a bill to outlaw all ammunition capable of penetrating soft body armor if fired from a handgun with a six-inch barrel. The standard would lead to a ban on most rifle ammunition, since most rifle ammunition will penetrate soft body armor, and many common types of rifle ammunition fit some handguns. Soft body armor is designed to stop handgun ammunition, not rifle ammunition.

When the fact was pointed out, media figures sneered that gun owners wanted to go deer-hunting with cop-killer Teflon bullets, as if deer were wearing body armor.

As the debated continued, the constant repetition of the phrase "cop-killer bullet" drove a wedge between Second Amendment groups and many police officers. The Fraternal Order of Police (FOP)—the largest rank-and-file police group in the U.S —had been an enthusiastic supporter of the McClure-Volkmer Firearms Owners' Protection Act (FOPA), a bill to reform abusive enforcement of the 1968 Gun Control Act.

But after the "cop-killer" controversy, the police group's director switched sides, and announced that FOPA was a grave threat to the lives of police officers. FOPA itself had nothing to do with KTW or Teflon ammunition, but the FOP director's broader point was his anger over the "cop-killer bullet" issue.

Many of the friends of the Second Amendment in Congress and the Reagan White House quietly insisted that something be done to get rid of the controversy.

Accordingly, the National Rifle Association and Representative Biaggi reached a compromise. Instead of a penetration standard (which would ban most rifle ammunition), a content standard was adopted. The sale or import of handgun ammunition with a significant amount of steel, titanium, or other metal core was outlawed. The relevant federal regulation specifies that "armor piercing ammunition" is a handgun bullet "constructed entirely" from "tungsten alloys, steel, iron, brass, bronze, beryllium copper, or depleted uranium," or with certain kinds of jackets on the bullet.

Biaggi pronounced that the compromise achieved everything he had wanted. The NRA spread the word that the vote for the compromise would not be scored as a "wrong" vote.

Severe mandatory prison sentences were enacted for use of federally defined "armor-piercing ammunition" in a violent or drug-trafficking crime. The rarity of the actual misuse of such unusual ammunition is demonstrated by the BATFE study of the first decade of the law, 1985-94, reporting that there had only been four prosecutions for use of the ammunition in a crime.

The 1997 BATFE report on the threat to police officers from criminal use of ammunition concluded: "Because the existing laws are working, no additional legislation regarding such laws is necessary. In this matter, to err on the conservative side of the existing status quo laws is to avoid any experimentation with police officer lives that could conceivably lead to numerous additional officer fatalities."

Unfortunately, gun-prohibition lobbies and their congressional allies have continued to call for such dangerous "experimentation."

Under current proposals, if a bullet can penetrate soft body armor (which is designed to stop handguns, not rifles), it could be outlawed. A law proposed by the late Senator Ted Kennedy and several colleagues refers to ammunition "designed" to have "armor-piercing capability." How can one know the inner mind of someone who designed a bullet, perhaps decades ago?

The Kennedy proposal refers to rifle ammunition that has more penetrating capability than "standard" ammunition of the same caliber. In other words, a bureaucrat could decide that "standard" ammunition in a certain caliber has a certain weight and velocity, and any round with a greater weight or velocity could be administratively prohibited.

As the Bureau of Alcohol, Tobacco, Firearms and Explosives urges, the safest approach is to leave existing laws in place—rather than frightening the public and endangering the police in order to score political points. The Fraternal Order of Police agrees, and opposes the Kennedy bill.

MISFIRING AT HARLON CARTER

In August 2000, the *Washington Post* ran a thoughtful and carefully-researched article about the internal politics of the National Rifle Association. Amazingly, the article dealt with the NRA's pro-freedom worldview in a respectful, nuanced manner, rather than with the shrill contempt which so often characterizes the old media.

The article did have some factual errors, such as mistakenly claiming that it was the 1995 Republican Congress, rather than the 1993 Democratic Congress, which passed the Brady Bill.

A much more serious error, however, was the description of the late Harlon Carter, the leading architect of the NRA's transformation into the most powerful civil liberties organization in the history of the world. According to the *Post*, "Asked in 1975 if he would rather let convicted violent felons and the mentally deranged buy guns than endorse a screening process for gun sales, Carter did not hesitate to say yes. That's the 'price we pay for freedom.'"

Not really. At the 1975 congressional hearing, a congressman asked the question described by the *Post*, but when Carter began to answer, the congressman cut him off, saying he wanted a different witness to answer. In the official transcript, Carter's answer is "The price we pay for freedom —".

The *Post's* inadvertent distortion of Carter's meaning was doubtless the product of an interview with someone from a Washington anti-gun lobby, where the politics of personal destruction has been the norm for decades.

Misrepresenting Carter's statement was pretty mild compared to other attacks that Handgun Control, Inc., (now known as the Brady Campaign) launched on Carter. One fundraising letter from HCI featured a picture of Harlon Carter on the envelope. The letter screamed that Carter "has seen to it that thousands of life-loving people like you and me DIE every year—shot with a handgun."

The Handgun Control letter continued: "50 years ago, Carter shot and killed a 15-year-old boy and was convicted of murder."

The letter omitted the fact that Carter was defending his mother's ranch against a gang of intruders led by the "boy," and that the "boy" was menacing Carter with a knife. At the trial, the judge was the prosecutor's father-in-law, and he refused to let Carter introduce evidence of self-defense.

43

Having left out the crucial facts about Carter's innocence, the Handgun Control letter complained that the conviction "was reversed on the technical grounds that the judge had not given the jurors adequate instructions about the law of self-defense." Actually, it wasn't just the instructions that were inadequate; all the evidence about self-defense had been excluded.

Most people would think that a citizen's shooting of a criminal should be judged by whether the citizen was acting in self-defense. But Handgun Control apparently considers innocent persons who shoot criminals to be as bad as common murderers—since self-defense is only a "technicality."

This fits rather well with Mrs. Sarah Brady's standard: "To me, the only reason for guns in civilian hands is for sporting purposes." (Tom Jackson, "Keeping the Battle Alive," *Tampa Tribune*, Oct. 21, 1993.) Vice-President Al Gore claimed that the NRA is against "family values" because the NRA opposes the anti-gun proposals which he copied from HCI, the nation's leading anti-defense lobby.

What kind of family values hold that a son shouldn't protect his mother from violent gangsters with knives?

THE FALLACY OF "43 TO 1"

Perhaps the most enduring factoid of the gun prohibition movement is that a person with a gun in the home is 43 times as likely to shoot someone in the family as to shoot a criminal. This "43 times" figure is the all-time favorite factoid of the gun-prohibition lobby. It's not really true, but it does tell us a lot about the gun-prohibition mindset.

The source of the 43-to-1 ratio is a study of firearm deaths in Seattle homes, conducted by doctors Arthur L. Kellermann and Donald T. Reay ("Protection or Peril?: An Analysis of Firearm-Related Deaths in the Home," *New England Journal of Medicine*, 1986). Kellerman and Reay totaled up the numbers of firearms murders, suicides, and fatal accidents, and then compared that number to the number of firearm deaths that were classified as justifiable homicides. The ratio of murder, suicide, and accidental death to the justifiable homicides was 43 to 1.

This is what the anti-gun lobbies call "scientific" proof that people (except government employees and security guards) should not have guns.

Of the gun deaths in the home, the vast majority are suicides. In the 43-to-1 figure, suicides account for nearly all the 43 unjustifiable deaths.

Counting a gun suicide as part of the increased risk of having a gun in the home is appropriate only if the presence of a gun facilitates a "successful" suicide that would not otherwise occur. But most research suggests that guns do not cause suicide.

In the book *Point Blank: Guns and Violence in America*, Florida State University criminologist Gary Kleck analyzed suicide data for every American city with a population more than 100,000, and found no evidence that any form of gun control (including handgun prohibition) had an effect on the total suicide rate. Gun control did sometimes reduce gun suicide, but not overall suicide.

Notably, Japan, which prohibits handguns and rifles, and regulates shotguns very severely, has a suicide rate more than twice the US level. Many of the northern and central European nations also have very high suicide rates to accompany their strict gun laws. (Of course, if you have any suspicion that anybody in your home might be suicidal, it would be wise for you to ensure that they do not have ready access to guns, tranquilizers, or other potentially lethal items.)

Putting aside the suicides, the Kellermann/Reay figures show 2.39 accidental or criminal deaths by firearm (in the home) for every justifiable fatal shooting. Now, 2 to 1 is a lot less dramatic than 43 to 1, but we still have more unjustifiable gun deaths than justifiable gun deaths in the home.

Yet just as many people who would commit suicide with a gun would use an equally lethal method if guns are unavailable, many of the people who kill themselves in firearm accidents may also be bent on destruction, regardless of the means. The people who cause gun accidents tend to have high rates of "arrests, violence, alcohol abuse, highway crashes, and citations for moving traffic violations." [Julian Waller & Elbert Whorton, "Unintentional Shootings, Highway Crashes, and Acts of Violence," 5 *Accident Analysis & Prevention* 351 (1973).]

Or, as another researcher put it, "The psychological profile of the accident-prone suggests the same kind of aggressiveness shown by most murderers." [Roger Lane, "On the Social Meaning of Homicide Trends in America," in *Violence in America*, vol. I, 1989.]

Without guns, many accident victims might well find some other way to kill themselves "accidentally," such as by reckless driving.

So by counting accidents and suicides, the 43-to-1 factoid ends up including a very large number of fatalities that would have occurred anyway, even if there were no gun in the home.

Now, how about the self-defense homicides, which Kellermann and Reay found to be so rare? Well, the reason that they found such a low total was that they excluded many cases of lawful self-defense. Kellermann and Reay did not count any of the cases where a person who had shot an attacker was acquitted on grounds of self-defense, or cases where a conviction was reversed on appeal on grounds related to self-defense. Yet 40% of women who appeal their murder convictions have the conviction reversed on appeal. ["Fighting Back," *Time*, Jan. 18, 1993.]

In short, the 43-to-1 figure is based on the implausible assumption that all the people who die in gun suicides and gun accidents would not kill themselves with something else if guns were unavailable. The figure is also based on a drastic undercount of the number of lawful self-defense homicides.

Moreover, counting dead criminals to measure the efficacy of civilian handgun ownership is ridiculous. Do we measure the efficacy of our police forces by counting how many people the police lawfully kill every year? The benefits of the police—and of home handgun ownership—are not measured by the number of dead criminals, but by the number of crimes prevented. Simplistic counting of corpses tells us nothing about the real safety value of gun ownership for protection.

Finally, Kellermann and Reay ignore the most important factor in assessing the risks of gun ownership: whose home the gun is in. You don't need a medical researcher to tell you that guns can be misused when in the homes of persons with mental illness related to violence; or in the homes of persons prone to self-destructive, reckless behavior; or in the homes of persons with arrest records for violent felonies; or in the homes where the police have had to intervene to deal with domestic violence. These are the homes from which the vast majority of handgun fatalities come.

To study these high-risk homes and to jump to conclusions about the general population is illogical. We know that possession of an automobile by an alcoholic who is prone to drunk driving may pose a serious health risk. But proof that automobiles in the hands of alcoholics may be risky doesn't prove that autos in the hands of non-alcoholics are risky. Yet the famous Seattle 43-to-1 figure is based on lumping the homes of violent felons, alcoholics, and other disturbed people with the population as a whole. The study fails to distinguish between the large risks of guns in the hands of dangerous people, with the tiny risks (and large benefits) of guns in the hands of ordinary people.

Then again, treating ordinary people according to standards appropriate for criminals and the violently insane is what the gun control movement is all about.

WHAT IF THE GOVERNMENT HAD TO OBEY GUN-CONTROL LAWS?

UCLA law school professor Eugene Volokh asked his weblog readers to "imagine that you had the superpower to add one amendment to the US Constitution...What would it be?"

Here's one proposal: the Goose and Gander Amendment. Since it works as a supplement to the Second Amendment, let's make it Amendment Two-and-a-Half:

> 1. No government agency, nor employee of any government agency, shall be allowed to possess firearms prohibited to the citizens of the state, county, or municipality in which they serve.

2. No government agency, nor any employee of any government agency, shall be exempt from laws and regulations regarding the possession or use of firearms which affect the citizens of the state, county, or municipality in which they serve.

3. All exemptions inconsistent with sections 1 and 2 shall be void beginning on the 30th day after the ratification of this amendment.

4. Nothing in this amendment shall be construed to exempt agencies and employees of the federal government from federal, state, or local laws and regulations related to firearms.

5. Nothing in this amendment shall apply to the Department of Defense or states' National Guards.

This amendment does not in any way restrict existing powers of the federal, state, and local governments to pass gun-control laws. Rather, the gun laws would be strengthened by being of more general applicability. Removing government exemption would provide an incentive for politicians and regulators to pass only those gun-control laws which are truly reasonable.

Suppose that a state wants to outlaw so-called "junk guns" (inexpensive handguns used by poor people for self-defense). The prohibitionists make sanctimonious claims about merely wanting guns to be safe and reliable. Yet the proposed bans always exempt police even though the police especially need safe and reliable handguns.

And in fact, "junk guns" are quite popular with many police officers, who carry them as back-up guns, often in ankle holster because the guns are compact and lightweight. Under the Goose and Gander Amendment, the prohibitionist legislators must explain to the police why guns that they like to carry for police work may no longer be carried—because legislators, after all, understand gun design and function much better than do police officers.

Alternatively, the legislators could admit that the reliability issue is a sham, and that the real goal is to deprive poor people of the only guns they can afford. This goal is so important, the legislators could argue, that it is worthwhile to deprive police officers of their backup guns—since the officers will still be able to carry their expensive primary guns.

Besides wanting to outlaw guns that are too small (inexpensive handguns), gun prohibitionists also want to outlaw guns that are too big—such as .50-caliber target rifles and so-called "assault weapons." (Unlike Goldilocks, the prohibitionists are unable to find any gun which is "just right.")

Under the Goose and Gander Amendment, cities will still be able to ban "assault weapons." Politicians will still be able to claim that the guns have no legitimate purpose, and are not suitable for target shooting (even though many of the banned guns are the primary firearms for rifle competition) or for hunting (even though some of the banned guns are particularly designed for game hunting, such as the Valmet Hunter) or for lawful self-defense (for which almost all the guns are quite effective). While enacting "assault weapon" bans, politicians can continue to assert that only mass murderers and drug dealers would want to own such guns, which are supposedly only good for spray-firing at crowds of innocent people.

Very well, then. We certainly don't want the police to spray-fire at crowds of innocent people. Nor do we want guns that are uniquely attractive to psychopaths to be available to police, since the possibility of owning such a gun might induce a clever psychopath to join the police force for purposes of obtaining extra weaponry.

While it is very, very rare for ordinary people or for law-enforcement officers to use an "assault weapon" in a crime, it is not unheard of. For example, in December 1992, an off-duty Bureau of Indian Affairs police officer opened fire and shot 50 rounds into a bar in Bemidji, Minnesota. He used the Colt AR-15 semiautomatic rifle he had been issued by the government, as well as his own 9mm handgun.

Advocates of a new federal ban on "assault weapons" are fighting for a new, tougher ban. A new ban should not contain the loophole form the old ban, which was codified in 18 US Code § 922(v)(4). The loophole allowed unlimited use and possession of "assault weapons" by law-enforcement officers, "whether on or off duty"—and even allowed possession and use by retired law-enforcement officers.

The gun-prohibition groups assure us that so-called "assault weapons" have no good purpose, that the mere presence of such an awful-looking gun can incite an otherwise law-abiding person to commit a mass murder, and that no amount of background checks or training can ensure that a person is safe enough to own an "assault weapon."

Will the gun-prohibition groups work to close the "assault weapon" loophole? Or will they cynically fight to protect the loophole which, by their own reasoning, is morally indefensible?

Opponents of the Goose and Gander Amendment will point out that police officers are better trained than ordinary citizens. While this may be true, there are plenty of citizens who have voluntarily taken defensive firearms training that is more extensive than what many police officers have received. Besides, allowing highly trained people to own guns whose only purpose is (allegedly) to murder a lot of people quickly would be especially dangerous.

In any case, the Goose and Gander Amendment would still allow governments to impose training for gun owners, or for people who want to possess certain types of firearms. The amendment would simply require that everyone who passes whatever tests and/or background checks the government mandates be treated equally.

The Goose and Gander Amendment would, of course, apply to more than just gun bans. If a state wants to impose a three-day wait to buy a handgun, then the police officers in that state would be required to wait three days before taking possession of a handgun, which is what happens to ordinary citizens. For example, in Illinois a gun owner must obtain a Firearms Owner Identification Card (FOID), which takes several weeks. Yet every time she buys an additional handgun, she still has to wait three days.

It's hard to see the public safety benefit of imposing a "cooling off" period on someone who already owns guns, but if this cooling off period is good for the general public, it would also make sense for government employees. Domestic-violence groups frequently point out that a not insignificant number of police officers are domestic abusers—precisely the kind of impulsive criminals that cooling off periods are supposed to thwart.

While many people think that police officers are the only government employees who carry guns, many other agencies also have armed agents, including the Environmental Protection Agency, the US Forestry Service, the Internal Revenue Service, agricultural inspectors, and others. Under the Goose and Gander Amendment, these employees would still be allowed to carry firearms while on duty—so long as they complied with state law.

In Wisconsin and Illinois, carrying a concealed handgun in a public place for protection is illegal under almost all circumstances—because the legislature has apparently determined that no matter what kind of background check and training one has, there is too great a risk that people carrying guns will shoot each other in traffic jams.

It would be difficult to argue that, simply by virtue of a person's employment by the US Forestry Service or the Department of Agriculture, he is immune to the surges of homicidal emotions that, we are told, strike anyone at any time.

Finally, the Goose and Gander Amendment is progressive, because it ensures that gun laws will sensibly keep up with changing social needs. Gun prohibition lobbies have begun pushing to outlaw the sale of all handguns except high-tech "personalized guns" that meet standards to be set by a bureaucratic commission. Although guns incorporating palm-print readers or similar technology are still in the unreliable prototype stage, the proposals would eventually outlaw all existing handguns.

Amazingly, these prohibition proposals, such as the one that is now law in New Jersey (and will go into effect once two companies put such guns on the market), also contain a government-employee exemption—even though the original reason the federal government began subsidizing personalized gun research was to protect police officers whose guns were snatched by a criminal.

The proponents of outlawing all current handguns and forcing citizens to buy only new-fangled gadgets quite accurately recognize that if the proposal were to apply to the police, the police lobbies would quash the proposal instantly. Police officers are not going to stand for being forced to rely on guns that won't work if the battery wears out, or if the palm-print reader has trouble recognizing a dirt-covered hand. Ninety-nine percent reliability isn't good enough for a gun that you are using against a violent criminal attacker.

Yet the gun-prohibition lobbies are ready to force everyone except government employees to use firearms of questionable reliability—because they consider defensive gun use by non-government employees to be immoral.

That antigun politicians and the lobbyists who support them are so willing to exempt the government from the gun laws suggests that many gun-control laws have less to do with protecting public safety than with disarming the citizenry and exalting the government. The policy reflects a philosophy that sovereignty belongs to the government rather than to the people—which is the opposite of what the Constitution says.

THE HIDDEN AGENDA BEHIND GUN STORAGE LAWS

Responsible gun owners store their guns safely. For over a century, the National Rifle Association and other civic groups have encouraged safe gun storage.

Partly as a result, the fatal gun accident rate for both kids and adults has fallen to an all-time low. Yet anti-gun politicians, and the anti-gun groups are working to turn "safe storage" into a tool for disarming the American public.

Gun owners who think they have nothing to lose from a government takeover of gun storage should look at what has happened in countries such as Canada and Great Britain. There, gun owner apathy has allowed "safe storage" to become the platform for abolishing gun ownership for home protection, for invading the privacy and the homes of gun owners, and for attacking even the simple possession of firearms.

British gun owners have a long tradition of going along with government proposals for "reasonable" restrictions on their rights. But as many Britons found out too late, a restriction that appears reasonable on paper may become quite unreasonable in practice.

British law merely mandates that guns be stored in "a secure place." But Britain has a national gun licensing system, similar to the American system proposed by the Brady Campaign. Because most police administrators in Britain are intensely opposed to citizens owning guns, they use the storage law to make acquiring a gun license as onerous as possible.

One effect of the heavy security costs is to reduce the ability of middle-income or poor people to legally own guns, a goal which has been a constant objective of gun control proponents throughout history. Of course, the requirement that guns be locked in safes makes it nearly impossible for the gun to be used for home protection, and the British police establishment despises the idea of defensive gun ownership.

The requirement that gun owners purchase safes was never democratically enacted by the British Parliament. Rather, the requirement was invented by police administrators, who correctly recognized that any system requiring government permission to buy a gun can be manipulated by anti-gun administrators.

In Canada, the Criminal Code prohibits "careless" storage of a firearm, and gives the government the authority to create storage regulations. What does this mean in practice? Consider some cases:

Hearing suspicious sounds, perhaps from a burglar, a husband took his unloaded rifle with him one night when he looked around his house. A few days later, the wife told a friend about the incident. Aghast, the friend called the police.

The police arrived at the couple's home and bullied their way in. Searching the home, they found the unloaded rifle under a mattress in the bedroom. No children lived in the home. The couple was charged with careless storage of a firearm.

A 67-year-old single woman ran a small boarding house in Ontario. A downstairs tenant began harassing and stalking her. Worried that the woman might pose a threat to the tenant, the police searched her apartment and found several unloaded guns in her closets. She was convicted of storage of a firearm in violation of government regulations. She had been attending school and studying to become a paralegal, but her conviction bars her from a job in the legal field.

In Winnipeg, a 72-year-old woman called a hospital to request that a visiting nurse come over and help her with some medication. Someone from the hospital asked if the woman had any firearms in the home. "Yes," she replied, "my husband has a couple of old hunting rifles down in the rec room."

The police came over immediately and began searching the home. They found several long guns, each with a trigger lock and locked to a rack in the basement. They also found a .25 caliber pistol locked in a bedroom closet, which they had broken into.

The 73-year-old husband came home in the middle of the search, and was immediately handcuffed, and accused of being violent. Other than the fact that he owned guns, there was no evidence that he was violent. His neighbors later signed statements saying they had known him for years, and he had always been peaceful. Eventually the police removed the handcuffs, and told the man that he had never been under arrest.

Gun storage laws sometimes provide a means for police to justify outrageously bad police work. In Medicine Hat, Alberta, a criminal who had charges pending against him tried to buy leniency by claiming that a man named Larry Davies was a marijuana dealer, with over a pound in his house. The Medicine Hat police did nothing to verify the informant's claim, other than looking up Larry Davies' address in the phone book.

The SWAT team, apparently having nothing else to do that day, broke into the Davies household, and forced Larry Davies and three friends to the floor, pointing submachine guns at their heads. A search of the house revealed: Mrs. Davies and her newborn baby, who had come home from the hospital that day; four grams of marijuana (weighing less than a United States 25-cent piece); and a disassembled FN/FAL rifle in a basement closet.

Apparently embarrassed but not repentant about the sloppy police practices and wanton show of force, the government charged Mr. Davies with unsafe storage of a firearm. Happily, a judge threw the charges out of court, noting that whatever Mr. Davies had done was much less of a threat to society than what the police had done.

Canadian courts have sometimes stopped other abusive prosecutions related to gun storage laws. But even then, the victim of the abusive prosecution must spend thousands of dollars in legal fees to avoid a prison sentence of up to two years.

As the late David Tomlinson, President of Canada's National Firearms Association, pointed out, gun storage laws are unenforceable without random police searches of the home. Canada's gun law gives the police the authority to "inspect" private homes to ensure that gun storage laws are being complied with.

Gun storage laws are like laws barring married couples from using birth control: they are unenforceable without massive government intrusions into the sanctity of the home. In 1965, the United States Supreme Court struck down a birth control ban for this very reason. (*Griswold v. Connecticut*, 381 U.S. 479). For the same reason, privacy-minded legislators and citizens should reject turning the government into the home gun storage enforcer.

Gun prohibition almost always moves by incremental steps. Restrictions that would have seemed outrageous if proposed by themselves can appear "reasonable" when they merely advance existing restrictions a few more steps.

In Canada, prohibitionists, such as then-Justice Minister Alan Rock, have used gun storage laws as a justification for imposing universal gun registration, since registration "will create a sense of accountability on the part of the firearms owner to comply with some of the safe storage laws that are in effect."

As the next step, the anti-gun lobbies in Canada have begun pushing for "community storage." Rather than keeping your guns in a safe in your home, you would have to keep your guns at a police station. When you wanted to use your gun for the day, you could check it out from the police station. In the Spring of 2007, Quebec's Prime Minister Jean Charest began a push to impose "community storage" on all handguns and many self-loading long guns.

The anti-gun groups point out that a gun in the home could be stolen, or could be misused in a domestic incident. There is no reason, they argue, for guns to be kept in a home 365 days a year, when the gun may only be used a few days a year.

To counter the anti-gun groups, gun owners in Canada can hardly argue that removing guns from the home makes it impossible to use the guns for home defense. They gave up the moral case for self-defense years ago by arguing that gun ownership was justified for sporting purposes, but not daring to assert that gun ownership is justified for defensive purposes. And by agreeing to "safe storage" laws, the Canadian gun owners gave up the practical ability to use a gun for self-defense in a sudden emergency.

With so much ground already surrendered, Canadian gun owners are reduced to arguing minor points, such as how a centralized gun storage repository might be more vulnerable to theft.

Even conceding on the "community storage" issue will do gun owners no good. In 1996, the British Parliament banned almost all handguns, but allowed owners of single-shot .22s to keep the guns locked in central repositories at gun ranges. The new restrictions only briefly sated the appetite of the British anti-gun lobbies. In 1997, community storage was replaced by its logical consequence, complete prohibition of all handguns.

Storing guns safely is the duty of every gun owner. What makes for safety depends very much on individual circumstances. Safety is, and always has been, the concern of organizations such as the National Rifle Association. In the hands of anti-gun lobbies and government bureaucrats, though, "safe storage" becomes an Orwellian term designed to negate the many safety benefits of the right to keep and bear arms. Home safety is the responsibility of the family, not the state.

RELIGIOUS PERSPECTIVES ON FREEDOM FROM THE ANCIENT WORLD

CHAPTER 5

TO YOUR TENTS, O ISRAEL

When the founders of the American republic grappled with the question of how to create government that was strong enough to protect the nation, but not so strong as to endanger the people's liberties, one of their most important sources of wisdom was the Old Testament's history of the nation of Israel. In our times, when Bible literacy (especially knowledge of the historical books of the Old Testament) is much more limited than it was in the 18th century, there are still important lessons to be learned from the history of an ancient people.

According to the Old Testament's narrative, the twelve tribes of Israel escaped from slavery in Egypt and conquered most of the Promised Land of Canaan, after which they continued to associate themselves in a loose confederation. They defended themselves with a militia rather than a professional army. The *Book of Judges* details a history of several hundred years in which the tribes often had to fight to resist or throw off foreign domination.

Soon after the Israelites began their invasion of Canaan by crossing the Jordan River from the east, Canaan came under assault from the west as well. The seafaring Philistines, who may have been a Greek-speaking people, had failed in an attempt to conquer Egypt. So they set their sights on Canaan. Technologically superior to the Israelites, the Philistines were outstanding smiths who equipped their soldiers with high-quality iron weapons. They established secure control over the territory of Gaza.

By the beginning of the history related in the first *Book of Samuel*, the Philistines had captured extensive territories from the disunited Israelite tribes. After defeating Judah (the largest tribe), which controlled the southern part of modern-day Israel, the Philistines imposed one of the first weapons-control laws in recorded history: "Now there was no smith found throughout the land of Israel: for the Philistines said, Lest the Hebrews make them swords or spears..." (1 Samuel 13:19. I quote from the King James Version, the most influential translation in 18th-century America, and today.) Even to sharpen a plow, the Israelites had to pay a Philistine ironsmith (1 Samuel 13:20–21).

Because of the iron-control laws, the Israelites had few good weapons to use against the Philistines, although a future leader named Saul and his son Jonathan apparently possessed some of their own: "So it came to pass on the day of battle, that there was neither sword nor spear found in the hand of any of the people that were with Saul and Jonathan: but with Saul and with Jonathan his son was there found" (1 Samuel 13:22).

As this passage shows, governments intending to prevent subjects from possessing arms must do more than outlaw arms; they must also find a way to prevent people from making their own. The Philistine ban on ironsmithing appears to have been largely effective in accomplishing its goal. Similarly, during the Tokugawa period in Japan, starting in the 17th century, the government imposed very restrictive controls on the small number of gunsmiths in the nation, thereby ensuring the almost total prohibition of firearms.

In the United States, the Brady Campaign (formerly Handgun Control, Inc., and before that the National Council to Control Handguns) has proposed similar legislation. In 1994, the group unveiled its the "Brady II" bill to control firearms parts and repair. Anyone owning an "arsenal" of 20 or more guns would be subject to three unannounced government inspections of his home every year. For purposes of establishing the existence of an "arsenal," all firearms, some spare parts of firearms, and all ammunition magazines would count as a "firearm." Thus, a person with four real guns, plus a normal-sized collection of spare parts and magazines, would be considered the proprietor of an "arsenal."

If Brady II became law, ordinary gun-owners would be encouraged to eliminate their supplies of spare parts, so as not to be subject to the special searches imposed on "arsenal" owners. As spare parts collections were diminished, practical knowledge of elementary gunsmithing (such as how to replace a worn-out barrel) would likewise diminish.

In countries such as the Philippines and Afghanistan that have long traditions of cottage gunsmithing, dictatorships have found it hard to disarm the populace. The Ferdinand Marcos dictatorship in the Philippines tried and failed to prohibit civilian gun ownership. The Taliban dictatorship in Afghanistan likewise outlawed gun ownership for everyone except Taliban supporters, yet did not succeed in disarming the country.

But let us return to Israel. Unifying leadership was provided by charismatic leaders, "judges," who told the Israelites what God wanted them to do. To speak in secular terms, these figures seem to have been selected for leadership by the consensus of the community, in recognition of their personal qualities. Samson was a judge. Deborah was a judge; the office was not restricted to males. Judges rendered legal decisions; they also led military resistance to foreign conquerors.

The last man to rule Israel as a judge was Samuel. Although the position was not hereditary, Samuel attempted to arrange for his sons to succeed him, even though they were notoriously corrupt and dishonest (1 Samuel 8:1–3). Samuel also seems to have failed as a military leader. The Philistines defeated Israel at the battle of Ebenezer, captured the Ark of the Covenant, and destroyed God's sanctuary at Shiloh (1 Samuel 4:1–11; Psalms 78:60–64; Jeremiah 7:12).

Understandably, the Israelites tired of the system of judges. They asked Samuel to ask God to appoint a king to rule over them (1 Samuel 8:6). Samuel replied by delivering a warning from God about the dangers of abusive government. One of the dangers was a standing army; another was conscription:

> "He will take your sons and appoint them for himself, for his chariots, and to be his horsemen; some shall run before his chariots. And he will appoint him captains over thousands, and captains over fifties; and will set them to ear [plow] his ground, and to reap his harvest, and to make his instruments of war, and instruments of his chariots." (1 Samuel 8:11–12)

In other words, military conscription for a standing army would lead to labor conscription, with Israelites forced to work for the king and his military.

Further, the prediction that the king would have chariots meant that as a monarchy Israel would abandon its policy of not developing a cavalry. The confederated Israel described in *Judges* did not use cavalry. Cavalry was expensive. It was better suited to wide-ranging wars of imperial conquest than to defending the hill country that was the core of Israelite settlement. Moreover, a cavalry force might—as in the case of imperial Rome, or the knights of the Middle Ages—turn itself into a social overclass, destroying an egalitarian militia system and enforcing a new system of political dominance.

Samuel issued more prophetic warnings. Besides the conscription of men, there would be conscription of women, and there would be taxes and confiscations. Women would be forced to serve as the king's cooks and bakers. The king would "take your fields, and your vineyards, and your olive-yards, even the best of them, and give them to his servants." He would take a tenth of the people's earnings, a tenth of the young men and servants, and a tenth of the sheep. "And ye shall be his servants. And ye shall cry out in that day because of your king which ye shall have chosen" (1 Samuel 8:13–18). Subsequent Bible history is full of examples of the truth of this prophecy. For example, wicked Queen Jezebel ordered that a farmer named Naboth be killed so that she and her husband could take his vineyard (1 Kings 21).

"Nevertheless the people refused to obey the voice of Samuel and they said, Nay; but we will have a king over us; that we also may be like other nations; and that our king may judge us, and go out before us, and fight our battles" (1 Samuel 8:19–20). So Samuel chose Saul as the first King of Israel, and the people ratified that choice.

Centuries later, political theorists were still debating the implications of the way Saul became king. In the famous book of 1644, *Lex Rex*, which justified Scottish Presbyterian resistance to the English king, Samuel Rutherford examined Saul's ascension to the throne, using it to argue that all lawful monarchies were founded on a consensual covenant between the king and the people. If the king violated the covenant, the people could remove him, by force if necessary, and choose a new government. The king was the people's delegate for enforcement of the law, but the people always retained the sovereignty. The ideas of Rutherford and other Calvinists about the nature of human government are an important link between biblical narrative and the English and American tradition of resistance to arbitrary political authority.

The Israelites had needed a strong, unified government to shake off Philistine rule. But just as Samuel had foretold, within a few generations their government became so strong that it took away the liberties and property of the Israelites themselves.

Saul was at first a successful and popular king. He mobilized the Israelites and led them on a series of campaigns against the Amorites and the Ammonites. Although militia comprised the bulk of the Israelite forces, Saul created the first Israelite standing army—a cadre of about 3,000 full-time professional soldiers. Unlike militia, the soldiers in the standing army did not return to farming, trade, or other civilian occupations when a campaign was over.

When they fought the Philistines at the battle of Michmash, the Israelites were once again greatly outnumbered. Saul's eldest son Jonathan and his shield bearer left the main force, sneaked up on a Philistine garrison, and caused it to panic and flee. As the panicked soldiers rushed toward a larger Philistine camp, they were mistaken for charging Israelites; Saul took advantage of their terror and confusion to rout them. Surprise and audacity carried the day—as they would again in Israel's 20th-century wars.

Later, 1 *Samuel* reports, Saul's young soldier David defeated the Philistine giant Goliath in single combat. Regardless of whether the story was literally true, it became a symbol of a small, resourceful nation—skilled in arms and trusting in God—defeating much larger, more arrogant foes. It became a symbol for America in its war against the world's strongest power, Great Britain.

But the incident also illustrated the instability of a political regime deriving its legitimacy from military leadership. As was the custom whenever an enemy army was defeated, "the women came out of all the cities of Israel, singing and dancing, to meet king Saul." But the women sang, "Saul hath slain his thousands, and David his ten thousands" (1 Samuel 18:6–7). Saul worried that David's sudden military fame would allow him to make a bid for the kingship. Indeed, unbeknownst to Saul, Samuel had already secretly anointed David as king (1 Samuel 16:12–13). Religion still played an important role in the state. Military success was important, but it was not the only thing that mattered.

After Samuel turned against Saul, Saul's fortunes declined. Abandoned by David and his followers, and, according to the Bible narrative, abandoned also by God, Saul was defeated at the Battle of Mount Gilboa, overwhelmed by Philistine chariots and archers (1 Samuel 31). Rather than be captured by the Philistines, Saul fell on his own sword. David assumed leadership of the Israelite military effort.

During a long reign, King David led Israel on enormously successful campaigns. He established direct rule in all the traditional territories of the twelve tribes—encompassing the 1948 borders of Israel, as well as Judaea and Samaria. He also conquered Damascus, and through vassal states established Israelite hegemony all the way to the northern tributaries of the Euphrates.

While the Israelites remained primarily an infantry force, King David encouraged the tribes to develop various specialties. The tribe of Naphtali were spearmen (1 Chronicles 12:34). The tribe of Issachar became expert in military intelligence (1 Chronicles 12:32). The Benjamites were already adept with slings, and became experts with bows and arrows (Judges 20:15–16; 1 Chronicles 12:2).

There were strict laws about children and weapons: children had to learn to use them well. Military training was universal and began early. As Mordechai Gichon and former Israeli President Chaim Herzog wrote in *Battles of the Bible*, "The tribal chiefs continued to train the young in the use of arms special to their clan, as well as in the maintenance of personal weapons." King David mandated that Judaean children be taught archery (2 Samuel 1:18).

The bulk of Israel's military was still the militia, including an active force for which each tribe contributed men to serve one month out of twelve. Settlements in border or contested regions were especially dependent on a home guard.

King David ordered a census, which the Bible describes as sinful. The Israelites probably feared a census as the first step towards centralized taxation and conscription into a standing army (2 Samuel 24; 1 Chronicles 21:1). Similar fears have been raised about censuses in other nations, and legitimately so. During World War I, for example, records from the 1910 US census were used to track down young American men who had not registered for the draft.

King David continued to strengthen the standing army. The military élite was built around two groups of 30 men each. Herzog and Gichon explain that these groups of 30 gave the Israelite army a strong foundation in unorthodox warfare against larger and technologically superior foes. Similarly, the modern

Israeli Defense Forces were built on the foundation of the Hagganah, which led the guerilla resistance to British occupation in the 1940s. The IDF has often excelled in unorthodox and daring tactics against numerically superior foes.

The capture of Jerusalem was an especially important strategic success for David. Recognizing that its terrain provided a very secure defensive position, he moved his capital there. The city, which had not historically belonged to any tribe, was a sign of national unity. But although David greatly centralized government power, the militia system remained intact. National consent was still required for most offensive wars. (An exception was made for wars involving the eight nations or tribal groups that scripture regarded as permanent enemies.)

David was succeeded by his son Solomon, under whose reign Israel achieved its greatest territorial and economic power. Solomon built a series of frontier fortifications, useful for offense as well as defense. He also built the first significant Israeli mobile force, composed of war chariots (1 Kings 10:26–29). And he became fabulously rich. Some of his military equipment was, like his throne and his drinking cups, literally made of gold: "And king Solomon made two hundred targets of beaten gold; six hundred shekels of gold went to one target. And he made three hundred shields of beaten gold" (1 Kings 10:16–18). It is likely that this equipment was more useful for ostentation than for war.

Although Solomon used his power to collect tribute from various vassal states, big government proved very burdensome to the Israelites. Empires and standing armies are expensive. Productive men were removed from the economy to serve in the armed forces and civil service, and other men had to be taxed to support them. The creation of an expensive corps of war chariots exacerbated the problem.

Significantly, the cabinets of King David and King Solomon each came to include a minister in charge of forced labor (2 Samuel 20:4, 23–26; 1 Kings 4:1–6), an office that was not present in David's original cabinet (2 Samuel 8:16–18). Some of the forced laborers may have been foreign captives from the imperial wars. One passage claims that non-Jews in Israel were conscripted into forced labor (1 Kings 9:20–22). Other passages suggest that the Israelites themselves were conscripted into Solomon's building projects (1 Kings 5:13, 11:28, 12:10–11).

As Samuel had warned, a large share of Israel's labor was being consumed by the monarchy. The heavy cost of government stretched the limits of Israel's ability to pay. The need for revenue led to an expansionist and imperialist policy, as Israel sought tribute from other nations to maintain its high-priced government. The cost of maintaining the empire then became an additional financial burden.

Far from being a recipe for security, Solomon's centralized and militarized big government was the recipe for revolution. The event waited only for the appearance of a very bad politician, Solomon's son and successor Rehoboam.

The people petitioned Rehoboam for tax relief. His older advisors suggested that he lie to the public, but he followed the advice of his younger ones: "And the king answered the people roughly...saying, My father made your yoke heavy, and I will add to your yoke: my father also chastised you with whips, but I will chastise you with scorpions" (1 Kings 12:13–14).

Incited by the prophet Ahijah (the spiritual and ideological entanglements of politics never went away), the ten northern tribes of Israel revolted and created an independent state of Israel. Their king was Jeroboam, who had previously failed in a revolt against King Solomon. The rallying cry of the rebellion was, "To your tents, O Israel" (1 Kings 12:16). It was the cry of a society that still recalled the time when government was small and localities were the foundation of political society. The rebels remembered the days before a centralizing government consolidated religious power by building the temple at Jerusalem. They remembered the days before the government, allied with a priestly hierarchy dedicated to religious uniformity, attempted to consolidate its economic power with high taxes and its military power with a standing army. They remembered the days when the Israelites said that their only king was God.

The divided kingdoms (Israel in the north, Judah in the south) won some wars in subsequent years, especially when they were allied with each other. But they usually failed to make an alliance. There were many domestic problems as well, especially those centering on their rival religious establishments. The policy of imperialism meant that Jewish royal families frequently took foreign wives (such as Jezebel) to cement alliances; the foreign wives and their local allies often supported nature religions (which included human sacrifice) in competition with Judaism.

It is interesting that although the religious conflicts within Israel and Judah were of the highest magnitude, involving, according to their partisans, a literal struggle for the nation's soul, there are no records of any faction, while in the ascendancy, ever attempting to disarm an opposing faction. Perhaps the memory of weapons prohibition under Philistine rule was just too strong.

Keeping arms in the hands of the people did help prevent government from sliding into absolute despotism. Checks and balances were often provided, especially in the northern kingdom, by people who knew how to use weapons to displace unruly kings. Religion acted as another check, especially when prophets arose to rebuke the king and his court.

So Israel under the monarchy always had an armed population (as the Second Amendment envisions for the United States). It also had powerful dissidents, the prophets, who were not afraid to use their freedom of speech to rebuke the government (as the First Amendment provides). Yet even though ancient Israel might be said to have usually protected both First and Second

Amendment rights, those rights were not sufficient to protect the full scope of liberty and prevent serious abuses by government. The concentration of national political power continued to have terrible consequences.

Today, some people naïvely claim that as long as their favorite right (free speech, for instance, or the right to arms) is protected, American liberty will always be secure. The experience of ancient Israel shows the folly of such claims. The First and Second Amendments make great contributions to safeguarding freedom, but they are not strong enough by themselves to shoulder the whole burden of safeguarding liberty from a government that consolidates too much political and economic power.

The first two generations of New Englanders saw themselves as Israel in the Wilderness (the 40-year period when the tribes wandered around the Sinai Peninsula, before entering the Promised Land). Around 1690, as increased population and the growth of towns made the Wilderness parallel untenable, the new ideology emphasized "Israel's constitution." The model of good government was Israel's unwritten constitution, which required that society be run according to published laws and fair and orderly procedures. New England's laws and customs should ensure that power could not be abused, as some kings of the Hebrews had abused their power, and should especially ensure that government would not suppress religion, as some Israelite monarchs had attempted to suppress or weaken the worship of Yahweh, while promoting nature religions.

Still later, as New England sought to convince the other colonies to revolt against George III, the dominant parallel to f Israel became the story of what historian Harry Stout called "the Jewish Republic." Israel had governed itself during the period of the judges, but had sinned against God by becoming a monarchy. America needed to throw off the monarchy and return to the only system of government that God approved: self-government.

To cite one example: Harvard College President Samuel Langdon's 1775 election sermon was built on *Isaiah* 1:26: "And I will restore thy judges as at the first, and thy counsellors as at the beginning; afterward thou shalt be called the city of Righteousness, the faithful city." Important sermons had a much broader audience than just the people who were in attendance when the minister spoke. Sermons were often reprinted and distributed throughout the colonies. By 1776, New England Congregationalist ministers were preaching at a record pace, over 2,000 sermons a week, and the number of Congregationalist pamphlets from New England exceeded the number of secular pamphlets from all the other colonies, combined, by a ratio of more than four to one.

Peter Whitney, in a 1776 sermon titled "American Independence Vindicated," summed up the attitudes of the New England Congregationalist ministers. He argued that the 13 "tribes" of Americans had been patient in their suffering under oppression, like the ten tribes of Israel under King Rehoboam, until they had no choice but to revolt. The form of government of an independent United States was uncertain, but the model should be pre-monarchic republican Israel.

Back in 1765, Stephen Johnson's sermon in Newport, Rhode Island, had pointed to Israel throwing off Rehoboam as analogous to Holland's throwing off the Spanish yoke in the late 16th and early 17th centuries, and he suggested that both rebellions provided good examples for Americans. In 1780, during the War of Independence, Simeon Howard preached a sermon to the Massachusetts legislators, reminding them that "the Jews always exercised this right of choosing their own rulers."

Even the deist Thomas Paine took up the theme in *Common Sense*, arguing that monarchy was inherently sinful, because the Israelites had rejected God when they asked for a king. Monarchs usurped prerogatives that belonged solely to God. A person could believe in the Bible or in kings, but not in both: "These portions of scripture are direct and positive. They admit of no equivocation. That the Almighty hath here entered his protest against monarchical government, is true, or the scripture is false."

Although the details changed with time, the intensity of New England's self-identification with Israel did not. In April 1776, when George Washington had just forced the British out of Boston, Samuel Cooper took the pulpit at the newly liberated First Church of Boston for a sermon that the congregation knew would be of great historical importance. Cooper explained that there was a "very striking Resemblance between the Condition of our Country from the beginning and that of antient Israel, so many Passages in holy writ referring to their particular Circumstances as a People, may with peculiar Propriety be adopted by us." Like the Israelites, the Americans were given their land by God, and would always possess it, as long as they stayed faithful to God.

In the famous 1780 "A Sermon on the Day of the Commencement of the Constitution," Cooper returned to the theme, pointing to "a striking resemblance between our own circumstances and those of the ancient Israelites." If Americans were virtuous, then they would build the New Jerusalem that is promised in the penultimate chapter of the last book of the New Testament: "Thus will our country resemble the new city which St. John saw 'coming down from God out of heaven, adorned as a bride for her husband.'"

Good Americans, like good Jews, needed to be ready to fight. Ministers warned of the ancient Israelite city of Laish, which was destroyed because it neglected to prepare defensively (Judges 18:27-28). "Curse ye Meroz," thundered the ministers, recalling the curse of Judge Deborah against a city that failed to arm itself and sat on the sidelines during Deborah's war of national liberation against a foreign king.

And good Americans, like good Jews, needed to be ready to overthrow tyrannical rulers. In the early 1770s, the most-read sermon was "An Oration Upon the Beauties of Liberty," delivered in 1772 by the Baptist John Allen, who cited the Israelite revolution against Rehoboam as justification for American resistance to England. He warned:

> "[T]he Americans will not submit to be SLAVES, they know the use of the gun, and the military art . . . and where his Majesty has one soldier, who art in general the refuse of the earth, America can produce fifty, free men, and all volunteers, and raise a more potent army of men in three weeks, than England can in three years."

The problem was—and remains—the challenge of maintaining a society that is strong enough to resist foreign enemies, yet whose government does not infringe domestic freedom. It is one thing to justify a revolution; it is another thing to maintain a system of limited government.

The writers of the Constitution knew how Israel changed from a decentralized militia society with a small government into a centralized, expensive monarchy with a large standing army. The story of Israel was consistent with what they had learned about England, France, Rome, and other great powers: centralism, monarchy, and standing armies created a vicious cycle of excessive growth and expensive government.

Yet as the founders also recognized, a decentralized, low-tax, militia-reliant society was difficult to sustain. During the era of the judges, the Hebrews had found the problem insurmountable. In times of peril, some tribes would sit out the conflict, leaving the fighting to others. Tribes might battle one another rather than working together against external dangers. Our American Constitution tries to balance the centralization necessary to national defense with the decentralization necessary to liberty; like the ancient Israelites, we have found that every generation must be vigilant in maintaining constitutional liberty.

ARMED JEWS WEEK

Hanukkah is an eight-day celebration of the Jewish revolution against Syria in the second century B.C. The Syrian government (a remnant of Alexander the Great's empire) attempted to wipe out the Jewish religion by forcing the Jews to conform to Greek culture. Some of them refused, and a tiny militia, led by Judah the Maccabee ("the hammer") began a guerilla war.

The Jewish militia grew in force, and repeatedly destroyed much larger Syrian armies which were sent to smash the revolution. Syria's King Antiochus decided that the Jewish people were so much trouble that he would just get rid of them entirely—slaughtering as many as necessary, and selling all the rest into slavery. But his wicked plans failed, and after years of war, the Jews won their independence.

During the years of Syrian tyranny, Syrian officers enjoyed the *droit du seigneur*—the authority to deflower virgin Jewish brides on their wedding nights, before they could join their husbands. So some stories which Jewish families retell at Hanukkah, such as the *Book of Judith*, extol brave Jewish women who went to the tent of enemy officers who were expecting sex—but who instead met their deaths as the hands of a Jewish woman.

During centuries of oppression in Christian and Moslem lands, many Jews adopted attitudes of passivity and helplessness. Those attitudes began to change in the late 19th century, with the growth of the Zionist movement.

Zionists believed that Jews had become disconnected from the physical world. That the Jews had no homeland was the most extreme manifestation of the disconnection, but the disconnect could be seen on many levels. Often pale and weak, Jewish boys were easy targets for bullies. Usually passive and timid, Jewish communities were easy targets for mobs. The root cause of Jewish physical weakness and of disrespect by gentiles was the Jewish lack of self-respect.

The Zionists set out to restore a Jewish homeland, and they recognized that such a project would require a widespread change in Jewish consciousness.

So in counties such as Russia and Israel (which was ruled by the Ottoman Empire and then by the British), Zionists organized Jewish self-defense groups. Many of the young Jewish men and women who would lead the resistance to Hitler were members of these Zionist self-defense youth groups in the 1930s in Eastern Europe.

Although there is a widespread myth that Jews in the Holocaust were passive, they were actually more active than any other conquered people. In 1942-43, Jews constituted half of all the partisans in Poland. Overall, about thirty thousand Jewish partisans fought in Eastern Europe. There were armed revolts in over forty different ghettos, mostly in Eastern Poland.

In other parts of Europe, Jews likewise joined the resistance at much higher rates than the rest of the population. Unlike in Eastern Europe, though, Jews were generally able to participate as individuals in the national resistance, rather than having to fight in separate units.

For example, in France, Jews amounted to than less than one percent of the French population, but comprised about 15-20 percent of the French Resistance.

In Greece too, Jews were disproportionately involved in the resistance. In Thessaly, a Jewish partisan unit in the mountains was led by the septuagenarian Rabbi Moshe Pesah, who carried his own rifle. The Athenian Jew Jacques Costis led the team which demolished the Gorgopotamos Bridge, thereby breaking the link between the mainland and Peloponnesian Peninsula, and interfering with the delivery of supplies to Rommel's *Afrika Korps*.

One of the great centers of resistance was Vilna, Lithuania, which before the Nazi conquest had been an outstanding center of Jewish learning, compared by some to Jerusalem.

Plans for resistance began in January 1942. The Jews' only weapons were smuggled in from nearby German arms factories where the Jews performed slave labor. Hopeful of liberation by the Russian army, many of the Vilna Jews did not support the partisans. Partisan resistance postponed by three weeks the German plans to transport all the inhabitants of the Vilna ghetto to death camps, but the deportation of 40,000 Jews was accomplished by the end of September 1943.

A young poet named Abba Kovner led the resistance movement known as the Avengers in the woods around Vilna. His lieutenants, and bedmates, were teenage girls, Vitka Kempner and Ruzka Korczak.

The Avengers were the first partisans in Nazi Europe to blow up a German train.

Towards the end of the war, the Avengers shepherded huge numbers of Jews to Palestine, in violation of the British blockade.

Before the war, Ruzka had belonged to left-wing Zionist youth group called "The Young Guard" (*HaShomer HaTza'ir*), which trained Jews in self-defense, and taught the older boys how to shoot. Abba was not religious, but he was a fervent Zionist, loving to read the Bible stories of Jewish warriors, and aiming to emulate the Jewish Bible heroes.

In the Vilna Ghetto, it was Abba Kovner who first saw that the tightening of the Nazi oppression was not just a temporary imposition by a local German official; it was a step towards the total destruction of the Jews. The only way out, he argued, was "Revolt and armed defense. This is the only way which promises any dignity for our people."

Other Jews countered that revolt was hopeless because the Germans were so strong, and that collective reprisals by the Germans would just lead to more Jewish deaths. Ruzka Korczak retorted that the stories of Jewish heroism could not remain only "a part of our ancient history. They must be part of our real life as well." The next generation of Jews must have something to admire. "How good will they be if their entire history is one of slaughter and extermination? We cannot allow that. It must also have heroic struggles, self-defense, war, even death with honor."

Vilna was typical, in that the young people were usually the ones who wanted to fight, and the elders usually counseled against causing trouble. Most of the partisan leaders and fighters were young.

Niuta Teitelbaum was a beautiful 24-year-old Jewish Polish woman who looked like she was sixteen. Known as "Little Wanda with the Braids," she was an expert smuggler of people and weapons, and instructed women's partisan cells. Her units blew up trains, artillery emplacements, and other German targets.

Once, wearing traditional Polish clothing and a kerchief on her hair, she talked her way past a series of Gestapo guards, whispering that she was going to see the SS commander on "private business." Alone with the commander in his office, she drew a revolver, shot him dead, and calmly left the building.

Because generation after generation after generation of Jewish families told their children the heroic Hanukkah stories of Judah the Maccabee and Judith, the spirit of freedom and resistance lived in modern heroes such as Abba Kovner and Niuta Teitelbaum.

At the annual Passover Seder, Jewish families say:

> "In every generation, each person must look upon himself or herself as if he or she personally had come out of Egypt. As the *Book of Exodus* says, 'You shall tell your children on that day: it is because of what the Eternal One did for me when I went forth from Egypt.' For it was not our fathers and mothers alone whom the Holy One redeemed. We too were redeemed along with them."

The point has a broader application than just for Jews at Passover. Hanukkah teaches that God's redemption of the Jewish people is a continuing act of history—and so does Jewish armed resistance during the Holocaust. The resistance proved to the world that Jews were active fighters, and not mere passive victims. That resistance (most famously, in the Warsaw Ghetto) was an indispensable step towards the rebirth of the modern state of Israel.

The *Books of Maccabees* and of *Judith* are part of the Roman Catholic, Episcopalian, and Orthodox Bibles; the stories of resistance to the Nazis are part of the heritage of freedom-loving people everywhere. So as Jewish families light Menorah candles during the eight days of Hanukkah, may people of good will, of all faiths, use the time as an occasion to teach their children about the inspiring Jewish and gentile men and women who, even in the darkest times, have kept alive the sacred light of freedom.

PERPETUA AND FELICITY

No saints were more uniformly honored in the early Christian era than Perpetua and Felicity. The two women were arrested and imprisoned, along with three other Christians, in Carthage in 203 A.D. Perpetua was a 22-year-old noblewoman with a son a few months old; Felicity a slave with a child not yet born. Their crime was defying Emperor Septimus Severus' prohibition of conversions to Christianity.

The account of their martyrdom and courage, *The Suffering of Perpetua and Felicity*, is one of the earliest historical accounts of Christianity, and one of the most feminist. Read in African churches for the next several centuries, it was treated as nearly equivalent to scripture. [A full English translation appears in Musurillo's *The Acts of the Christian Martyrs* (Oxford, 1972); Butler's unabridged *Lives of the Saints* contains lengthy excerpts.]

While the five Christians (along with their instructor in faith) were being held awaiting execution, Perpetua's father urged his favorite child to save her life and life of her baby by renouncing her faith. "Father," she answered, "do you see this vessel—waterpot or whatever it may be?...Can it be called by any other name than what it is?"

"No," he replied.

"So also I cannot call myself by any other name than what I am—a Christian."

At a trial shortly thereafter, Perpetua refused to offer a sacrifice for the prosperity of the emperors. When the court asked "Are you a Christian?" she answered, "Yes, I am," thereby condemning herself to death.

A few days before the festival games, at which the martyrs would face wild beasts in the coliseum, Perpetua had a dream in which she was transformed into a man, and engaged in unarmed combat with an Egyptian (signifying the devil). "I was lifted up into the air and began to strike him as one who no longer trod the earth...I caught hold of his head and he fell upon his face; and I trod on his head," she dreamt. The other captives also had visions which fortified their courage.

Felicity, meanwhile, had been afraid that she would not suffer with the rest, because Roman law forbade the execution of pregnant women. In answer to her prayers, her child was born while she was in prison, and was promptly adopted by a Christian couple.

Perpetua had managed to convert their jailer to Christianity, and so the captives were treated well in their final days.

The prisoners turned their last meal into an *agape*, a lovefeast, and spoke of the joy of their own sufferings—thereby astonishing most witnesses, and converting some.

When the day of the Games arrived, Perpetua and Felicity went to the amphitheater "joyfully as though they were on their way to heaven," as Perpetua sang a psalm of triumph. The guards attempted to force the captives to wear robes consecrated to Roman gods, but Perpetua resisted so fiercely that they were allowed to wear their own clothes. The three male martyrs threatened the crowd, including the procurator who had condemned them, with the judgment of God, thereby enraging the crowd.

One of the men, Saturnius, although prepared for martyrdom, was terrified of bears. Saturnius was first exposed to a wild boar, which turned upon its keeper, and promptly killed him. Saturnius was then tied up, and exposed to a bear, which refused to come out of its den. As Saturnius had hoped, he was quickly killed by a single bite from a leopard. As he died, he said to his newly-converted jailer, "Farewell: keep the faith and me in mind, and let these things not confound but confirm you."

A wild heifer was sent against the women. The heifer tossed Perpetua, who got up, straightened her hair, and helped Felicity regain her feet. Absorbed in ecstasy, Perpetua was unaware that she had been thrown, and did not believe it until Felicity showed her the marks on her body.

Having survived the animals, the women were to be executed. They exchanged a final kiss of peace. A nervous gladiator tried to kill Perpetua, but failed to finish the job until she guided the knife to her throat. "Perhaps so great a woman...could not else have been slain except she willed it," the *Passion* observes.

Although the execution in the Coliseum was intended as entertainment, and enjoyed as such by most of the jeering crowd, some of the spectators, inspired by the martyrs' fearlessness, became converts; nor were these spectators the last people who would be encouraged by Perpetua and Felicity, who, even at the cost of their lives, worshipped God and not the state. They are celebrated on March 7.

Religious Perspectives on Freedom from the West

John of Salisbury

Who said "Rebellion to tyrants is obedience to God"? Pat yourself on the back if you answered "Thomas Jefferson and Benjamin Franklin." They proposed placing the motto on the Great Seal of the United States. Pat yourself even harder if you knew that the phrase was created by John Bradshaw (1602–59), the lawyer who served as President of the Parliamentary Commission which sentenced British King Charles I to death. But who thought up the idea?

The idea is implicit in much of the Old Testament, which is full of righteous Hebrews overthrowing tyrants. And certainly the history of Republican Rome and classical Greece has many similar stories. But in the first millennium of Western Christianity, Christians fell under the sway of the law of the Roman Empire, which claimed that the Emperor was above the law. Cicero, who lived in the last days of the Republic, was the last great Roman writer to articulate the right of revolution.

The man who restored the right of revolution in Western political thought was an English bishop named John of Salisbury. In 1159, he wrote *Policraticus* ("Statesman's Book"), which became the best-seller of the century. Although *Policraticus* is mostly forgotten today, it is one of the few books which truly changed the world.

In 1075, Pope Gregory VII had started the Investiture Contest, by claiming that the Pope, not monarchs, had the sole authority to appoint Bishops. He further announced that he had the authority to depose monarchs.

In the decades of war that followed the assertion of Papal authority, a variety of pro-pope writers articulated theories supporting the Pope's position. For example, Manegold of Lautenbach, a scholar at a monastery destroyed by the Holy Roman Emperor Henry IV, argued that the Pope had the authority to release subjects from their obedience to a ruler, as Gregory VII had done. Manegold analogized a cruel tyrant to a disobedient swineherd who stole his master's pigs, and who could be removed from his job by the master. So:

> "[I]f the king ceases to govern the kingdom, and begins to act as a tyrant, to destroy justice, to overthrow peace, and to break his faith, the man who has taken the oath is free from it, and the people are entitled to depose the king and to set up another, inasmuch as he has broken the principle upon which their mutual obligation depended."

But the book that changed Western political thought forever was *Policraticus.*

John of Salisbury was a cosmopolitan and very well-educated English bishop, and "the most accomplished scholar and stylist of his age." (David Knowles, *The Evolution of Medieval Thought*).

Policraticus was perhaps the most influential book written since Byzantine Emperor Justinian's legal code had been compiled six centuries before. *Policraticus* "created an immediate sensation throughout Europe," explains Harold Berman in *Law and Revolution: The Formation of the Western Legal Tradition.* Berman observes that "For over a century *Policraticus* was considered throughout the West to be the most authoritative work on the nature of government."

In the 13th century, Thomas Aquinas, whose work displaced Salisbury's, consciously built on Salisbury's foundation. Throughout the Middle Ages, John of Salisbury's writings were carefully studied by political reformers, lawyers, priests, and scholars.

As an English bishop, John of Salisbury saw first-hand the tremendous Church vs. State struggle then underway in England. English King Henry II (1154-89) was determined to rule the church. Although *Policraticus* did not mention Henry II by name, the book was dedicated to Thomas Becket, the great English bishop with whom Salisbury served for many years.

Policraticus was published around 1159, as the English struggle was intensifying.

In 1162 the King appointed Thomas Becket as Archbishop of Canterbury, the highest position in the English church. In 1164, King Henry forced Becket and other leaders to proclaim the Constitutions of Clarendon, which reasserted extensive royal authority over the church. The Constitutions of Clarendon were contrary to canon law (church law), Becket later asserted, and he repudiated the Constitutions. He publicly declared that King Henry was usurping power.

A bitter conflict ensued, and in 1170 an enraged Henry roared, "Will no one rid me of this pestilential priest?" Four knights heard the King's remarks, and promptly rode off to assassinate Becket, at Canterbury Cathedral. (The story is retold in the play *Murder in the Cathedral*.) Eleven years after *Policraticus* was published, John of Salisbury was present in Canterbury Cathedral when Becket was murdered

The murder of Becket horrified public opinion, and Henry accurately saw that his throne was in grave danger. He did penance, allowing himself to be scourged by some monks. He worked out a compromise with the Church in which he revoked the Constitutions of Clarendon, was allowed to claim that he never wanted Becket killed, but did take responsibility for indirectly inciting Becket's death by proclaiming the Constitutions in the first place.

Before Becket's death, *Policraticus* was already the bestseller of the century. Even so, the author's personal witness to the most infamous tyrannical crime of the twelfth century doubtless caused even more interest in what John of Salisbury had to say about resistance to tyranny.

Policraticus broke away from the old Two Swords debate, in which monarchs and the church argued with each other about who had supreme power—that is, whether the temporal sword was supreme over the church's sword, or vice versa. The Two Swords metaphor came from Jesus's Last Supper instructions to the disciples, telling them to start carrying swords. They responded, "Lord, lo, here are two swords." (Luke 22). *Policraticus*, though, turned the discussion to the rights and duties of government, and to people's remedies when the government exceeded its rights and failed to perform its duties.

The book was a direct shot at contemporary monarchs who oppressed the Catholic Church: Holy Roman Emperor Frederick Barbarossa (the *teutonicus tyrannus*), Roger II (the harsh Norman king of Sicily), Stephen of Blois (who ruled England, more or less, from 1136 to 1154 after starting a civil war to usurp the throne from his cousin Matilda, and who plundered the church and threw bishops in prison), Eustace (Stephen's son, who was killed while pillaging the abbey of Bury St. Edmunds), and Henry II (Matilda's son).

"All tyrants reach a miserable end," John announced. To prove this, he pointed to contemporary examples, such as Eustace, Geoffrey de Mandeville (the plundering Earl of Essex, who was killed in 1144), and Ranulf of Chester (another participant in the Stephen/Matilda war, killed in 1153).

And then there were plenty of stories from the past: the anti-Christian Roman Emperor Julian the Apostate was said to have been stabbed to death with a lance by the martyr Mercurius "on the command of the Blessed Virgin." The Danish tyrant Swain, who imposed the Danegeld (a tax) on the British was slain by "the most glorious martyr and king Edmund." And "Where is Marmion [another contemporary Briton] who, pushed by the Blessed Virgin, fell into the pit which he had prepared for others? Where are the others whose mere names would consume a book? Their wickedness is notorious, their infamy is renowned, their ends are unhappy..."

John of Salisbury lauded the military arts, and described Christian knighthood as an especially holy vocation.

Citing Bible examples, he explained that "one may frequently kill and still not be a man of blood nor incur the accusation of murder or crime." Citing King David and the prophet Samuel, he wrote, "This is indeed the sword of the dove, which quarrels without bitterness, which slaughters without wrathfulness and which, when fighting, entertains no resentment whatsoever." This is similar to what St. Augustine had written in the fifth century about the proper attitude for just war; in the thirteenth century, Thomas Aquinas would elaborate along similar lines.

Hunting, theatre, gambling, and music were all approved as forms of recreation, provided that they were pursued in moderation.

John explained that a good Christian should not be expected to obey the law or a superior's order in all circumstances, for "Some things are...so detestable that no command will possibly justify them or render them permissible." For example, a military commander might order soldiers to deny the existence of God or to commit adultery.

Similarly, if a prince "resists and opposes the divine commandments, and wishes to make me share in his war against God, then with unrestrained voice I must answer back that God must be preferred before any man on earth."

John argued that intermediate magistrates—such as local governors—had a duty to lead forcible resistance, if necessary, against serious abuses by the highest magistrate—such as the king. Interestingly, the theory of "inferior magistrates" not being bound, under all circumstances, to obey the supreme magistrate was also developing in canon law, as many bishops argued that they were not in all circumstances required to obey the Pope.

Policraticus drew heavily on Bible stories, and on examples from ancient Rome. John announced "That by the authority of the divine book it is lawful and glorious to kill public tyrants..."

John of Salisbury was the first Western writer to provide a detailed theory of tyrannicide. He went even further, and made tyrannicide a positive duty:

> "[I]t is not only permitted, but it is also equitable and just to slay tyrants. For he who receives the sword deserves to perish by the sword.
>
> "But 'receives' is to be understood to pertain to he who has rashly usurped that which is not his, now he who receives what he uses from the power of God. He who receives power from God serves the laws and is the slave of justice and right. He who usurps power suppresses justice and places the laws beneath his will. Therefore, justice is deservedly armed against those who disarm the law, and

the public power treats harshly those who endeavor to put aside the public hand. And, although there are many forms of high treason, none is of them is so serious as that which is executed against the body of justice itself. Tyranny is, therefore, not only a public crime, but if this can happen, it is more than public. For if all prosecutors may be allowed in the case of high treason, how much more are they allowed when there is oppression of laws which should themselves command emperors? Surely no one will avenge a public enemy, and whoever does not prosecute him transgresses against himself and against the whole body of the earthly republic."

In short, "As the image of the deity, the prince is to be loved, venerated, and respected; the tyrant, as the image of depravity, is for the most part even to be killed." Thus, tyrannicide was "honorable" when tyrants "could not be otherwise restrained."

There were two important limits: First, poison could not be used. Second, a person could not rebel against a person to whom he legally owed fealty.

The political theory of the Dark Ages had insisted that obedience to God required obedience to any ruler, no matter how awful. John of Salisbury turned this theory on its head: "it is just for public tyrants to be killed and the people to be liberated for obedience to God."

At great length, *Policraticus* denounced tyranny and justified tyrannicide. A few passages did counsel patient reliance on deliverance by God, warned against taking drastic actions based on small or isolated offenses, and urged prayer as the method of ending tyrannical oppression. These cautionary lines, however, did not undermine the revolutionary impact of the book.

Going beyond political tyranny, John of Salisbury explained that tyranny could occur in many forms; "many private men are tyrants." "[E]veryone is tyrant who abuses any power over those subject to him which has been conceded from above." A father, a land-owner, or a merchant could be a private tyrant, to those over whom they abused their power.

An ecclesiastical tyrant was a priest, bishop, or other church official who abused his power, harming rather than protecting the people in his spiritual care.

One of the problems of the tyranny of petty officials was that it was illegal to resist their depredations, even though, according to Justinian's code of Roman law, "it is otherwise lawful to repel force with force without blame if one has safeguarded moderation." However, tyrannicide was appropriate only for actual rulers of governments, not for private tyrants.

Over the next half-millennium, the right of revolution would be defended by Scholastics such as Thomas Aquinas and Francisco Suárez. Lutherans and Calvinists would initially adopt a limited form of the theory. Then the Calvinists, acknowledging that they were building on the Catholic intellectual heritage, would advance the full right of revolution. The "black regiment" of New England preachers would bring the right to its greatest fruition, exhorting their congregations to their sacred duty to overthrow King George and establish a free republic.

John of Salisbury never knew that there was a Western Hemisphere. But he did know that God wants man to be active and free, not passive and enslaved. All of us who enjoy civil liberty in the New World owe a debt of gratitude to the intellectual revolution set off by John of Salisbury.

THE VIRGIN OF GUADALUPE

If you don't know who she is, you might as well learn, because she is well on the road to becoming an all-American icon like St. Patrick and St. Nicholas.

You don't have to believe that there really was an escaped slave who spearheaded the Christianization of Ireland in order to acknowledge that St. Patrick's Day is an inescapable element of American culture.

And you don't have to believe that the 4th century's Bishop Nicholas in southwestern Turkey gave presents to poor people—especially to impecunious young women, so that they would have a marriage dowry, and thereby be saved from a life of prostitution. But there's no doubt that the St. Nicholas story traveled west, becoming especially popular with Catholics in the Netherlands.

And from there, the story jumped the Atlantic when Washington Irving and Clement Moore morphed St. Nicholas into Santa (the Spanish word for "holy") Claus in the early 19th century.

The Virgin of Guadalupe started out as a Mexican icon in 1531, but she has already come to your hometown. And she has a very good chance of becoming a much bigger figure in American culture than St. Patrick, because she represents, in part, all-American values.

Let's start at the very beginning.

Thanks to political correctness, the average American knows just a few things about the Aztecs: They had colorful feather costumes which re-enactors wear today in multicultural festivals. They were very good at astronomy/astrology. Their astrologers had long foretold that the end of world would occur in precisely the year that Hernando Cortez and his conquistadores actually did arrive in Mexico, and began to demolish the Aztec Empire.

Oh, and the Aztecs had a custom of human sacrifice. History textbooks tend to elide the details of the sacrifices, and some students get the impression that the sacrifice victims were pious volunteers. Or as Neil Young sang in

Cortez the Killer: "They offered life in sacrifice, so that others could go on. Hate was just a legend. And war was never known."

Not exactly. The priests of Aztec Empire murdered about a quarter million people per year by ripping out their living hearts. The main victims were not Aztec volunteers, but other Indian tribes who had been conquered by the Aztecs during the Flower Wars. The Aztec gods received the beating heart; according to anthropologist Marvin Harris in *Cannibals and Kings: The Origins of Culture*, the Aztecs ate the rest of the body.

Children were the favorite sacrifice of these bloodthirsty priests. According to Aztec religion, nothing pleased the gods more than the tears of children who were being killed. The priests also liked to flay their victims alive, so the priests could wear the victims' skins.

Sacrifices (that is, murders) were perpetrated on a massive scale. For example, during the 1487 rededication of the Great Temple in Tenochtitlan (modern Mexico City), the Aztecs gloated that over 80,000 victims were slaughtered in just four days.

One of the most important reasons that the evil Aztec Empire fell to Cortez was that other Indian tribes of Mexico allied with the Spanish, and provided the great bulk of the anti-Aztec military force.

Spanish rule over Mexico was sometimes harsh, although Spain, which was a preeminent center of Catholic scholarship in the 16th century, did have influential voices which had some success in insisting that the Indians be treated decently. Bartolomé de las Casas is the best known, but there was also professor Francisco de Vitoria, who argued that the Spanish had no legal or moral right to enslave Indians. That the Indians were pagans did not deprive them of their natural rights, including their right of self-defense. Vitoria, who was one of the founders of international law, also argued that the Spanish had a moral duty and a legal right to intervene to protect the Indians who would otherwise become victims of cannibalism or human sacrifice.

Around the Winter Solstice in December 1531, ten years after the Spanish had conquered the Aztecs, a Catholic Indian peasant named Juan Diego was walking past Tepeyac hill, several miles outside of Mexico City. He heard what seemed like unusually beautiful songbirds at the top of the rocky hill. When he went up to investigate, "he saw a Lady, who was standing there and told him to come hither. Approaching her presence, he marveled greatly at her superhuman grandeur; her garments were shining like the sun; the cliff where she rested her feet, pierced with glitter, resembling an anklet of precious stones, and the earth sparkled like the rainbow. The mezquites, nopales, and other different weeds, which grow there, appeared like emeralds, their foliage like turquoise, and their branches and thorns glistened like gold."

He recognized her as Mary. She addressed him affectionately as her child, and told him to tell the Bishop to have a church for her built at the top of the hill.

He walked several miles to the Bishop's office, and, after a long wait, met with the Bishop, who thought Juan Diego to be a fraud.

The next day, he again saw Mary at the top of the hill, and she requested him to keep trying with the Bishop, despite Juan Diego's feeling that he was a poor messenger. After another long walk and long wait, Juan Diego found the Bishop no less skeptical. The Bishop asked Juan Diego to supply some kind of sign if he were really speaking the truth.

Back at Tepeyac hill the next day, Mary promised Juan Diego that she would supply a sign tomorrow, and told him to come back in the morning.

The next morning, Tuesday, December 12, Juan Diego stayed away from the hill's summit, and instead walked around the base of the hill, so that he could avoid meeting Mary. He was more concerned with hurrying to get a priest for his uncle, who was gravely ill. Partway around the hill, he saw Mary walking down from the top, and she soon met him on the path. He explained his hurry, and promised to come back to her tomorrow. She told him not to worry and that his uncle would be alright (which was true).

She told him to go up to the top of the hill, and gather flowers. There, at the top of the craggy, rocky, weed-ridden hill, he found roses which were blooming in the dead of winter, and he placed them in an apron made from his tilma. (The tilma was the common peasant clothing, made from cactus fibers, and worn sort of like a Roman toga.) He carried the roses back to the base of the hill, where she arranged them carefully on the tilma.

Again, he walked the miles back to the Bishop's office, and waited at length. He would have waited even longer, but some of the Bishop's assistants spotted the roses through a fold in the tilma. When the Bishop finally saw him, Juan Diego opened the apron, and the roses fell to the floor. So did the Bishop and all his staff, who dropped to their knees. On Juan Diego's tilma was a painting of the woman he had met.

Her cape was spangled with stars, a traditional garb of an Aztec princess. She was standing on the moon and in front of the sun, which emitted brilliant rays behind her.

The church was promptly built on the spot that Mary had designated, former site of a pilgrimage temple to the Aztec earth and corn goddess Tonantzin. Like Mary, Tonantzin was addressed as "Our Holy Mother," and was associated with the moon. The original church is no longer there, but a basilica and museum have been built in its place, where the tilma and its painting are viewed by large crowds every day.

A normal tilma should have decayed into tatters after about 20 years, but this one is well-preserved, even though it was frequently kissed, touched, and had objects placed on it for the first century after the painting appeared. (Today, the tilma is behind glass.)

Scientists have investigated the painting several times, most recently in 1979. While, it is possible that some of the materials on the outer part of the painting may have been added in the early 1600s, there has not yet been a good explanation for how a Mexican Indian, with the paint materials available at the time (or any other painter in 1531) could have produced the picture.

Microscopic examination of the painting of Mary's eyes reveals (at least to some observers) details which would have been impossible from a 16th century painter to create: matching images of a bearded man who appears to be kneeling.

There is no serious dispute that the Guadeloupe story is nearly five centuries old. A colonial Mexican codex from 1548 refers to the incident. The *Nican Mopohua*, Juan Diego's recorded version of the Guadeloupe events, provides the details of the story as it is known today.

In any case, tens of millions of people believe the painting to be an authentic miracle, and (for purposes of assessing the painting's impact on society), that's all that matters.

There have been many, many reports of public apparitions of the Virgin Mary (perhaps an order of magnitude greater than the number of reported public apparitions of Jesus or any other religious figure), but the Virgin of Guadalupe is by far the most famous and influential Marian apparition ever in the Western hemisphere.

The reason is found in the painting itself. To begin with, Mary is not white. She is either Indian, or perhaps Mestizo (a mix of Indian and Iberian). Although she wears a traditional European dress and headscarf, her clothing is resplendent with Aztec symbols.

For example, in Aztec numerology, the numeral 4 symbolizes plentitude, and a four-petal flower appears directly over her womb. The 10 eight-petaled flowers symbolize the planet Venus, which was what the hero-god Quetzalcoatl became. (Quetzalcoatl opposed human sacrifice.)

To a Spanish Christian from the Old World, the painting's celestial imagery had obvious ancestors. The *Book of Revelation*, the apocalyptic conclusion to the New Testament, describes the final battles between good and evil: "And a great sign appeared in heaven: a woman clothed with the sun, and the moon under her feet, and on her head a crown of twelve stars..." Biblical critics have identified her with the church, with the community of believers, with Israel, and in various other ways. But the most common identification is that she is Mary.

The *Revelation* image was re-capitulated in a Spanish statue of the Virgin; the statue was lost for six centuries, and then re-discovered in 1326 near Guadalupe, Spain. It was credited with miraculous victories of the Christian Spaniards against Muslims.

The beautiful lady who spoke to Juan Diego told him her name in Nahuatl, the Aztec language, and whatever she said sounded to the Spanish Bishop to be something like "Guadalupe," which is unpronounceable in Nahuatl. (Scholars are still undecided about what the Nahuatl phrase was; my favorite is "She who proceeds from the region of light like a fire eagle.")

To the Aztecs, the celestial images in the painting had a very direct and personal meaning. The black crescent moon was a prime symbol of the Aztec religion. The conquerors' sacred lady was standing (or perhaps dancing and clapping) on the Aztec moon, dominating it—as she dominated every celestial object. The constellations were mere ornaments on her dress. The dress constellations are a depiction of the celestial globe on the Winter Solstice of 1531. (Before the calendar reform of the 17th century, the solstice took place on December 12.)

And so the painting depicted the triumph and supremacy of Christianity over the Aztec religion. But this triumph was not of whites over Indians, or the Old World over the New. To the contrary, the Virgin had appeared to the Indians as one of them, wearing their clothes, and presenting religious messages using Aztec symbols in almost every inch of the painting. The day on which the Virgin appeared for the final time, December 12, was the earth goddess Tonantzin's festival day.

The syncretistic Virgin of Guadalupe thus prefigured the Mexican nation itself, in which Iberian whites and native Indians intermarried, to create a new people.

Over the centuries, the Virgin never lost her place as the preeminent symbol of the Mexican people—notwithstanding the hostility of anti-clerical governments after 1910.

The Virgin has been misused by people who try to make her into an argument that Mexican women should let men treat them like doormats ("Be like the Virgin; her eyes are humble and downcast"). Nevertheless, for many women the Virgin of Guadalupe has been a source of strength and empowerment.

And what has all this to do with the United States? Well, she is the "Mother of the Americas," not just of Mexico (according to Pope John XXIII, in 1961). The massive Mexican immigration to the US in the last several decades is not going to be undone, as many of those Mexicans, or their children, are now legal American citizens. And if you start keeping an eye out for the Guadalupe image, you'll see that it's already very common in pick-up truck rear windows, behind the counter in family stores, ubiquitous in Catholic churches with a large Mexican congregation, and often seen even in American Catholic churches which have very few Mexicans. Much of the mainstream American press now pays far more attention to the Virgin of Guadalupe than to any other religious event of the last 500 years.

In the United States, Santa Claus has long since forgotten his Turkish/Dutch roots, while St. Patrick is still clearly Irish. A few decades from now, the Virgin of Guadalupe in the US will probably still be associated with Americans whose ancestors came from Mexico. Even *Chronicles* magazine (which definitely does not celebrate non-European immigration) acknowledges that the Guadalupe quincentenary in 2031 is going to be a very big deal in the US.

But I don't think that the Virgin of Guadalupe is going to help the multiculturalists. They abhor the melting pot, and work assiduously to divide Americans into mutually exclusive tribes, with each tribe clinging to its old culture. The centripetal forces of America, however, are too strong for the divisive multi-cultural scheme to succeed. On college campuses, engineering students whose parents came from Taiwan date communications majors whose parents came from Nigeria.

And the Virgin herself is a uniter, not a divider. In the entire history of the world, the Virgin of Guadalupe has been one of the greatest symbols (and causes) of the mixture of white and non-white, of indigenous and immigrant, of east and west, of old and new.

By 2031, the United States may have a thriving community of Mexican immigrants who are contributing to the American dream, adding to American culture in constructive ways—as did the Germans, Irish, Italians, and other groups, after their own massive waves of immigration. Or the US in 2031 could have an angry and unassimilated lower-class population which despises the nation which welcomed them—like the Arab Muslims in the suburban ghettoes around Paris. The enduring power of the Virgin of Guadalupe gives us good cause to hope for the best.

NICHOLAS OWEN: GOD'S CARPENTER

In some parts of the world, persons who wish to exercise the fundamental human right to keep and bear arms must sometimes resort to hiding their guns or knives. In China, as in many other countries, people must hide illegal Bibles. But suppose that instead of hiding a handgun or a Bible, you had to hide your religious leaders?

Several hundred years ago, a small man named Nicholas Owen made himself an expert in constructing hiding places for clergymen. Owen's life is the story of the great things that even the most wretched person can accomplish.

In the late 1500s and early 1600s in England, during the reigns of Queen Elizabeth I and then King James I, everyone was legally required to attend and participate in the services of the Church of England. The head of the Church of England was the monarch.

Even the possession of Catholic religious objects, such as rosaries, was illegal, and smuggling a Catholic priest into the country was punishable by death.

The vast majority of the English people sheepishly followed the government's religious laws, and practiced the Anglican religion, just as their parents had sheepishly followed the government's requirement to practice the

Catholic religion, when Catholicism had been the state's monopoly religion a few decades earlier.

But history is made by determined minorities, rather than by docile majorities, and England was blessed with a good number of people for whom following God was more important than keeping out of trouble with the government.

During the reign of Queen Mary I (1553-58) England was officially Catholic, and Protestants were viciously suppressed. The great deeds of the Protestant English martyrs resisting "Bloody Mary" are recounted in *Foxe's Book of Martyrs* which was, next to the Bible, the most influential book in the development of the Protestant religion in the English-speaking world.

Mary was succeeded by her Protestant half-sister, Queen Elizabeth I. Elizabeth convinced Parliament to pass the Act of Supremacy and the Act of Uniformity in 1559, which turned England into an exclusively Anglican religious nation, by law.

Most English people went along with the change. Elizabeth, for her part, asked only for external shows of conformity, and rejected advice to persecute persons who remained secret Catholics. She had no desire to make "a window into men's souls," she explained.

Unfortunately, the Catholic powers of continental Europe, led by Spain and encouraged by the Pope, plotted to assassinate Elizabeth, and attempted to overthrow her by force. The defeat of the Spanish Armada in 1588 removed the military threat, but the Protestant majority turned intensely suspicious of the small Catholic minority. Persecution of the Catholics grew severe.

In 1603, King James I succeeded Elizabeth. In the years before taking power, he had dropped hints that he might tolerate Catholics. Indeed, his Danish wife, Queen Anne, was a quiet Catholic. But upon becoming King of England, James made it clear that there would be no relaxation of the stringent anti-Catholic laws or their enforcement.

And this is where the hero Nicholas Owen enters the story.

Owen was born in approximately 1550 to a fervently Catholic family. When Anglicanism was established as the state religion, the Owen family became "recusants"—meaning that they paid hefty fines rather than attend Anglican church services.

Two of Owen's brothers entered the priesthood as Jesuits. The third, Henry Owen, ran a covert Catholic printing press. When he was sent to prison for his continued recusancy, he managed a secret press from prison.

Nicholas Owen was only a little taller than a dwarf. This was just one of his medical problems; because of a hernia, his stomach had to be held together by a metal plate. After a packhorse fell on him in 1599, he was further disfigured, and walked with a limp for the rest of his life.

Most Englishmen of Owen's time thought that a twisted body was an outer sign of a twisted character. But as Antonia Fraser observes in her book *Faith and Treason: The Story of the Gunpowder Plot*, Owen's "great soul and measureless courage" offered "the strongest possible refutation of the contemporary prejudice."

Trained as a carpenter and a mason, Owen became perhaps the greatest builder of hiding places in man's history.

The English Catholic community needed priests, both for spiritual leadership, and for administration of the sacraments. Yet harboring a priest was a capital offense.

So in the large country mansions owned by England's crypto-Catholics, Owen constructed ingenious hideouts for priests.

Mansions were built of stone in those days, so Owen's task was especially difficult. The English government's priest-catchers ("poursuivants") would carefully tap on walls, and a hollow sound would immediately betray a room that was hidden through mere use of an empty space.

So Owen's hiding places were much more sophisticated. For example, at the Baddesley Clinton mansion, Owen contrived secret trapdoors in the turrets and stairways, connecting them with the mansion's sewer system. During a 1591 search, several priests stood up to their waists in water, hidden from searchers for four hours. In some cases, priests survived several searches of the same house.

Owen ran feeding tubes into the rooms, so that priests hidden therein could receive food for the days or weeks they might spend inside. Sometimes he built an easily-discovered outer hiding place which concealed an inner hiding place.

While Owen completed scores of hiding places, the exact number is unknown; some remained undiscovered until the 20th century, and others still remain hidden. (Perhaps some of the hideouts that are still secret are being used to conceal guns these days.)

So that the mansion's servants would not know about the hidden chambers, Owen would do ordinary house carpentry work during the daytime. But at night, Owen would build his secret spaces, always working alone—thus minimizing the number of persons who would know about a given hiding place and be susceptible to revealing it under torture. Breaking through heavy stone walls to build complex rooms would have been difficult for any construction crew, but it was difficult in the extreme for a small man working alone. He always worked for free, and received communion before starting a new project.

Nicholas Owen used a variety of names to conceal his identity as he traveled around England: Little John, Little Michael, Andrewes, and Draper.

Owen was chosen as one of the first laypersons to be inducted in the Jesuit Order. When his fellow Jesuit Edward Campion was arrested, Owen spoke openly about Campion's innocence, so Owen himself was arrested. He was arrested again in 1594, tortured on the infamous Topcliffe rack, and hung for three hours from iron rings, with heavy weights on his feet. But he revealed nothing, and was released after a wealthy Catholic paid a ransom. The English jailers who took the bribe to let Owen go thought he was just an insignificant friend of a priest—rather than the master builder of England's underground railroad for priests.

Three years later, Owen masterminded Father John Gerard's escape from Tower of London.

In November 1605, Guy Fawkes and a small band of Catholic conspirators made plans to blow up Parliament, kill King James, and place James' Catholic daughter on the throne. The discovery of the Gunpowder Plot led to a severe crackdown on all suspected Catholics, which led to Owen's arrest in early 1606.

Owen had been secreted in one of his hiding places for two weeks, while poursuivants searched a Catholic home. But when he came out of hiding and attempted to sneak off the premises, he was captured. Immediately he claimed to be a priest—a claim which amounted to condemning himself to death, but which he hoped would distract the poursuivants from the search for the priests who remained hidden in the building.

But this time, the English authorities knew that they had captured the one person who knew enough to bring down the entire network of covert Catholics in England.

At first, Owen was held under light confinement, with visitors allowed, in the hope that some secret priests would reveal themselves by coming to visit him. Owen, however, was too cautious to be tricked, and spent his time in solitary prayer.

Soon, Owen was transferred to the infamous Tower of London, so that he could be tortured. Yet he remained calm and fearless.

The English law of the time forbade torturing anyone to death. For this reason, any person who was already maimed (as Owen had been since the horse fell on him) was not supposed to be tortured at all, due to the risk of death. Nevertheless, Owen was tortured in a particularly gruesome manner, in light of his already-ruptured hernia.

Nicholas Owen was racked for day after day, six hours at a time. An iron band was tightened around his hernia.

While the reliability of confessions obtained under torture was dubious, England's law enforcement authorities never had a problem getting some kind of confession from a torture victim. Except for Nicholas Owen.

He refused to answer the interrogators' questions about anything important, and never revealed a single fact about any of his hiding places. Instead, he constantly invoked the aid of Jesus and Mary.

Perhaps all the physical suffering which Owen had endured since the birth of his deformed body helped him cope with tremendous levels of pain.

Owen died from the torture on March 2. Since Owen's treatment had been unconscionable even by the standards of the time, the government claimed that Owen had committed suicide by stabbing himself twice with a dinner knife. Actually, Owen's hands had been so disfigured by the torture that he could not even hold a pen or a knife, or feed himself.

In 1970, Nicholas Owen as canonized as a saint by the Catholic Church. His feast day is March 22, and he is counted as one of the Forty Martyrs of England and Wales, from the time of the anti-Catholic persecutions.

Father John Gerard, one of England's leading secret priests, wrote that no-one had accomplished more than Owen: "I verily think that no man can be said to have done more good for all those who laboured in the English vineyard. For, first, he was the immediate occasion of saving the lives of many hundreds of persons, both ecclesiastical and secular, and of the estates also of these seculars, which had been lost and forfeited many times over if the priests had been taken in their houses." (A hidden priest then, like illegal drugs or guns today, was cause for forfeiture of an entire home.) The modern edition of Butler's *Lives of the Saints* states, "Perhaps no single person contributed more to the preservation of the Catholic religion in England during penal times."

Regardless of whether one is a Catholic, a Protestant, or anything else, the decision of England's Catholics to maintain their faith, no matter how great the threats from the government, was highly admirable. The Catholics who illegally received communion, or otherwise resisted the government's effort to stamp out their religion, affirmed that the God and the individual are more important than the government. The survival of Catholicism in England, and the failure of the Church of England to establish a complete monopoly of faith, helped sow the seeds for the long-run development of religious toleration in England, and in the rest of the Western world.

Nicholas Owen was one of the pivotal figures of English history, and, indirectly, one of the fathers of modern religious freedom. He was not born to wealth or nobility or normality, and few people who stared at his small and twisted body would have predicted that he would be remembered as one of the greatest Englishmen of his time.

Jonathan Mayhew, and the Catechism of the American Revolution

"The Revolution was effected before the war commenced. The Revolution was in the minds and hearts of the people; a change in their religious sentiments of their duties and obligations." So wrote John Adams, looking back on the American Revolution from the perspective of 1818. The date when the revolution of hearts and minds began was January 30, 1750, and the leader was Congregationalist minister Jonathan Mayhew, who preached perhaps the most important sermon in American history. That sermon was only one highlight of a life dedicated to human rights.

Like most New Englanders, Mayhew (1720-66) was a Congregationalist, an intellectual descendant of the English Puritans. Because Congregationalists held that God's word, as contained in the Bible, is the supreme authority, they believed that a balance of powers within human government is essential, so that misuse of power could never interfere with the preaching of God's word. In their view, separation of church and state was critical, in the sense that the church must be free of control by the state.

In the rival Church of England (the state church) priests were under the authority of bishops, who were under the authority of the king and Parliament. By contrast, individual Congregational churches were accountable to no higher human power, not even an assembly of their fellow churches. Within a Congregational church there was a careful balance of power between the minister and the congregation, so that neither could dominate the other. The congregants knew the Bible very well, and could discipline ministers who misused it.

Three years after graduating from Harvard, the premier training ground for the Congregational clergy, Jonathan Mayhew was called to the pulpit by the congregation of the Old West Church in Boston. Right from the start, he was a theological liberal. Congregationalists had always emphasized the importance of the individual in religion. In "Seven Sermons," preached in 1748 and published thereafter, Mayhew took Congregational principles to their logical conclusion, arguing that everyone has the right and duty to make personal judgments in matters of religion and conscience.

Congregationalists were among the many intellectual heirs of John Calvin, the Protestant reformer of the sixteenth century who argued that a person's salvation or damnation was predestined by God, with salvation based solely on the person's God-given faith. Calvin agreed with the orthodox Roman Catholic theory of original sin—that man was inherently depraved.

Mayhew rejected the Calvinist principles in favor of modern, Enlightenment views. Indeed, he even rejected the orthodox Christian doctrine of the Trinity (that the Godhead is composed of three persons—Father, Son, and Holy Spirit). Mayhew contended that God was One—which implied that Jesus was not God, but instead was simply mankind's mediator and advocate with God.

Thus, Mayhew was one of the most influential forerunners of Unitarianism in America. Yet he always considered himself a Congregationalist, as did the members of the Old West Church, which could have dismissed him if they chose. They did not. And Harvard was so impressed with Mayhew that he was named a lecturer in 1765. His insistence on the importance of the individual conscience became not only a Unitarian doctrine but also a cornerstone of broader American cultural beliefs about religious freedom.

Mayhew is most famous, however, for preaching the principles of political freedom. His preaching appealed to theological conservatives as well as theological liberals—indeed, to persons of all religious persuasions, all over America, and abroad.

January 30, 1750, was the centennial of the execution of Charles I of England, condemned by Parliament for treason and other crimes. He had repeatedly and infamously abused the rights of Englishmen, had attempted to destroy the checks and balances of England's government, and had claimed a divine right to rule with near-absolute powers.

Charles's son was later restored to power, and Charles was proclaimed a martyr by the Church of England. Although a second son was overthrown in the Glorious Revolution of 1688, in Mayhew's time the Church of England still promoted the cult of Charles with a major feast day every January 30. Each year, priests of the Church of England venerated Charles's martyrdom and propounded the duty of submission to government. The New England Congregationalist ministers—whose Puritan ancestors had helped to execute Charles I—generally tried to ignore the topic in their own January 30 sermons.

Mayhew did not. He took the pulpit and preached "A Discourse Concerning Unlimited Submission and Non-Resistance to the Higher Powers." The historian Bernard Bailyn declared this the "most famous sermon preached in pre-Revolutionary America." John Adams called it his personal "Catechism" of revolution. Adams remembered, "It was read by everybody; celebrated by friends, and abused by enemies...It spread an universal alarm against the authority of Parliament. It excited a general and just apprehension, that bishops, and dioceses, and churches, and priests, and tithes, were to be imposed on us by Parliament."

According to Mayhew, God had created hierarchical authorities, and people were expected, under ordinary circumstances, to obey the government, just as children were expected to obey their parents—for their own good. On the other hand, if a father lost his mind and tried to slit his children's throats, the children should not obey him. A tyrannical government was like a father trying to murder his children, and must not be obeyed.

Mayhew expounded the natural law theory of government: "God himself does not govern in an absolute arbitrary and despotic manner. The Power of this almighty King is limited by law—by the eternal laws of truth, wisdom, and equity, and the everlasting tables of right reason." (The "tables" was an analogy to the Twelve Tables, stone tables where the fundamental laws of Republican Rome were written for all to read.) Because God is no arbitrary tyrant, no human tyranny can comport with his eternal laws. Therefore, "disobedience is not only lawful but glorious" if it is against rulers who "enjoin things that are inconsistent with the demands of God."

The "Discourse Concerning Unlimited Submission" presented a popularly accessible form of John Locke's analysis of Paul's *Epistle to the Romans*. Locke's central idea is that the Christian duty to submit to just governments creates a correlative duty to resist and overthrow tyrannical governments, because unjust government is the antithesis of true Christian government. Like most other Congregationalist ministers, Mayhew had studied Locke at Harvard, and considered him a Christian intellectual ally.

Particularly among adherents of the Church of England, there were some Christian authoritarians who warned that a person who resisted tyranny would be damned. To the contrary, Mayhew announced, a people must use the means "which God has put into their power, for mutual and self-defense. And it would be highly criminal in them, not to make use of this means. It would be stupid tameness, and unaccountable folly..." It would "be more rational to suppose that they that did NOT *resist*, than that they who did, would *receive to themselves damnation*."

In sum, to resist a just government was "rebellion" against God. To resist tyranny was "self-defense," which was required by God, because tyranny was not real government.

In 18th-century America, notable sermons were often printed and sold all over the colonies, and overseas. The publication of Mayhew's January 30 sermon added to his already significant international prestige. As Adams recalled, Mayhew "had raised a great reputation both in Europe and America, by the publication of a volume of seven sermons in the reign of King George the Second, 1749, and by many other writings, particularly a sermon in 1750, on the 30th of January."

In Adams' opinion, the January sermon deserved its fame; it was "seasoned with wit and satire superior to any in Swift or Franklin." He believed that in the period 1760-66, the person most influential in arousing the American spirit of liberty was "James Otis; next to him was Oxenbridge Thacher; next to him, Samuel Adams; next to him, John Hancock; then Dr. Mayhew... This transcendent genius threw all the weight of his great fame into the scale of his country in 1761, and maintained it there with zeal and ardor till his death." It was in 1760-61 that the British government began a serious attempt to raise "a national revenue from America by parliamentary taxation."

Mayhew was alive to the threat. Five years later, he was a staunch advocate for American interests during the Stamp Act crisis. He was also active in a closely-related political crisis: the threat of the appointment of an Anglican (that is, Church of England) bishop for America.

Although most American Anglicans (who comprised most of the American ruling élite) lacked the protesting spirit of the Congregationalists and the Presbyterians, the Church of England had never exported its hierarchy to America. As a result, local Anglican churches tended to be controlled by wealthy land-owners, who enjoyed their independence from British oversight. Fears that the King was preparing to send bishops to America, to administer the Anglican church and interfere with other Protestant churches, sent Americans into an ecumenical rage. Adams wrote that no issue was more important in making common people question the authority of Parliament than the controversy over American bishops.

As Adams explained, "The objection was not merely to the office of a bishop, even though that was to be dreaded, but to the authority of Parliament, on which it could be founded." If Parliament had the authority to appoint a bishop for America, Parliament would also have the authority to "introduce the whole hierarchy, establish tithes, forbid marriages and funerals, establish religions, forbid dissenters, make schism heresy..." Americans who favored the appointment of a bishop for America promised that the official would exercise power only on spiritual matters, not temporal ones. But the promise had little credibility, because bishops in England exercised extensive temporal power and were plainly agents of the government.

On May 23, 1766, Mayhew celebrated the repeal of the Stamp Act by preaching a sermon ("The Snare Broken. A Thanksgiving Discourse Preached at the Desire of the West Church in Boston") that recalled American fears that Stamp Act revenues were "partly intended to maintain a standing army of bishops, and other ecclesiastics." Fear of oppressive standing armies was part of the right-to-bear-arms ideology, and would eventually become one of the ideological foundations of the Second Amendment. Mayhew borrowed the proto-Second Amendment philosophy to make a point about freedom of religion that would later become part of the First Amendment: a government-controlled corps of bishops and their minions could trample the freedom of the people, just as could a government-controlled corps of professional soldiers. A standing army of soldiers and a standing army of bishops threatened liberty in the same way, by centralizing and monopolizing power.

"The Snare Broken" is one of many examples of the way in which pre-revolutionary Americans identified connections between religious rights and other rights. It is not a coincidence that the constitutional amendment guaranteeing freedom of religion was placed adjacent to the constitutional amendment guaranteeing the right to keep and bear arms.

In gratitude for repeal of the Stamp Act, Mayhew praised King George and extolled William Pitt, the British Prime Minister who had urged a policy of moderation and conciliation with America. He warned, however, that Americans would always need to be vigilant about their liberties, for "Power is of a grasping, encroaching nature...Power aims at extending itself, and operating according to mere will, where-ever it meets with no balance, check, controul, or opposition of any kind." Americans must "oppose the first encroachments" on liberty, because "after a while, it will be too late." He reminded his congregation of Jesus' parable: "The kingdom of heaven is like to a man that soweth good seed, but while he slept, his enemy cometh, and soweth tares among the wheat" (Matthew 13: 24-25). Because the man had slept, it was impossible to uproot the tares without also uprooting the wheat.

To Mayhew, it was obvious that the kingdom of heaven was a kingdom of rights and liberty. He recalled that in his youth he had studied Plato, Demosthenes, Cicero, and other ancients, and among the moderns, had liked Algernon Sidney, John Milton, and John Locke, all advocates of individual freedom. The Bible taught Mayhew that the Israelites angered God when they asked for a king, and that "the Son of God came down from heaven, to make us 'free indeed'." Mayhew's own father taught him "the love of liberty" with "a chaste and virtuous passion." In middle age, he was proud to say that he was unable "to relinquish the fair object of my youthful affections, liberty; whose charms, instead of decaying with time in my eyes, have daily captivated me more and more."

Mayhew had grieved at the promulgation of the Stamp Act, when liberty "seemed about to take her final departure from America, and to leave that ugly hag slavery, the deformed child of Satan, in her room." Now, however, he was "filled with a proportionable degree of joy in God, on occasion of her speedy return, with new smiles on her face, with augmented beauty and splendor. Once more then, Hail! Celestial maid, the daughter of God, and, excepting his Son, the first-born of heaven!" Liberty was "the delight of the wise, good and brave; the protectress of innocence from wrongs and oppression, the patroness of learning, arts, eloquence, virtue, rational loyalty, religion!"

Mayhew's scripturally-influenced view of history was optimistic. Although the Stamp Act had been dreadful, "God often bringeth good out of evil," just as Joseph's enslavement in Egypt led to his rescue of his family. American liberties were like an oak tree growing stronger roots and broader branches after being buffeted by "storms and tempests." "And who knows," he said, "our liberties being thus established, but that on some future occasion, when the kingdoms of the earth are moved, and roughly dashed one against another...we, or our posterity may even have the great felicity and honor to 'save much people alive' and keep Britain herself from ruin"—precisely what would happen during World War II.

"The Snare Broken" was Mayhew's last great sermon. He died six weeks later, at the age of 46, an inspired and devoted servant of Liberty.

Schools and Children

CHAPTER 7

"Zero tolerance" is a thought-control program

On May 9, 2001, a fifth-grader was handcuffed at Oldsmar Elementary School near Tampa, and taken into custody by police. "That's normal procedure in a situation like this," said school district spokesman Ron Stone.

What crime could this youthful offender have committed to warrant such treatment? His dastardly deed, ferreted out by an alert teacher, had been to draw some pictures of weapons. The punishment meted out, aside from the trauma that comes from being treated like a violent criminal, was suspension from school—the same punishment he would have received had he actually brought a firearm to school. Said principal David Schmitt, "the boy probably won't return for the rest of the year and probably would be moved to another school." Added Schmitt reassuringly, "The children were in no danger at all. It involved no real weapons."

Many adult Americans today smugly contrast themselves with their narrow-minded, intolerant ancestors. Back in the 1890s, for example, there were many parents and teachers who forbade young people to dance, play cards, or attend the theater. In the middle decades of the twentieth century, teenage schoolgirls were warned against wearing patent leather shoes, because the shoes might reflect their underwear.

While it's easy to smirk at hyper-fearful parents and teachers who pestered children about whist or patent leather shoes, less amusing is the realization that many of today's educators have surpassed their ancestors in imposing absurd restrictions on young people.

Today's restrictions go by the name of "zero tolerance," and for once, this is a government program aptly named. To have "zero tolerance" is the same as to have "no tolerance," which is the same as being "intolerant" or "bigoted"—

the precise opposite of "celebrating diversity" or "embracing tolerance." And just as we might expect as much from programs that revel in intolerance, "zero tolerance" is used by many so-called "educators" to suppress the behavior of students who deviate from political correctness.

As originally conceived in the 1980s, "zero tolerance" had nothing to do with expelling children from school for thought crimes involving art projects. Rather, "zero tolerance" meant setting strict rules against bringing guns, knives, or other potentially dangerous items to school, and imposing automatic and uniform discipline for violators. The inflexible system was meant to protect schools against discrimination complaints by racial minority students who violated the rules.

"Zero tolerance," however, has morphed into a thought-control program that would have impressed Chairman Mao. In an August 2000 report, Prof. Russell Skiba, Director of Indiana University's Institute for Child Study, noted that, "School punishments greatly out of proportion to the offense arouse controversy by violating basic perceptions of fairness inherent in our system of law."

A perfect example was reported by the Associated Press on January 31, 2001, when "an 8-year-old boy was suspended from school for 3 days after pointing a breaded chicken finger at a teacher and saying 'Pow, pow, pow'. The incident apparently violated the Jonesboro [Ark.] School District's 'zero tolerance' policy against weapons."

South Elementary principal Dan Sullivan said that, "The school has zero-tolerance rules because the public wants them." After Jonesboro's 1998 school shootings, said Sullivan, "People saw real threats to the safety and security of their students."

How silly must school administrators become in order to convince the public that children playing with a chicken finger are "real threats" to "safety and security"?

Sullivan declared that punishment for a threat "depends on the tone, the demeanor, and in some manner you judge the intent. It's not the object in the hand, it's the thought in the mind. Is a plastic fork worse than a metal fork? Is a pencil a weapon?"

On March 24, 2001, the Associated Press reported that a third-grade honor student at Lenwil Elementary School in West Monroe, La., was suspended for three days because he drew a picture of a soldier holding a knife and a canteen. The picture also included a fort filled with appropriate gear, including rifles, handguns, knives, and first-aid kits. The school's principal defended the suspension because the school "can't tolerate anything that has to do with guns or knives."

In fact, the school could tolerate drawings of soldiers, Civil War battle scenes, police officers, and lots of other things that involve guns or knives. They're present in our history books and our monuments all across America, which honor heroes who have sacrificed their lives for the liberty we Americans now enjoy. The school simply chose to be intolerant. Punishing a third-grader for drawing a picture of soldier doesn't make anyone safer.

Willie Isby, director of Child Welfare and Attendance for the Ouachita Parish School System, called the student's picture "a violent arrangement here"—even though the picture simply depicts a standing soldier, and contains no violence.

"The punishment is not that bad in this case," Isby continued, "in light of the fact that we have been having all these killings in schools."

Isby's quote gets to the heart of modern "zero tolerance" policies, under which third-graders are turned into scapegoats and punished (even though they did nothing wrong) because the real criminals (e.g., school shooters) are beyond the power of school officials to punish.

Put another way, the schools themselves are perpetrating classic bullying behavior. Emory University primatologist Frans de Waal observes that most monkey or ape species have designated scapegoats, who get picked on when the group is under stress. De Waal explained, "The scapegoat also gives the high-ranking individuals in the group a common enemy, a unifier. By uniting against the scapegoat in moments of tension, it creates a bond."

Thus, when the high-ranking individuals in a school (administrators, psychologists, and teachers) are under stress (because of highly publicized school violence), they can unite by bullying the scapegoat—namely the children who commit thought crimes.

Late in 2000, a third-grade boy in Pontiac, Mich., was suspended because he brought a one-and-one-half inch "gun-shaped medallion" to school. It wasn't a real gun, or a even a toy gun, only the symbol of a gun. Punishing a child for a wearing a medallion is—like punishing a child for artwork—a form of thought control.

The reason that's usually given for zero-tolerance policies in schools is the reduction of aggressive behavior. But does denying civil rights to children create a safer learning environment? Does administrative bullying really reduce aggression? Not according to Prof. Skiba, who concluded from a comprehensive review of the literature that there is an "almost complete lack of documentation linking zero tolerance with improved school safety...Zero Tolerance is a political response, not an educationally sound solution....The most extensive studies suggest a negative relationship between school security measures and school safety."

Concluded Rand Institute behavioral scientist Jaana Juvonen in the March 9, 2001, issue of *Salon*, solutions to combat juvenile violence "may not only be ineffective but may actually backfire." Juvonen singled out "zero tolerance" policies as the worst example.

The zeal to bully scapegoats might be diminished if school administrators believed in the existence of Hell (a concept which was popular in the late

19th and mid-20th century, but one which is not taken seriously among the so-cial classes from which today's government school administrators are drawn). If school bureaucrats could picture the Columbine murderers spending eter-nity (or at least a long time) in Hell, would they devote so much psychic en-ergy to punishing children who are merely exhibiting normal development by drawing pictures of soldiers, or by wearing trench coats?

What of the original core of "zero tolerance": weapons in school? Even here, the enforcement has gone insane. Brooklyn high school student Reginald McDonald was suspended for carrying a 12-inch metal ruler, which the school labeled a "weapon"—even though his shop class required him to have a ruler.

In Pennsylvania, a six-year-old was expelled because he carried a nail clipper in his backpack. The capriciousness of the nail-clipper expulsion is a central feature of totalitarian criminal "justice": Anyone can be punished for anything. Random punishment for innocent acts creates a sense of learned helplessness in the victim as well as in those who witness the punishment. Did this youngster have any more reason to believe he was committing a crime than Joseph K. did in Franz Kafka's *The Trial*?

Zero tolerance isn't a program to make our children safer. Instead, it's a program to enable the bullying of children by intolerant adults.

THE RESISTANCE: TEACHING COMMON-SENSE SCHOOL PROTECTION

Since the Columbine murders in 1999, several important steps have been taken to prevent or thwart school shootings. Much more still needs to be done.

The good news is that, since Columbine, police tactics in school attacks have dramatically changed. At Columbine, the armed "school resource officer" refused to pursue the killers into the building, and kept himself safe outside while the murders were going on inside. Even after SWAT teams arrived, and while, via an open 911 line, the authorities knew that students were being me-thodically executed in the library, the police stood idle just a few yards outside the library.

To this day, the authorities in Jefferson County, Colorado, have success-fully covered up who made the decision not to fight the killers.

Fortunately, police tactics have changed since that disgraceful day. Now, the standard police response to an "active shooter" is speedy counter-action. For example, at a March 2001 attack on Santana High School in Santee, California, the police response was immediate, and saved lives. It was the first time ever that a school shooting had been met with prompt police use of force.

A second form of progress post-Columbine has been greater news me-dia responsibility. *Time* and *Newsweek* put the Columbine killers on the front cover—giving them the posthumous infamy which motivates many mass murderers. As Clayton Cramer has documented, massive publicity given to mass murderers plays a significant role in encouraging more mass murders. ("Ethical Problems of Mass Murder Coverage in the Mass Media," *Journal of Mass Media Ethics*, vol. 9, Winter 1993-94.)

In the 21st century, the mainstream media have been somewhat more responsible about focusing coverage on the victims, rather than the perpetrator. While stories are still written about perpetrators, the killers are less likely to be rewarded (in effect) with a big picture on the front of a magazine or newspaper. The mass attention given to pictures and the video-taped rantings of the Virginia Tech killer in April 2007 was an unfortunate exception to the trend towards greater media responsibility.

After Columbine, there was a great push for anti-bullying programs and the like. Whether bullying was or is a major cause of shootings is debatable. The older of the Columbine killers likely suffered from a superiority complex; his problem was excessive self-esteem. Indeed, many criminals have excessively high self-esteem, and one cause of their criminality is the large gap between how most people see them (accurately, as mediocre losers) and their own self-image. Self-esteem programming in the schools, whatever its other merits, might be counterproductive to school safety.

One important value of anti-bullying programs, however, is that most of them strongly encourage students to come forward and report a problem. Much more so than in the pre-Columbine period, students and other community members who hear rumors or threats of a school attack have been willing to warn the authorities. There have been many attacks which have been prevented only because someone did so. The willingness of people to speak up has been the most significant post-Columbine step forward in safety, and has likely saved many dozens of lives.

Compared to the Columbine aftermath, there is much less inclination among the political classes, and, even much of the media, to use school murders as a pretext for irrelevant anti-gun laws. If it were actually possible to ban all guns, and confiscate all of the more than 200 million firearms in America, school killers would be deprived of their most effective weapon—since most killers do not have the skills to build bombs, and a criminal cannot use a knife or sword to control two dozen people at a distance.

But it is pretty clear that the kinds of laws which were pushed after Columbine (one-gun-a-month in California, special restrictions on gun shows in Colorado and Oregon) are of little value in keeping guns away from people who plan their attacks a long period of time in advance.

The attacks in the fall of 2006 highlighted a problem that was forgotten in the post-Columbine frenzy. There are lots of attacks which are not perpetrated by disaffected students. We knew this in 1988, when a 30-year-old woman attacked a second-grade classroom in Winnetka, Illinois. Or when a pederast killed 16 kindergarteners and a teacher in Dunblane, Scotland.

One reason why adult sociopaths so often choose to attack schools—schools to which they have no particular connection—is that schools are easy targets. It is not surprising that police stations, hunting-club meetings, state-side army bases, NRA offices, and similar locations known to contain armed adults are rarely attacked.

Because of the spread of reasonable concealed-handgun licensing laws, now in 40 out of 50 states, whenever you walk into a place with a large crowd of people—a restaurant, a theater, a shopping mall—you can safely assume that several people in the crowd will have a license to carry a concealed handgun, and some of them are currently carrying.

Schools are one of the few places in the United States where the government has guaranteed that there will be no licensed, trained adults with a concealed firearm that could be used to resist a would-be mass murderer.

Since the fact is apparently obvious to random psychopaths, it would be very dangerous to assume that the fact is not obvious to terrorists also. Beslan, Russia, shows that terrorists with al Qaeda connections consider schools to be good targets. There is also the danger of self-starting jihadis, such as the man who attacked the Jewish community center in Seattle. Every Jewish school and community center should very seriously consider having at least one full-time security guard.

Like many states, Utah enacted a concealed-handgun licensing law in 1995. Unlike many other states, Utah did not make schools an exclusion zone for lawful carrying. Not only a teacher on duty, but also a parent coming to pick up a child from school, can lawfully carry a concealed handgun in a Utah school building—after, of course, passing a background check and safety training. (Utah Code § 76-10-505.5.) In 2003, the legislature expanded the law, by allowing principals to authorize firearms possession by individuals who do not have a concealed-handgun carry permit.

After years of experience in Utah, we now have exactly zero reported problems of concealed handgun licensees misusing guns at school, or students stealing guns from teachers, or teachers using their licensed firearms to shoot or threaten students. During the same period, we also have had exactly zero mass murders in Utah schools.

My proposal, however, is not that other states go as far as Utah. Rather, I simply suggest that teachers and other school employees be allowed to carry if they obtain a handgun carry permit. If a school wants to require special additional training for school carry, that's fine.

Some people who do not like the idea of teachers being armed to protect students simply get indignant, or declare that armed teachers are inconsistent with a learning environment. I suggest that dead students—and the traumatic aftermath of a school attack—are far more inconsistent with a learning environment than is a math teacher having a concealed handgun.

"Teachers don't want to carry guns!" some people exclaim. True enough, for most teachers. But there are about six million teachers in the United States, and it would be foolish to make claims about what every teacher thinks. The one thing that almost all teachers have in common is that they have passed a fingerprint-based background check, meaning that they are significantly less likely than the general population to have a criminal history.

There are plenty of teachers who have served in the military, or the police, or who have otherwise acquired familiarity with firearms. And there will be other teachers who would willingly undergo the training necessary to learn how to use a firearm to protect themselves and their students. After all, almost all the teachers in southern Thailand are Buddhists, and even they have chosen to carry handguns because of Islamic terrorist attacks on schools; so it would be ridiculous to claim that American teachers, as a universal category, would never exercise the choice to carry.

We know that school shootings have been stopped by armed citizens with guns. In 1997, a Mississippi attack was thwarted after vice principal Joel Myrick retrieved a handgun from his trunk. The killer had already shot several people at Pearl High School, and was leaving that school to attack Pearl Junior High, when Myrick pointed his .45 pistol at the killer's head and apprehended him. A few days later, an armed adult stopped a school rampage in Edinboro, Pennsylvania.

It is commonly, but incorrectly, believed that the federal Gun-Free School Zones Act creates an insurmountable barrier to arming teachers. Not so. The Act has a specific exemption for persons who have a concealed handgun carry permit from the state where the school is located, if the state requires a background check before issuance of a permit.

It is state laws, not the federal law, which are in need of reform to allow schools to be protected.

Pending legal reform, there are several steps that school districts can take to improve school safety. Almost all teachers spend several days a year in continuing professional education programs. Every school district should begin, at least, offering self-defense training as an option to teachers on in-service days.

These programs should explain the critical importance of decisive action by teachers in the very first moments when an armed intruder has entered a room. The faster that students get out, the more lives that can be saved. Allowing an intruder to take control of the room, and line students up, or tie them up, is extremely dangerous. If students flee immediately (especially if the room has at least two exits), the criminal will have a much harder time obtaining control and taking hostages.

Undoubtedly, the criminal might begin shooting immediately. But if the victim is moving and is constantly getting further from the shooter, it is much harder for the shooter to deliver a critical hit. In contrast, when the victims are

95

stationary and under the shooter's control, the killer has an easy time delivering a fatal head shot from a foot away. At Columbine, some fleeing students were wounded, some of them very seriously. But almost all the fatalities were the result of up-close executions of stationary victims.

Defensive training for teachers can also include how to quickly disarm a person with a gun, especially when his attention is distracted. This can be a dangerous move, and it does not always work. If it does, perhaps everyone's lives can saved. If it does not, the killer has no greater power than if the move were never attempted.

At a more advanced level, there are programs such as Krav Maga ("contact combat")—a technique of unarmed self-defense currently used by some US police departments, and the Israeli Defense Forces. It was originally created by Jews in Bratislava during the 1930s, for self-defense against anti-Semitic thugs who might have weapons. Every school district should offer to pay half the tuition for a teacher who takes classes in Krav Maga or similar programs. Introductory versions of these programs could also be offered for free on in-service days.

Of the teachers who would never choose to carry a firearm, some would choose to carry non-lethal defensive sprays. Basic training in defensive spray-use takes an afternoon. Schools could offer more sophisticated training as well, focused on the situations most likely be encountered in a school.

Pepper sprays are not always a panacea (they do not work on some criminals, especially ones who eat a lot of spicy foods), but they can save lives. While a predator is writhing in excruciating pain, he will lose control of the situation, allowing students to flee, and giving the teacher a good chance of taking the gun.

And what about self-defense for students? Incorporating several days of self-defense into the annual physical education curriculum would be sensible anyway, even if there were no problems with school shootings. Self-defense training will make students less vulnerable at isolated bus stops, and everywhere else. The core of all self-defense training is greater awareness of one's environment, so that a person can get away from potential trouble before it becomes actual trouble.

Self-defense training also teaches that it is dangerous to let a criminal take control of your surroundings; even if a criminal is pointing a gun at you, you are probably better off to try running away, than to let him put you in a car where he can transport you to an isolated location.

Teachers and students would also learn that it is sometimes better to submit; if you can surrender your purse to a mugger, and protect yourself from injury, that is often the safe choice. We know, however, than when an armed criminal attempts to take over a school, there is no realistic hope that the criminal will be satisfied with stealing some money.

Consider a 12th-grade classroom containing 15 healthy males, several of whom are athletes. If the males rush the perpetrator en masse, some of them might be shot, but it is also likely that the perpetrator would be quickly subdued, all the more so since most school shooters are not physically powerful. The school shooting in Springfield, Oregon, ended when several brave students, including wrestler Jake Ryker, rushed the shooter; Ryker was shot, but recovered.

To some people, the notion that teachers like Joel Myrick or students like Jake Ryker should engage in active resistance is highly offensive, and the idea that teachers and students should be encouraged to learn active resistance is outrageous.

Our nation has too many people who are not only unwilling to learn how to protect themselves, but who are also determined to prevent innocent third persons from practicing active defense. A person has the right to choose to be a pacifist, but it is wrong to force everyone else to act like a pacifist. It is the pacifist-aggressives which have turned American schools into safe zones for mass murderers.

School shootings are the ultimate form of bullying, and long experience shows that the more likely and more effective the resistance, the less the bullying.

If a trained teacher carries a concealed defensive tool, such as pepper spray, there is no downside except an offense against the self-righteous sensibilities of pacifist-aggressives. Except for criminals, everyone would be a lot safer—and not just at school—if teachers and students were encouraged to learn at least basic unarmed self-defense.

FOLLOW THE LEADER: ISRAEL AND THAILAND SET AN EXAMPLE BY ARMING TEACHERS

Islamist terrorists in Beslan, Russia, took over a school and murdered 334 people, including 186 children. It could have been prevented. Decades ago, Israel adopted a policy that swiftly ended terrorist attacks against schools. In 2004, Thailand adopted a similar approach. It is politically incorrect, but it does have the advantage of saving the lives of children and teachers. The policy? Encourage teachers to carry firearms.

Muslim extremists in Thailand's southern provinces of Narathiwat, Yala, and Pattani have been carrying out a terrorist campaign, seeking to create an Islamic state independent of Thailand, whose population is predominantly Buddhist.

Most teachers are Buddhists, and they have been a key target of the terrorists, who have also perpetrated arsons against dozens of schools.

As reported by the Associated Press on April 27, 2004, "Interior Minister Bhokin Bhalakula ordered provincial governors to give teachers licenses to buy guns if they want to even though it would mean bringing firearms into the classrooms when the region's 925 schools reopen May 17 after two months of summer holiday."

The AP article explained: "Pairat Wihakarat, the president of a teachers' union in the three provinces, said more than 1,700 teachers have already asked for transfers to safer areas. Those who are willing to stay want to carry guns to protect themselves, he said."

Gun-control laws in Thailand are extremely strict, and were tightened even more because of three school shootings (perpetrated by students) that took place in a single week in June 2003. Two students were killed.

But though Thailand's government is extremely hostile to gun ownership in general, it has recognized that teachers ought to be able to safeguard their students and themselves.

A similar strategy worked in Israel, as David Schiller detailed in an interview with Jews for the Preservation of Firearms Ownership. (Available on jpfo.org.) Schiller was born in West Germany and moved to Israel, where he served in the military as a weapons specialist. He later returned to Germany, and was hired as a counterterrorism expert by the Berlin police office, as well as by police forces of other German cities. For a while he worked in the terrorism research office of the RAND corporation, and for several years he published a German gun magazine.

Schiller recalls that Palestine Liberation Organization attacks on Israeli schools began during Passover 1974. The first attack was aimed at a school in Galilee. When the PLO terrorists found that it was closed because of Passover weekend, they murdered several people in a nearby apartment building.

Then, on May 15, 1974, in Maalot:

> "Three PLO gunmen, after making their way through the border fence, first shot up a van load full of workers returning from a tobacco factory (incidentally these people happened to be Galilee Arabs, not Jews), then they entered the school compound of Maalot. First they murdered the housekeeper, his wife and one of their kids, then they took a whole group of nearly 100 kids and their teachers hostage. These were staying overnight at the school, as they were on a hiking trip. In the end, the deadline ran out, and the army's special unit assaulted the building. During the rescue attempt, the gunmen blew their explosive charges and sprayed the kids with machine-gun fire. 25 people died, 66 wounded."

Israel at the time had some strict gun laws, left over from the days of British colonialists who tried to prevent the Jews from owning guns.

After vigorous debate, the government began allowing army reservists to keep their weapons with them. Handgun carry permits were given to any Israeli with a clean record who lived in the most dangerous areas: Judea, Samaria, and Gaza.

All over Israel, guns became pervasive in the schools:

> "Teachers and kindergarten nurses now started to carry guns, schools were protected by parents (and often grandpas) guarding them in voluntary shifts. No school group went on a hike or trip without armed guards. The Police involved the citizens in a voluntary civil guard project 'Mishmar Esrachi,' which even had its own sniper teams. The Army's Youth Group program, 'Gadna', trained 15 to 16-year-old kids in gun safety and guard procedures and the older high-school boys got involved with the Mishmar Esrachi. During one noted incident, the 'Herzliyah Bus massacre' (March '78, hijacking of a bus, 37 dead, 76 wounded), these youngsters were involved in the overall security measures in which the whole area between North Tel Aviv and the resort town of Herzlyiah was blocked off, manning roadblocks with the police, guarding schools kindergartens, etc."

After a while, "When the message got around to the PLO groups and a couple infiltration attempts failed, the attacks against schools ceased."

This is not to say that Palestinian terrorists never target schools. In May 2002, an Israeli teacher shot a suicide terrorist before he could harm anyone.

Then on May 31, 2002, as reported by Israel National News, a terrorist threw a grenade and began shooting at a kindergarten in Shavei Shomron. Instead of closing in on the children, he abruptly fled the kindergarten and began shooting up the nearby neighborhood. Apparently he realized that the kindergarten was sure to have armed adults, and that he could not stay at the school long enough to make sure he actually murdered someone.

Unfortunately for the terrorist, "David Elbaz, owner of the local minimarket, gave chase and killed him with gunshots. In addition to several grenades and the weapon the terrorist carried on him, security sweeps revealed several explosive devices that he had intended to detonate during the thwarted attack."

People can spend months and years studying the root causes of terrorism, and pondering the merits of the grievances of Islamic terrorists in Malaysia, Israel, and Russia. But it's fair to say that schoolchildren and teachers are not legitimate targets even of people who have legitimate grievances.

No one knows if civilized nations will ever eliminate the root causes of terrorism. But we do know that terrorist attacks on schools and schoolchildren could be greatly reduced—if every nation at risk of terrorist attacks on schools began following the lead of Thailand and Israel.

Adults have a duty to protect children. In Beslan, 186 children died because the teachers lacked the tools to stop the evildoers. If we are really serious about gun laws that protect "the children," then it seems clear that—whatever other gun laws a society adopts—every civilized nation at risk of terrorist attack ought to ensure that armed teachers can protect innocent children.

INTERNATIONAL FREEDOM

CHAPTER 8

HOW THE UNITED NATIONS HELPS MASS MURDERERS

"The spread of illicit arms and light weapons is a global threat to human security and human rights," insisted United Nations secretary-general Kofi Annan. But it would be more accurate to say: "The UN's disarmament policy is a global threat to human security and human rights." It was the UN's lethal policy that was responsible for the deaths of thousands of innocents in Srebrenica in 1995.

For orchestrating a vicious ethnic-cleansing campaign that included the slaughter in Srebrenica, ex-Yugoslav president Slobodan Milošević was prosecuted for genocide and crimes against humanity before the International Criminal Tribunal for the Former Yugoslavia (ICTY) at the Hague. Milošević, the first head of state to be charged with war crimes, faced a maximum sentence of life imprisonment, and died in prison before a verdict was rendered.

The massacre of more than 7,500 men and boys at Srebrenica garnered worldwide publicity after Bosnian Serb general Radislav Krstić, the senior commander charged with genocide there, was found guilty by the ICTY on August 2, 2001. As CNN explained, Krstić "planned and led a week-long rampage in July 1995 in the UN declared 'safe zone' of Srebrenica in eastern Bosnia, where Muslims had been promised protection by U.N. soldiers." Krstić was given a 46-year prison term. (Although the terms "safe area," "safe haven," and "safe zone" are often used interchangeably, there are legal distinctions between them; Srebrenica was supposed to be a "safe area.")

A large share of the blame for Srebrenica was placed on the Dutch government and ill-prepared Dutch "peacekeepers," as detailed in an April 2002 report by the Netherlands Institute for War Documentation. Dutch prime minister Wim Kok—and his entire cabinet—resigned in shame a week later.

Located near the eastern border of Bosnia-Herzegovina, the silver-mining town of Srebrenica was once part of the Republic of Yugoslavia. Yugoslavia had been created by the Treaty of Versailles in 1919, and until the country broke up in 1991, it was the largest nation on the Balkan peninsula, approximately the size of the state of Virginia.

Yugoslavia was turned into a Communist dictatorship in 1945 by Marshal Tito. When Tito died in 1980, his successors feared civil war, so a system was instituted according to which the collective leadership of government and party offices would be rotated annually. But the new government foundered, and in 1989, Serbian president Milošević began re-imposing Serb and Communist hegemony. Slovenia and Croatia declared independence in June 1991.

Slovenia repelled the Yugoslav army in ten days, but fighting in Croatia continued until December, with the Yugoslav government retaining control of about a third of Croatia. Halfway through the Croat-Yugoslav war, the UN Security Council adopted Resolution 713, calling for "a general and complete embargo on all deliveries of weapons and military equipment to Yugoslavia" (meaning rump Yugoslavia, plus Croatia and Slovenia). Although sovereign nations are normally expected to acquire and own arms, Resolution 713 defined such arms as "illicit" in the eyes of the UN

It was universally understood that the Serbs were in control of most of the Yugoslav army's weaponry, and that the embargo therefore left them in a position of military superiority. Conversely, even though the embargo was regularly breached, it left non-Serbs vulnerable. The UN had, in effect, deprived the incipient countries of the right to self-defense, a right guaranteed under Article 51 of the UN Charter.

Macedonia seceded peacefully from Yugoslavia in early 1992, but Bosnia-Herzegovina's secession quickly led to a three-way civil war between Bosnian Muslims ("Bosniacs"), Serbs (who are Orthodox), and Croats (who are Catholic). The Bosnian Serbs received substantial military support from what remained of old Yugoslavia (consisting of Serbia and Montenegro, and under the control of Slobodan Milošević).

Security Council Resolution 713 made it illegal for the new Bosnian government to acquire arms to defend itself from Yugoslav aggression.

The Bosnian Muslims were told by the UN that they did not need weapons of their own; instead, they would have immediate access to the upper echelons of UN and NATO "peacekeeping" forces. As noted in UN documents, Bosnia-Herzegovina president Izetbegović "was in favour of the UNPROFOR [United Nations Protection Force] proposal, which, as he understood it, meant that the Bosniacs would hand their weapons over to UNPROFOR in return for UNPROFOR protection."

The Bosniacs subverted the UN embargo by importing arms from Arab countries while the US winked. At the same time, the Bosniacs also tried to play the part of good guys, under the theory that they would garner more territory in the long run by being the party that did what the UN said. Not until 1995 did the Bosniacs begin to achieve arms parity with the Serbs—and it was the prospect of impending parity that convinced the Serbs to make a final grand offensive, to acquire as much territory as possible before losing their military advantage. Srebrenica was one result of the final Serb campaign.

The other disastrous policy was the creation of "safe areas" pursuant to Resolution 819, adopted by the Security Council in April 1993. Safe areas were "regions, which should preferably be substantially free of conflict beforehand, where refugees could be offered a 'reasonable degree of security' by a brigade of peacekeeping troops."

The concept of a "safe area," however, was a fantasy. Even the UN forces were not safe; they could not protect themselves, let alone anyone else. In fact, they were taken hostage, casually, at will, without resistance—sometimes in hundreds at a time. The UN hostages would then be used by the Bosnian Serbs to deter the UN and NATO from taking more aggressive action.

While the UN peacekeepers had collected some of the Bosniacs' weapons, the Bosniacs retained the better ones. With those weapons, they attacked Bosnian Serb villages and civilians, returning afterwards to Bosniac "safe areas." Each successive raid left the Serbs more infuriated. The UN was aware of these raids, and was aware that the Bosniacs had kept some weapons; but it took no steps to ensure the safety of Bosnian Serb civilians.

By the summer of 1995, the population of Srebrenica, a designated safe area, had swelled with refugees. By the time of the massacre, it was an island of Bosniacs in Bosnian Serb territory—an island the UN had sworn to protect.

But the UN would not honor its pledge. As the BBC later reported, "A former United Nations commander in Bosnia has told a Dutch parliamentary inquiry into the Srebrenica massacre that it was clear to him that Dutch authorities would not sacrifice its soldiers for the enclave."

And, indeed, on July 11, 1995, Bosnian Serb forces entered Srebrenica without resistance from Bosniac or UN forces; not a shot was fired. (The Bosniac general in Srebrenica had recently been recalled by his government, leaving the Bosniac forces leaderless.) Ethnic cleansing and genocide followed. The men and boys were separated from the women, then taken away and shot.

Knowing that remaining in the UN "safe area" would mean certain death, some ten to fifteen thousand Bosniac males fled into the surrounding forests, escaping to the Bosniac-held town of Tuzla. Only about three to four thousand were armed, mostly with hunting rifles; these were the men who survived what has since become known as the six-day "Marathon of Death." And the rest? Laura Silber and Allan Little, in their book *Yugoslavia: Death of a Nation*, describe the slaughter in the forest:

"Some were killed after having surrendered, believing the UN would protect them...Serb soldiers, some even dressed as UN peace-keepers driving stolen white UN vehicles, would guarantee the Muslims' safety. Then they would shoot."

The Serbs killed over 7,500 Bosniac males.

Three months after the massacre at Srebrenica, a unanimous Security Council rescinded its arms embargo against the nations of former Yugoslavia.

The UN can hardly claim ignorance of Serb intent. Prior to Srebrenica, the international body had knowledge of other mass killings committed by the Serbs against the Bosniacs between 1991 and 1994. One of the largest was perpetrated in April 1992 in the town of Bratunac, just outside Srebrenica. There, approximately 350 Bosnian Muslims were tortured and killed by Serb paramilitaries and special police.

Given that the UN was fully aware of Milošević's designs for a "Greater Serbia" (incorporating portions of Bosnia), and that the UN was fully aware of the disparity in military capabilities between Milošević and his intended victims, the UN had every responsibility to defend the Muslims; if the UN itself could not, it at least had a duty to lift the arms embargo immediately and allow Bosnia's Muslims to defend themselves.

Nor can the UN claim ignorance of what happens when victims are abandoned to their oppressors. The Srebrenica scenario is reminiscent of the 1994 genocide in Rwanda, when promises by the UN to protect Rwandan civilians proved just as empty. There, too, UN personnel knew that the victim groups had been previously disarmed—in this case, by laws enacted in 1964 and 1979. Early in the genocide, thousands of Rwandan civilians, thinking they would be protected, gathered in areas where UN troops had been stationed. The victims were not protected. If the Rwandans had known that the UN troops would withdraw, they would have fled, and some might have survived. "The manner in which troops left, including attempts to pretend to the refugees that they were not in fact leaving, was disgraceful," an independent report later concluded. (The 1999 report was commissioned by the UN, and led by Ingvar Carlsson, Han Sung-Joo, and Rufus M. Kupolati.)

In short, the UN was aware of Milošević's propensity for ethnic cleansing, and had ample reason to know that its actions would create a situation ripe for genocide. The atrocities at Srebrenica could not have been perpetrated by the Serbs on such a grand scale had not the UN and its policies first prepared an enclave of victims, most of them disarmed.

While Radislav Krstić and Slobodan Milošević were prosecuted, upper-echelon UN policymakers have escaped accountability for their role in the tragedy. Kofi Annan, who served during this period as undersecretary-general for peacekeeping operations, was presented with the Nobel Peace prize on

December 10, 2001. Likewise unscathed is Boutros Boutros-Ghali, who presided as secretary general at the time of the Srebrenica massacre.

In 1998, three years after the Srebrenica massacre, Kofi Annan offered an apology:

> "The United Nations...failed to do our part to help save the people of Srebrenica from the Serb campaign of mass murder...In the end, the only meaningful and lasting amends we can make to the citizens of Bosnia and Herzegovina who put their faith in the international community is to do our utmost not to allow such horrors to recur. When the international community makes a solemn promise to safeguard and protect innocent civilians from massacre, then it must be willing to back its promise with the necessary means. Otherwise, it is surely better not to raise hopes and expectations in the first place, and not to impede whatever capability they may be able to muster in their own defense."

Just months after the show of contrition, Kofi Annan and the UN were back at work preventing prospective genocide victims from defending themselves. This time, the victims were the people of East Timor. Left unprotected because their firearms had been sequestered at the behest of the UN, the Timorese were attacked by the Indonesian military.

The fraud of UN "protection" was underscored yet again in May 2000. As Dennis Jett explains in *Why Peacekeeping Fails*, Sierra Leone "nearly became the UN's biggest peacekeeping debacle" when 500 peacekeepers there were taken hostage by rebels of the Revolutionary United Front (RUF). The RUF has been described by Human Rights Watch as a "barbarous group of thugs," who "lived off the country's rich diamond fields and terrorized the population with its signature atrocity of chopping off arms and hands of men, women and often children."

Jett continues: "The RUF troops are unspeakably brutal to civilians, but will not stand up to any determined military force. Yet the UN peacekeepers, with few exceptions, handed over their weapons including armored personnel carriers and meekly became prisoners." It was only the deployment of Britain's troops to the former colony that saved civilian lives and averted a "complete U.N. defeat."

It would be difficult to find an organization in recent history whose work has facilitated government mass murder of more people, in more diverse locations around the world, than the United Nations. And the UN's current campaign to disarm the world's peoples suggests that the genocides of the previous decade are to be repeated in many other places in the years to come.

An e-mail from a reader encapsulates the consequences of the UN's program to disarm everyone but the government:

"In 1999 I spent a year with the peacekeeping mission in Bosnia. I was stationed in the former 'safe' area Gorazde. I learned a lot about that war and how the civilians were massacred. One day we were discussing guns and private ownership. In response to the statement that the U.N. believes only the police and military should have guns, a Bosnian exasperatedly asked: 'Who do you think slaughtered everyone?'"

GLOBAL GUN POHIBITION LOBBY: BAN ARMS SALES TO ISRAEL

The international gun prohibition movement is making good progress in its push for Arms Trade Treaty. The proposed treaty is currently being discussed at the United Nations by the First Committee (Disarmament and International Security) of the General Assembly.

The leading NGO lobbying for the Arms Trade Treaty is Control Arms, an organization created and directed by IANSA (International Action Network on Small Arms), Amnesty International, and Oxfam. A Control Arms report, *Arms without Borders*, makes the case for the Arms Trade Treaty.

The report offers examples of arms transfers which, according to Control Arms, would be stopped by a global Arms Trade Treaty. Among the examples cited is the sale of Apache AH-64 helicopters to Israel (page 12). Control Arms notes an incident in which an Apache helicopter shot an automobile in Tyre, Lebanon, and that, according to Human Rights Watch, there was no evidence of Hezbollah activity in the vicinity. In response, Prof. Gerald Steinberg of Bar-Ilan University states that the HRW/Control Arms claims "contradict clear evidence of heavy Hizbullah presence and use of vehicles for transporting missiles and armed personnel."

Page 25 of the Control Arms report declares:

"Helicopters, combat aircraft and air-to-surface missiles supplied to Israel primarily by the USA, but often incorporating components supplied by other countries, have been used in the Occupied Territories resulting in hundreds of deaths and thousands of injuries, in apparent violation of international humanitarian law. According to Amnesty International, many of the 190 Palestinians killed in 2005 were 'killed unlawfully', including as a result of deliberate and reckless shooting, or attacks in densely populated residential areas. At the same time, Palestinian armed groups have used rockets, explosive belts and other bombs to kill and injure hundreds of Israelis."

Page 4 of the report includes a half-sentence criticizing Hezbollah for firing rockets at civilian targets in Israel. The Control Arms paper does not mention any problem about the international flow of arms to Syria. Iran is criticized for its arms sales to Sudan, but not for its supplying of arms to Hezbollah and to terrorist organizations in Iraq and Afghanistan.

The Control Arms paper presents, at best, a moral equivalence between Israel, Hezbollah, and Palestinian terrorists—all three of whom would, under the Arms Trade Treaty, theoretically be prevented from acquiring arms.

In future discussions of the Arms Trade Treaty, everyone should acknowledge that the Treaty is intended, according to its leading NGO sponsor, to create an arms embargo against Israel. A person who wants arms sales to Israel to remain legal under international law would be foolish to support the Arms Trade Treaty.

It is true that Israel has a robust domestic military industry, and therefore could survive an arms import embargo. The Control Arms folks are one step ahead; their paper emphasizes that the Arms Trade Treaty must include control of components as well as finished products. Control Arms is also very clear on requiring that the trade in dual-use materials (e.g., titanium which could be used for civilian products, or for arms) be banned, unless there are strong safeguards that the material will not be used for human rights violations—such as, in the view of Control Arms, Israel's self-defense against Hezbollah, Hamas, Islamic Jihad, and al Aqsa.

Off target: Canada's gun registry was created to stop massacres, but failed again

Several school shootings in late 2006 in the United States led the anti-gun groups and their media allies to renew their demands for more American gun control. But a tragedy in Montreal, Canada, shows how dangerous the anti-gun agenda can be—for students and for everyone else.

Because of the copycat effect, a single highly-publicized attack on a school tends to beget others. Sometimes, attacks are thwarted before they begin because a concerned citizen tells the authorities when she has good reason to believe that someone poses an imminent danger.

Sadly, nobody in Canada spoke up about Kimveer Gill.

On Sept. 13, 2006, the 25-year-old implemented an attack he had been planning for more than a month, when he shot two people near the entrance of Dawson College, a community college in Montreal. Then, armed with a handgun, a carbine and a shotgun, he walked to a cafeteria known to be popular with Jewish students and began shooting at random. He fired 50 shots, killing 18-year-old Anastasia De Sousa and wounding 19 others, putting two of them into a coma.

By coincidence, two police officers were visiting the Dawson campus that day. They responded immediately, as did reinforcements. Gill used a pair of hostages as human shields. After being wounded in the arm by the police, Gill fatally shot himself.

A review of security camera tapes revealed that Gill had been staking out the school since August 10.

A few days later, police in the town of Hudson, Quebec, arrested a 15-year-old male who had threatened to shoot up a local high school. Hunting rifles were confiscated from his home.

Those firearms were properly registered in accordance with Canadian law, as were all of Gill's guns.

Ironically, it was a mass murder at another Montreal college in 1989 that led to enactment of Canada's present repressive and ineffective gun registration laws.

Marc Lépine (whose birth name was Gamil Gharbi) was the son of an Algerian immigrant who was an alcoholic, woman-hating, violent domestic abuser. Lépine was also a big fan of Corporal Denis Lortie, who in 1984 had perpetrated a triple homicide in the Quebec National Assembly.

On December 6, 1989, Lépine—who blamed women for the many failures of his life, including rejection by the Canadian armed forces—attacked a computing class at the École Polytechnique, the engineering school at the University of Montreal. After ordering the men out of the room, he fatally shot 13 women, fatally stabbed another and wounded eight women and four men, roaming the building at will before a long-delayed and incompetent police response finally resulted in his demise.

Like Lépine, Kimveer Gill was a bundle of hatred. On the VampireFreaks. com website, Gill dubbed himself "Fatality666" and expressed his desire to be the "angel of death." He said he wanted to die "in a hail of bullets," and snarled that "anger and hatred simmers within me." He described himself as a Satanist, and he posted pictures of himself in menacing and malicious poses with knives and firearms.His neighbors were afraid of him, and his friends reported that "he had a big problem with humanity in general."

After the 1989 Montreal massacre, the Progressive-Conservative government responded with a harsh new gun law that, among other things, banned many self-loading guns and classified many other self-loaders as "restricted weapons." In Canada, all handguns were already "restricted weapons," requiring a special licensing procedure and registration; the process takes about three months. Kimveer Gill's Glock pistol, his Norinco HP9-1 short-barreled 12-gauge shotgun and his Beretta CX4 Storm self-loading carbine were all legally registered as "restricted weapons."

The Progressive-Conservative anti-gun law helped alienate the party's base of support; the party was demolished in the next election and no longer exists. However, the PC anti-gun laws were not nearly enough for Canada's anti-gun lobby.

Heidi Rathjen, who had been a student at Polytechnique during Lépine's attack, co-founded the Coalition for Gun Control, which used the 1989 crime to demand vast new anti-gun laws.

Their efforts were supported by many feminists who had not a word of criticism for the misogynist Algerian culture that had spawned Lépine, but who were instead enraged at traditional Canadian values of masculinity. For example, in *The Montreal Massacre* (gynergy books, 1991), Quebec feminists called for a complete reconstruction of masculinity, decried masculinity as inherently anti-women and pro-death, and traced the pathologies of men to violent entertainment and rough sports

In 1995, Rathjen and company got almost everything they had demanded when the new Liberal government passed a law making gun license applications subject to the *de facto* veto of the applicant's spouse or former girlfriends, and abolished privacy for gun owners by making every gun owner's home open to warrantless, unannounced police inspection. The capstone of the law was the creation of a registry for all rifles and shotguns.

Proponents promised that the registry would cost only two million dollars (Canadian). Now the cost has reached over two billion and is still climbing. The two billion that was wasted on the registry could have been spent on putting police on the street (rather than shuffling paperwork). Or it could have upgraded forensics laboratories. Or it could have paid for social worker outreach to potentially violent people.

After the Dawson attack, Wendy Cukier—who was Rathjen's co-founder of the Coalition for Gun Control—said, "The argument for gun control has never been based on individual cases."

Calgary Sun columnist Ian Robinson responded: "Her statement is disingenuous to say the least. 'Disingenuous' is a fancy word for 'lie.'"

He reminded readers, "The entire gun control and registry debate in this country is, and always has been, based on an individual case," the École Polytechnique shooting. After 1989, gun control became "part of the nation's ongoing gender wars and was framed in precisely those terms." He remembered, "Anyone who objected to the content of the legislation—citing practicality, lack of efficacy, civil rights—was written off as some kind of psychopathic redneck."

The problem with the gun registration fiasco is not just that it didn't work at preventing precisely the type of crime that had led to the creation of the registry in the first place. Rather, the registry made Canada much less safe by wasting enormous criminal justice resources.

In January 2006, Canadians dumped the Liberal government, which had set up the gun registry, and elected Conservative Prime Minister Stephen Harper. He has announced plans to put more police on the street, and to impose tougher sentences for violent crime and for crimes such as stealing or smuggling firearms.

Even after the Dawson shootings and a renewed cry by gun-haters to save the long gun registry, Prime Minister Harper refuses to back away from his proposal to abolish it.

He told the House of Commons, "What this last government did is that instead of worrying about insane people or criminals, they simply went after farmers."

However, Harper heads a minority government, meaning that it is the largest party in Parliament, but it does not have a majority. Accordingly, it will be difficult to get rid of the registry unless the Conservatives win an outright majority in a future election.

Although abolishing the registry for ordinary long guns would have nothing to do with Gill's firearms (all of which would still be registered as "restricted weapons"), opportunistic leaders of the Liberal Party and the Bloc Québécois used the Dawson murders to declare that parliamentary members of their party would be "whipped" (required) to vote against scrapping the long gun registry.

Canadian Member of Parliament Garry Breitkreuz is the leader of pro-rights forces in the House of Commons. He is also co-chair of the Outdoor Caucus, a multi-party group of MPs who support Canada's traditions of hunting, fishing and conservation. Breitkreuz suggests that Canada get rid of the gun registry and replace it with a registry of people who are prohibited from possessing firearms.

This would include, he says, "all persons prohibited from owning guns by the courts, all persons with an outstanding criminal arrest warrant, all persons with restraining orders against them, all persons with refused or revoked firearms licenses and all individuals who have threatened violence."

Breitkreuz points out that it is ridiculous that a licensed firearm owner must report a change of address to the government's Canadian Firearms Centre, yet a person who is legally barred from owning guns is subject to no such requirement.

The reactions to the Dawson shooting reflect an important cultural divide in Canada. On one side are people such as columnist John Robson, who wrote in the *Ottawa Citizen*, "The most notable thing about the Dawson College shooter is not that he was armed but that he was wicked. If Canadians, like Americans, have been rodded up for centuries, yet mass shootings are a recent phenomenon, then maybe we need moral rearmament, not material disarmament."

On the other side are Canadians who also see a moral problem—namely that Canadians think too much like Americans. James Laxer, a political science professor at York University, calls for gun confiscation. He complains that Canada has "a watered-down version of the gun culture in the United States."

As an example of the "rancid" American gun culture, Laxer quotes, accurately, from a magazine article I wrote, observing that "A homeowner who never has to use his gun for self-defense still possesses something his unarmed next-door neighbor does not: he has made the decision that he, personally, will take responsibility for defending his family."

Canada's anti-gun culture warriors have not yet succeeded in eradicating the Canadian culture of outdoor sports, but they have almost entirely destroyed the legal right of Canadians to be armed for legitimate defense. It is even illegal to carry self-defense sprays for protection against crime.

Such sprays are, technically, allowed for defense against bears, but of course nobody on a Montreal college campus would be allowed to carry bear pepper spray.

Writing in the *Toronto Star*, Canadian journalist Rondi Adamson described herself as "a latte-drinking urbanite who has no interest in owning a gun of any kind." She has concluded, though, that there is "no societal benefit" to gun registration.

Her solution: "Had all, or many, students and faculty at L'École Polytechnique, or Dawson College, been armed, Marc Lépine and Kimveer Gill would have been taken out quickly."

Should college and graduate school adult women and men who are attacked by hate-filled killers be allowed to resist and thereby save lives? Or would that be "too American"?

GUN BANS & AFRICAN GENOCIDE: THE DISARMING FACTS

The international gun prohibition lobbies and their United Nations allies insist that there is no personal right of self-defense—that people should be forced to rely exclusively on the government for protection. The prohibitionists also insist that there is no human right for people to possess the means of self-defense, such as firearms. But what are people supposed to do when the government itself starts killing people? The genocide in Darfur, Sudan, is the direct result of the types of gun laws which the United Nations is trying to impose all over the world. Millions of people have already died because of such laws, and millions more may die unless the UN is stopped.

Like Iran today and Afghanistan under the Taliban, Sudan is ruled by a totalitarian, Islamist government. The current regime took power in a military coup in 1989, and immediately began imposing Islamic law throughout the country and perpetrating genocide. The genocide targets have varied: people in the central highlands were the first victims. Then the black Africans of south Sudan, who are mainly Christians or Animists. The most recent genocide victims are the people of Darfur, a Texas-sized region in western Sudan.

The Darfuris are Muslims, but like the majority of Sudan's population, they are black Africans, in contrast to the Arabs who control the government.

The foundation of Sudan's genocide is, as with almost every other genocide in world history, the disarmament of the victims.

In Sudan, it is virtually impossible for an average citizen to lawfully acquire and possess the means for self-defense. According to the national gun-control statutes, a gun licensee must be over 30 years of age, must have a specified social and economic status, and must be examined physically by a doctor. Females have even more difficulty meeting these requirements because of social and occupational limitations.

There are restrictions on the amount of ammunition one may possess, making it nearly impossible for a law-abiding gun owner to achieve proficiency with firearms. A handgun owner, for example, can only purchase 15 rounds of ammunition a year. The penalties for violation of Sudan's firearms laws are severe, and include capital punishment.

The practical application of the gun laws is different. If you are someone the government wants to slaughter—such as all the black Africans of southern and western Sudan, regardless of religion—then you are absolutely forbidden to possess a firearm. A US Department of State document notes: "After President Bashir seized power in 1989, the new government disarmed non-Arab ethnic groups but allowed politically loyal Arab allies to keep their weapons."

So if you are an Arab who wants to kill blacks, then Sudan's gun control laws became awfully loose. In Darfur, there has been a long rivalry between camel-riding Arab nomads and black African pastoralists. The Arabs consider the blacks to be racially inferior, and fit only for slavery. In *Darfur Rising*, the International Crisis Group explains: "Beginning in the mid-1980s, successive governments in Khartoum inflamed matters by supporting and arming the Arab tribes, in part to prevent the southern rebels from gaining a foothold in the region....Arabs formed militias, burned African villages, and killed thousands. Africans in turn formed self-defense groups, members of which eventually became the first Darfur insurgents to appear in 2003."

The report states that what provoked the black African to rise up against the Khartoum tyranny was "the government's failure to enforce the terms of a tribal peace agreement requiring nomads of Arab background to pay blood money for killing dozens of Zaghawas [one of the African tribes in Darfur], including prominent tribal chiefs."

Likewise, Peter Verney, of the London-based Sudan Update, writes that the government armed the Arabs "while removing the weapons of the farmers, the Fur, Masalit and Zaghawa." He points out that the disarmament of the Africans has been enforced ruthlessly: "Since 2001, Darfur has been governed under central government decree, with special courts to try people suspected of illegal possession or smuggling of weapons...The security forces have misused these powers for arbitrary and indefinite detention."

While the blacks are forbidden to possess arms, the Arabs are given arms by the government—five or six guns per person according to Amnesty International. The Arabs are then formed into terrorist gangs known as Janjaweed, literally, "evil men on horseback" or "devil on a horse".

In both south Sudan (Christian and Animist Africans) and western Sudan (Darfur, inhabited by Muslim Africans) there were armed rebel groups. That these resistance groups had been able to acquire weapons illegally was a great affront to the United Nations and the gun prohibition lobbies, who denounce any form of gun possession by "non-state actors." A "non-state actor" is any person or group whose arms possession is not approved by the government; examples include the Sudanese fighting the genocidal dictatorship in their country, the Jews in the Warsaw ghetto, and the American revolutionaries.

The Sudanese resistance movements, although able to acquire some arms for their own operations, did not have the resources to protect the many isolated villages in the vast nation.

So with the black villagers disarmed—thanks to Sudan's strict gun laws—and the Arab gangs well-armed (thanks to the government), the stage was set for genocide. Typically, the mounted Arab gangs would attack a village on the ground, while the Sudanese military provided air support and bombed the village.

In the south Sudan, the genocide program killed 2.2. million victims, and drove 4.5 million from their homes. Victims who were not killed were often sold into slavery. Rape was extensively used as an instrument of state terror.

Darfur was the next target

There, the Janjaweed have caused the deaths of hundreds of thousands of black Sudanese, raped many thousands, and forced over two million black Sudanese into refugee camps. After a village has been softened up by bombardment from the Sudan Air Force, the Janjaweed enter and pillage, killing and raping in order to displace the population and steal the land.

In the December 2004 issue of *Commentary* magazine, Roger Sandall writes that the Janjaweed attackers "unmistakably hurl racial abuse at their victims, alleging in particular that Africans are born to be slaves: 'Slaves, run! Leave the country. You don't belong; why are you not leaving this area for Arab cattle to graze?'"

Notably, the majority of villages bombed were villages where there were no armed rebels. Thus, the destruction of the villages should be seen not as an overzealous form of counter-insurgency warfare, but rather as a deliberate attempt to destroy an entire society. The ethnic cleansing of Darfur has been so thorough that there are no villages left to burn.

The victim villagers are generally unarmed. Amnesty International reported the testimony of a villager who complained: "none of us had arms and we were not able to resist the attack." One under-armed villager lamented: "I tried to take my spear to protect my family, but they threatened me with a gun, so I stopped. The six Arabs then raped my daughter in front of me, my wife and my other children."

In cases when the villagers were able to resist, the cost to the marauders rose. Human Rights Watch reported that "some of Kudun's residents mobilized to protect themselves, and fifteen of the attackers were reportedly killed."

The Pittsburgh *Tribune-Review* asked a US State Department official why there were no reports of the Darfur victims fighting back. "Some do defend themselves," he explained. But he added that the perpetrators have helicopters and automatic rifles, whereas the victims have only machetes.

Darfur is one of those places where the government has implemented the Rebecca Peters(Peters is the head of IANSA) principle that crime victims should not use arms to protect themselves. The Sudan Organisation Against Torture (a human rights group based in London) reported on March 20, 2006 about an incident which took place on March 7:

> "Two men in military uniform attacked four girls from Seraif IDP [refugee] camp, Hay AlGeer, West Nyala, Southern Darfur. The girls were attacked whilst collecting firewood outside the camp at 11:30. During the attack, one of the men assaulted one of the girls and attempted to rape her. The armed man touched the girl's breasts and attempted to forcefully remove her underwear. When she resisted, the man began to beat her. In defence she grabbed a knife that she had been using to cut the firewood and stabbed the attacker in the stomach.
>
> Following the stabbing, the girls managed to escape and returned to Seraif camp where they reported the incident to police officers inside the camp. The police refused to file the case."

One of the rapists died from a knife wound. "Following the news of the death, the officers immediately arrested the four girls inside the camp on suspicion of murder." They faced execution by hanging. The teenage girls were: Amouna Mohamed Ahmed, Fayza Ismail Abaker, Houda Ismail Abdel Rahman, and Zahra Adam Abdella. International pressure led to the release of the latter three, while Miss Ahmed was kept in prison to face murder charges. Her fate is unknown.

The United Nations has done nothing meaningful to stop the genocide in Sudan. An African Union "peacekeeping" force was dispatched, but that small and low-quality force was only assigned to protecting international aid workers at refugee camps. The AU was not supposed to protect the actual victims.

One reason for UN inaction is that the Chinese, Russians, and French—each of whom have Security Council veto power—are apparently determined to protect their own lucrative commercial and oil development relations with Sudan's tyrants.

Because the international community has utterly failed to protect the Darfuris, they have every moral right to protect themselves. In an article in the *Notre Dame Law Review*, Paul Gallant, Joanne Eisen, and I argue that the Genocide Convention gives the Darfuris a formal legal right to arms.

A teenage girl with a gun might not be the ideal soldier. But she is certainly not the ideal rape victim. It is not particularly difficult to learn how to use a firearm to shoot a would-be rapist from a distance of five or twenty-five feet away. Would every one of the Janjaweed Arab bullies who enjoy raping African girls be brave enough to dare trying to rape a girl who was carrying a rifle or a handgun?

The United Nations, however, is hard at work to make sure that genocide victims in Sudan, and anywhere else in Africa, will not be able to resist.

Sudan is covered by a UN-backed treaty called the "The Nairobi Protocol for the Prevention, Control and Reduction of Small Arms and Light Weapons in the Great Lakes Region and the Horn of Africa." The protocol was signed on in 2004, by representatives of Burundi, Democratic Republic of the Congo, Djibouti, Eritrea, Ethiopia, Kenya, Rwanda, Seychelles, Sudan, Uganda, and Tanzania.

The treaty requires universal gun registration, complete prohibition of all civilian-owned semi-automatic rifles, "heavy minimum sentences for...the carrying of unlicensed small arms," as well as programs to encourage citizens to surrender their guns, widespread searches for firearms, educational programs to discourage gun ownership, and other policies to disarm the public.

Even more extreme UN gun prohibitions are being imposed in the Economic Community of West African States (ECOWAS). Among the ECOWAS states where the UN has successfully pushed victim disarmament are the Ivory Coast (Côte d'Ivoire) and Guinea. According to Genocide Watch, Ivory Coast has entered the final pre-genocide phase of "preparation."

In Guinea, the National Alliance for Democracy and Development warns that, "There is a looming Rwanda-type genocide..."

The prohibition lobbies and their UN allies will tell you that people never need guns for protection—not for protection from rapists, and not for protection from genocidaires. Governments and the United Nations will protect everyone. The tragedy of disarmed victims in the Sudan, and all over Africa, shows the deadly falseness of the prohibitionist promise. For decades, millions of Africans have been slaughtered by genocidal tyrants while the rest of the world stood idle. Now, the United Nations has become objectively complicit in genocide, by trying to ensure that never again will anyone targeted for genocide be able to use a firearm to save herself or her family.

GENOCIDE IN ETHIOPIA

The world should pay attention to the genocide which the Ethiopian government has been perpetrating in southwestern Ethiopia, in the state of Gambella.

The Anuak people of Ethiopia, a minority tribe, have historically been enslaved by other Ethiopians. The slavery persisted into the late 20th century. Today, the Anuak are being exterminated, while the central government of Ethiopia tells the world to ignore the violence, claiming that it is merely an inter-tribal conflict.

Gambella is in southwestern Ethiopia, bordering Sudan. It has been the home of five ethnic groups: the Anuak, Nuer, Majangir, Opo and Komo. The Anuaks and the Nuer are the largest groups and have long feuded over the land and its resources. The Anuaks, who live atop gold and oil reserves, number approximately 150,000.

A mainly agricultural people, the majority of Anuak inhabit Gambella, although some live in eastern Sudan, and some have recently been displaced to Kenya and the US. Gambella also hosts UN refugee camps, for people who have fled the decades-long genocide in south Sudan.

The central government, in Ethiopia's capital Addis Ababa, has disarmed most of the Anuak, and even disarmed Anuak police officers. Ethiopia is among the East African nations which have promised to conduct campaigns against civilian gun ownership, as part of the United Nations-sponsored Nairobi Protocol. Like several other signers of the Nairobi Protocol (Rwanda, Uganda, Congo, Sudan), Ethiopia already had a well-established record of genocide against disarmed victims.

On December 13, 2003, eight UN workers were ambushed and killed. Although the perpetrators were never caught, the blame for their deaths fell on the Anuaks; the subsequent massacre of Anuaks was blamed on the Nuer.

The Ethiopian government vehemently and persistently denies its participation in the violence against the Anuaks. But consider the following:

With the expectation of the discovery of oil in the state of Gambella, the government in Addis Ababa has developed a keen interest in exploiting the region.

After the massacre of the UN workers, an Anuak police officer, Ojo Akway, observed tracks leading from the crime scene, yet he was not permitted to investigate. Instead, he was arrested and then shot dead.

Seven months later, another investigator was also shot and killed. The humanitarian group Genocide Watch wonders why the UN has not investigated the deaths of its own personnel. Who benefits the most from this cover-up? Have UN workers been warned that if they speak up, they will be expelled?

According to a report by Genocide Watch, at an Ethiopian cabinet meeting in September 2003 government officials and military officers discussed ethnic cleansing of the Anuak, and the benefits of destroying Anuak leadership. A military official told Genocide Watch that he was present at a subsequent meeting on December 11, 2003, just two days prior to the murders of the UN personnel. At that meeting, government officials discussed eliminating Anuaks in a military campaign in Gambella, code-named "Operation Sunny Mountain."

Subsequent behavior of the Ethiopian army is consistent with a plan to destroy the Anuak. As detailed in a statement by an Anuak representative that was delivered to the Office of the United Nations High Commissioner for Human Rights, the Ethiopian army is perpetrating extrajudicial killings, beatings, torture, rape, sexual slavery and the destruction of Anuak properties. As a result, half the Anuak population has been displaced.

The pattern of rape described by the victims appears to be systematic, and designed to create pregnancies that would produce non-Anuak children. Such use of rape to deliberately destroy an ethnic group is considered, under international law, to be a type of genocide.

And of course, directly killing people is also a method of genocide. An anonymous Anuak spokesperson told the UN's Office of High Commissioner for Human Rights that from 2003-2005, up to "15,000 Anywa [Anuak] people have been killed in different villages by the Ethiopian national defence force militaries in trying to clear the area from the indigenous Anywa people and to facilitate the ongoing oil exploration in the land of the indigenous Anywa people...."

Government guilt became especially evident in April 2006, when there was an attempt to capture eighteen Anuak resistance leaders who had fled to a refugee camp in south Sudan. These leaders could render potentially damaging eye-witness accounts of the 2003 massacre of Anuak by the Nuer. The Ethiopian army, under the guise of a disarmament exercise (that is, gun confiscation), rampaged through numerous villages on both sides of the Ethiopia-Sudan border. The "disarmament" campaign was accompanied by rape, pillaging, and murder.

As the Ethiopian army advanced towards the Alari Refugee Camp in Pochalla, Sudan, surviving Anuak villagers warned the refugees in the camp. Then, the tribal leader of the Anuak in Sudan, King Adonga, vowed that the Sudan Anuak would protect the refugees "with whatever it takes, even spears." The refugees moved the vulnerable in their camp to a safer location, while they and King Adonga's forces prepared for a violent confrontation.

The Anuaks contacted several people in the international community and alerted them to the imminent slaughter. With the plan exposed to potential donor governments, the Ethiopian regime aborted the invasion, and denied any hostile intention.

But in August 2006, over a dozen villages in Gambella were ethnically cleansed. The villagers were suddenly ordered to leave, to just go away, by the Ethiopian National Defense Forces. The Anuak Justice Council claims that there is extreme hardship for these new refugees because of a lack of clean water, food, and shelter, and that Anuaks are killed with impunity almost daily.

Human Rights Watch accuses the Ethiopian government of "human rights abuses so severe that they may rise to the level of crimes against humanity."

It's not surprising that hardly anyone has heard of what the Ethiopian government has been doing to the Anuak. The world has barely paid attention even to the human rights atrocities perpetrated in Ethiopia's capital of Addis Ababa and other cities, after the disputed elections of May 2005. A leaked report by Ethiopian judge Wolde-Michael Meshesha revealed that police killed 193 protesters, injured 763, and arrested over 100 others. These opposition leaders and journalists were put on trial for treason. And for attempted genocide!

Ana Gomes, the European Union observer at the 2005 elections, said that European leaders remain silent because "they want to continue dealing as usual with the Ethiopian regime."

Ethiopian journalist Habtamu Dugo (who is now in the US, and was granted asylum with the support of the Independence Institute) explained that the government has created so many enemies that he predicts the current regime will be overthrown. He adds that in Ethiopia, "millions live in fear and their mouths are gagged."

UGANDA GOVERNMENT USES UN GUN CONTROL MANDATE TO TERRORIZE UGANDANS

Ugandan army troops are garrisoned in the northeast part of the country under orders to disarm the local populace—pastoral, cattle-herding tribes known as the Karamojong. The army is attempting, and failing, to quash an uprising which was caused by a prior attempt to disarm the same tribes.

To "disarm" the tribes, the Ugandan army, supported by tanks and helicopter gunships, is burning down villages, sexually torturing men, raping women, and plundering what few possessions the tribespeople own. Tens of thousands of victims have been turned into refugees. Human rights scholar Ben Knighton has used the term "ethnocide" to describe the army's campaign.

Persecution of the Karamojong by the central government in Kampala, Uganda, is nothing new. During the Idi Amin regime, the Karamojong were selected as special targets for genocide. Against Amin's armies, their traditional bows and arrows were futile. So it is understandable that the Karamojong will not surrender their firearms.

This time, the pretext for the "disarmament" of the Karamojong is United Nations gun control. The Ugandan military is trying to round up every last firearm in Karamoja, supposedly for the Karamojong's own good.

The procedure is euphemistically called "forcible disarmament." It works like this: The misnamed Uganda People's Defence Force (UPDF) will torture and rape Karamojong, after which some Karamojong might disclose the location of some hidden guns. Or the army will burn down a village,and then find some guns in the ashes.

If the pastoral tribespeople's bloody history with Amin were not enough, they have no reason to trust the current government of Uganda, either. The current government has repeatedly broken its promises of goods, services, and personal protection for tribespeople who voluntarily disarmed.

According to David Pulkol, the former Director of External Security Organisation (part of the Ugandan government's intelligence agency), the disarmament process is a tactic to facilitate robbing the Karamojong of their resources. The *Daily Monitor* newspaper, for example, reports that the Ugandan government has announced plans to confiscate "about 1,903 sq km out of the total area of 2,304 sq km of the Pian Upe game reserve" for private investment purposes.

This government predation has naturally sparked resistance. More and more Karamojong are wearing traditional ethnic garb—not only as a symbol of solidarity, but also because the loose clothing makes it easy to conceal weapons. The tribes are also uniting and improving their tactical skills. The weapons that had been taken by the government have been replaced by better ones from the ubiquitous black market. The helicopters that have been bombing the populace and burning their villages are now at risk from high-powered rifles.

The Karamojong women are not remaining passive while their families suffer, starve, and die. Some Karamojong widows have taken their husband's firearms and are actively defending themselves, their families, and their cattle.

In 2006, the Ugandan army's atrocities led the United Nations Development Programme to cut off its disarmament aid to Uganda. But the outrage did not last long, and the "aid" was restored. Although the United Nations does not fund the Ugandan army, the UN does provide a public relations sanction for the disarmament. In November 2006, Louise Arbour, United Nations High Commissioner for Human Rights, stated: "The actions of the UPDF do not comply with international human rights law and domestic law." But, she also stipulated, "the decision of the Government to undertake renewed efforts to eradicate illegal weapons in Karamoja is essential." Never mind that the disarmament campaign also eradicates *people*.

If the Karamojong did not have to worry about the central government targeting them for genocide, or stealing their land, one could possibly make an argument that they would be better off without guns. The various tribes have a long tradition of inter-tribal cattle rustling, and the cattle-raiding would undoubtedly be less dangerous if perpetrated with stone-age weapons instead of AK-47s. But as a practical matter, there have been numerous instances of civilians who have voluntarily disarmed, and were then—despite government promises of protection—robbed by the competing tribes who remained armed. And the loss of even a small number of cattle can place a subsistence level family at risk of starvation. Of course, cattle-rustling never led to the deliberate destruction of entire villages, turning thousands of people into refugees. Nor has it ever paved the way for government theft of the land the tribespeople need to survive.

The number of illegally possessed firearms prior to the disarmament campaign had been estimated at between 50,000 and 150,000. On November 10, 2007, the newspaper *New Vision* reported that "since this year began, they have recovered 4,500 guns." So the Ugandan government is wiping out the very people the government ostensibly claims to protect, and that "protection" amounts to taking just 3 to 9 percent of unauthorized weapons. All the while, the Ugandan government is using its own guns to destroy Karamoja, burn villages, slaughter the defenseless, and perpetrate ethnocide.

Seems like the kind of "protection" the Karamojong could live without.

UNRWA AND PALESTINIAN SUFFERING

November 29 is the United Nations "International Day of Solidarity with the Palestinian People." It occurs on the anniversary of the 1947 date that the United Nations voted to partition the British Mandate of Palestine between Jews and Arabs. Many Palestinians and other Arabs rejected the UN partition, and started a war to exterminate the infant state of Israel a few months later. So by choosing November 29 as Palestinian Day, the United Nations is in effect rewarding the aggressors who refused to comply with the UN plan. A much better date for the United Nations to acknowledge the suffering of the Palestinian people would be December 8, the anniversary of the 1949 creation of the organization that, for over half a century, has done more than anyone to immiserate the Palestinian people. That organization is UNRWA, the United Nations Relief and Works Agency for Palestine Refugees in the Near East.

That there is 21st-century refugee problem from a war that ended in 1949 is primarily because of UNRWA's decision to maximize Palestinian suffering for political advantage.

Established in December 1949, UNRWA began operations the next May. The Agency's job was to help settle the Palestinians who had left Israel because of the 1948-49 war. According to General Assembly resolution 302(IV), UNRWA's mandate was that "constructive measures should be undertaken at an early date with a view to the termination of international assistance for relief."

Over half a century later, UNRWA's annual budget is nearly half a billion dollars, including nearly $150 million from US taxpayers. As UNRWA's website explains, "In the absence of a solution to the Palestine refugee problem, the General Assembly has repeatedly renewed UNRWA's mandate." Stated another way, UNRWA's bureaucratic existence depends on making sure that the Palestinian refugee problem is not solved, and that "international assistance for relief" is not terminated at an "early date," or ever.

In 1950, the United Nations created the United Nations High Commissioner for Refugees (UNHCR), which began work in 1951. UNHCR tries to help refugees all over the world. It has worked on behalf of refugees in more than a hundred nations. UNHCR, whose work is governed by the Convention Relating to the Status of Refugees, has helped more than 25 million refugees begin new lives.

In terms of organizational behavior, UNHCR has no incentive to try to obstruct the solution of any particular refugee problem. To the contrary, UNHCR can work to solve one problem, secure (bureaucratically) in the knowledge that new problems with other refugees will occur soon enough.

But in 1949, there was no UNHCR, so UNRWA was created solely to deal with the Palestinians. UNRWA is the only UN entity dedicated solely to serving a single ethnic group.

The creation of UNRWA turned out to be a catastrophe, particularly for the Palestinians, and also for the Israelis. Because the suffering of Palestinians has been used so effectively by terrorists to build support for attacks on the United States, Americans are also victims of UNRWA. America's naïve good intentions in providing billions for UNRWA, while Arab governments contribute only a pittance, has obviously not bought America good will in the Middle East.

In retrospect, it is clear that once the UNHCR was created, the UN should have merged UNRWA into UNHCR. Then UNHCR could have aided the Palestinian refugees the same way that it has aided refugees in so many other countries: by helping them find new, permanent homes, so they could begin a fresh start.

Wars often produce refugees. People who choose to initiate a war must accept responsibility for the creation of refugees as a result of the war.

From the end of World War I until 1948, "Palestine" (a name invented by Roman imperialists) was governed by the United Kingdom, as the result of a mandate from the League of Nations. Formerly part of the Ottoman Empire, Palestine (consisting of the modern nations of Jordan and Israel) was acquired by the UK as part of the spoils of World War One.

The reason that the League of Nations awarded Palestine to the UK was the 1917 Balfour Declaration, which promised to establish a Jewish homeland there. The Declaration was part of a British effort to win Jewish support during the war.

But the British government broke its promise and failed to carry out the League of Nations mandate. Even after World War II and the Holocaust, Britain refused to create a Jewish homeland. The exasperated Jewish population's war of national independence finally led to Britain announcing in 1947 that it would abandon its mandate in Palestine in 1948. In late 1947, the United Nations partitioned Palestine: over 80 percent would be given to the new nation of Jordan, whose population was, and still is, majority-Palestinian. The new Jewish state would be given only territory which was already owned by Jews, or which was Crown property, owned by the United Kingdom.

On the day in May 1948 that Israel declared its indepdence, the new state was granted diplomatic recognition by American President Harry Truman. The same day, five Arab states, joined by many Palestinians, launched a war of extermination.

The war lasted from 1948 to 1949, when the Arabs gave up trying to destroy the Jews immediately, and accepted an armistice, although they did not renounce their state of war.

During the Arab war of aggression, several hundred thousand Arabs left Israel. Some left because they listened to the Arab propaganda urging Palestinians to get out of the way of the Arab armies. Some left without prompting because they just wanted to get away from the fighting. Some were pushed out because they were part of Palestinian villages that were fighting to eliminate the Jews.

Many Arabs, however, chose to stay in Israel, and today they constitute one-sixth of the Israeli population. For over half a century they have enjoyed the rights denied almost everywhere in the Arab world: complete freedom of religion, freedom of speech, the right to vote, the right to be elected to government (as many Israeli Arabs have been), the right to due process of law under a fair judicial system, and many other fundamental human rights. The Middle East nation with by far the best record for protecting the rights of Arab citizens is Israel.

During war, Israel urged the Arabs to stay, and after the war Israel welcomed back a hundred thousand who did return.

At about the same time—from 1947 to 1950—over three-quarters of a million Jews were forced out of Islamic nations where they had lived for many centuries. Intensified persecution in Iraq, Yemen, Morocco, Syria, and other Islamic countries made life intolerable. The United Nations did nothing for the Jewish refugees.

Most of the Jewish refugees went to Israel, where they were welcomed, and the new government worked hard to integrate them into society. Israel has always accepted Jewish refugees from anywhere, and today Israel is one of the most successful multi-racial and multi-ethnic societies in the world.

The Palestinian Arab refugees did not receive similar treatment from their Arab brethren. Except for Jordan, none of the Arab countries would grant them citizenship. Instead, the Arab governments decided to make them permanent refugees. By preventing them from resettling, the Arab dictatorships could create a human rights problem which could be used to distract the subjects of the Arab dictatorships from the massive human rights abuses of those dictatorships.

As Ralph Galloway, a disillusioned former director of UNRWA observed in 1958: "The Arab states do not want to solve the refugee problem. They want to keep it as an open sore and as a weapon against Israel. Arab leaders don't give a damn whether the refugees live or die." [Terrence Prittie, "Middle East Refugees," in Michael Curtis et al., eds., *The Palestinians: People, History, Politics* (Piscataway, N.J.: Transaction Books, 1975), p.71.]

Today, many of the children, grandchildren, and great-grandchildren of those Palestinians who left Israel in 1948 still live in refugee camps. They are the only refugee population in the world for whom the United Nations has actively prevented resettlement.

Because of pressure from Arab countries, UNRWA was, from its very inception, given almost unlimited autonomy. It sends one report per year to the General Assembly, and is subject to essentially no checks or balances on its operations. There are no outside audits; just an audit performed by the notoriously corrupt UN itself.

UNRWA has used its autonomy in the manner favored by its prime UN sponsors, "the Arab bloc," to ensure that as many people as possible are classified as "Palestinian refugees."

For all refugees in the world—except the Palestinians whom UNRWA "serves"—the key international law is the 1951 United Nations Convention Relating to the Status of Refugees. The UN's High Commissioner for Refugees follows the standards of the Refugee Convention.

The UNCHR defines its objective as finding solutions, which often means working to ensure that "everyone can exercise the right to seek asylum and find safe refuge in another state." The goal of UNHCR, in accordance with the 1951 Convention, is to help people stop being refugees.

UNRWA does just the opposite. For example, the 1951 Refugee Convention defines a "refugee" as a person who "is outside his/her country of nationality or habitual residence; has well-founded fear of persecution because of his/her race, religion, nationality, membership in a particular social group or political opinion; and is unable or unwilling to avail himself/herself of the protection of that country, or to return there, for fear of persecution."

The UNCHR definition means that, at the least, a refugee must be someone who has left his "country of nationality or habitual residence." If an American businessman lived in China for three years, and then the businessman tried to help India and Russia invade China, and then the American businessman fled China after China won the war, the American businessman would not be "refugee" according to UNCHR's common-sense definition.

Likewise, if a Jewish or Ukrainian family fled from Communist persecution in the Soviet Union in 1948, and came to the United States, then the

American children, grand-children, and great-grand-children of the Soviet refugees would, obviously, not be refugees according to UNCHR. The children, grand-children, and great-grand-children, having been born and spent all their lives in the United States, could hardly be "habitual" residents of Russia.

UNCHR's practical definition of "refugee" is designed to identify true refugees, while preventing other people from making false claims about refugee status for political purposes.

UNRWA works in exactly the opposite way, awarding refugee status to people who are not real refugees.

Although Jews have lived in Israel continuously for over three thousand years, a surge of Jewish immigration to Israel began in the late 19th century, when the area was ruled by the Ottoman Empire. Immigration continued during the period of British rule, and the formerly torpid economy of the region began to blossom. The Zionist immigrants drained swamps, reclaimed wasteland, started small businesses, and made the desert bloom. The economic growth resulting from Jewish immigration attracted many Arabs, who sought to participate in the economic opportunities that had been created by Zionist initiative.

Many of the Arabs who left Israel because of the 1948-49 war had not been there very long. So UNRWA fabricated the definition that refugees were "persons whose normal place of residence was Palestine between June 1946 and May 1948, who lost both their homes and means of livelihood as a result of the 1948 Arab-Israeli conflict." By UNRWA's definition, the American businessman who left China after living there three years (or an illegal alien in the United States who got deported after living in the US for more than two years) would be a refugee.

Similarly, UNRWA pretends that any descendant of a refugee is a refugee. By UNRWA's theory, if your ancestors fled from someplace 150 years ago, then you are still a refugee. In fact, the descendants of many of the Arabs who chose to leave Israel after 1948 have permanently settled in other countries and become citizens. The largest number settled in Jordan, the only Arab country to grant them citizenship. Many others moved to Europe. Yet UNRWA still issues refugee cards to all of these people, and their children, and their children's children.

In contrast, the 1951 Convention does not include any descendants of refugees—let along the third or fourth generation of descendants—as "refugees."

Similarly, the 1951 Convention specifies that if a refugee acquires a new nationality and the protection of a new government (e.g., a refugee from Russia becomes a US citizen), she is no longer a refugee. In contrast, UNRWA claims that a "Palestinian refugee" who becomes a citizen of the United States, France, Jordan, or any other nation is still a "Palestinian refugee" forever—and so are his children, his grandchildren, and his great-grandchildren.

UNRWA has been so eager to increase the number of refugees that it can claim to serve that it has given out enormous numbers of refugee cards to people whom it knew were not refugees. (And then, of course, all the descendants of the person with the original refugee card are also counted as refugees.) UNRWA admits that it gave out at least a hundred thousand improper refugee cards (entitling card-holders to UN welfare) in its early days, although the actual number of improperly-issued cards may be much larger.

So today, you may hear that there are over four million "Palestinian refugees," a figure that has grown from the 914,000 refugees that UNRWA claimed in 1950. Most of them are not refugees, but are descendants of people whom UNRWA labeled as "refugee" many years ago.

Of the "refugees," about two-thirds have found their own housing, while one-third live in one of the 59 housing facilities that UNRWA operates in five countries. Some of the housing is UNRWA-owned row houses in cities that have grown around or near the camps. Other housing is more primitive. Rarely are the housing facilities well-maintained. Their Palestinian residents do not own them; they belong to UNRWA, so no-one in a housing unit has a financial incentive to conduct preventive maintenance, let alone invest in improvements.

Moreover, UNRWA insists on the fiction that the housing units—which have been occupied from 1950 until the present—are merely "temporary" because the residents will be going "home" to Israel. So UNRWA too performs little upkeep or improvement, lest UNRWA be seen as deviating from its official pretense that the housing is temporary.

When Israeli troops entered Gaza in 1967, they were appalled at the squalid conditions in the UNRWA camps there. The Egyptians had forbidden residents to work outside the camps, and had not allowed electricity or running water inside the camps. Israel attempted to ameliorate conditions there, including medical care, and to replace shacks with small houses, but UNRWA blocked the improvements. UNRWA is often reluctant to allow conditions in the camps to improve, because such improvements might diminish the desire of "refugees" to "return."

In 1985, Israel offered to give 1,300 permanent homes near Nablus to refugees. Israel did not even ask the people who would receive the charity housing to renounce their so-called "right of return." But the UN blocked the housing program, and claimed that "measures to resettle Palestine refugees in the West Bank away from the homes and property from which they were displaced constitute a violation of their inalienable right of return."

Similarly, after the Israelis withdrew from Gaza in 2005, the United Arab Emirates donated one hundred million dollars to the Palestinian Authority to build a new city in Gaza, for the benefit of people who have been harmed by the Arab-Israel conflict. Yet the PA refused to allow the refugees to live in this new city.

Under international law, there is no such thing as a right of return. If your ancestors left France, or Russia, or anywhere else (regardless of whether they were forced out, or they just wanted to live somewhere else), then you have no right of return to France or Russia. Nor do your grandchildren.

Nevertheless, UNRWA tells the "refugees" that they have a "right of return" to Israel—that the grandchild of someone who moved to Tel Aviv to work as a janitor from 1946 to 1948 has a right to live in Israel, and to take back whatever real property their ancestor abandoned when he left Israel.

The pretext for the claim of an "inalienable right of return," is General Assembly Resolution 194, which says, "the refugees wishing to return to their homes and live at peace with their neighbours should be permitted to do so at the earliest practicable date..."

In fact, Israel did allow one hundred thousand Arabs who had fled the fighting to return to Israel.

The General Assembly Resolution itself indicates that the only refugees who should be allowed (not who have a "right") to return are those who wish to "live at peace with their neighbours." It is the Palestinians who have the obligation to prove—against a record of many decades of aggression—that they have changed, and are now willing to live in peace with their Jewish neighbors.

In 1974, at the height of the period when the UN was dominated by the Soviets and anti-Semites, General Assembly Resolution 3236 declared "the inalienable right of return" of the Palestinians, and formalized the UN's relationship with what was then the world's foremost terrorist organization, the PLO.

Yet in international law, General Assembly resolutions have no legal force. In contrast to Security Council resolutions, GA resolutions express nothing more than the sense of the General Assembly, and cannot, by themselves, create legal rights.

The notion of a right of return is preposterous not only as a matter of international law, but as a matter of common sense. Israel was established to be the Jewish homeland. To allow immigration by over four million people—the vast majority of whom have never lived in Israel, and whose ancestors rejected the opportunity for Israeli citizenship—would destroy Israel as a Jewish state. Even worse, more than half a century of anti-Israel propaganda education at UNRWA-run schools have turned many of the four million "refugees" into anti-Semites and supporters of terrorism.

UNRWA schools follow the curriculum in the host country, so UNRWA schools in Egypt and Syria are now, and always have been, schools for indoctrination in extreme anti-Semitism. In 1995, the Palestinian Authority was granted authority over UNRWA schools in the West Bank and Gaza, pursuant to the Oslo Accords. According to the Oslo treaty between Israel and the Palestine Liberation Organization, both sides were required to carefully revise their educational curricula, so that schools did not foment hatred. Israel complied with the Oslo Accords, while Arafat and his PLO did not. So beginning in

1995, UNRWA schools in the West Bank and Gaza adopted the hate curriculum developed by the Palestinian Authority.

The Committee for Monitoring the Impact of Peace (CMIP) analyzed the UNRWA/PA curriculum, based on general guidelines from the United Nations Educational, Cultural, and Scientific Organization (UNESCO). The analysis revealed massive lies about Middle-East history and the present, all of them geared towards fomenting anti-Semitism and encouraging terrorism.

The schools' maps do not even acknowledge the existence of Israel. Among the features of the PA hate education are: covering up the extensive historical and archeological record of Jewish habitation of Israel and nearby areas from ancient times until the present; using the Koran to incite hatred of Jews; refusing to acknowledge the existence of Israel; presenting Zionism as a western colonial movement (even though it was resisted by Western colonial powers); ignoring the existence of Jewish holy sites; depicting Jews as uniformly evil; propagandizing for the destruction of Israel; blaming the status of Palestinian refugees solely on Israel, with no hint of responsibility for the Palestinians and other Arabs who started the war against Israel; and extolling jihad and terrorism.

A study of fourth and ninth grade textbooks by the Israel/Palestine Centre for Research and Information (the only joint Palestinian-Israeli public policy think-tank) also found extensive historical misrepresentation, including maps which denied Israel's existence, and the promotion of jihad. Although the textbooks did promote "tolerance" in the abstract, the concept was not directly applied towards modern-day tolerance of non-Muslims.

As a practical matter, no-one but the deluded victims of UNRWA and terrorist propaganda actually expects that Israel would honor the fictive right of return. But by making sure that as many Palestinians as possible remain refugees incensed about the continuing denial of their "right of return," UNRWA fulfills the objective of Arab dictatorships in making sure that the Arab-Israeli conflict is never resolved.

As with so much that the UN does, the "Palestinian right of return" is presented to the world as a high moral principle—but it is a principle that applies only when it can be used against Israel. Consider the many Palestinian guest workers who lived in Kuwait before Saddam Hussein invaded in 1990. Many of these guest workers been there for much longer than two years (the period that UNRWA claims entitles a Palestinian and every one of his descendants to the right to "return" to Israel).

When Saddam invaded, many of the Palestinians in Kuwait supported him, as did Yassir Arafat's Palestine Liberation Organization. After US-led forces drove Saddam out of Iraq, the Kuwaitis promptly expelled the entire Palestinian population.

If Kuwait were treated like Israel, the expelled Palestinians would be housed in special camps run by a UN agency created just for their benefit. The

United Nations would incessantly denounce Kuwait for violating the "inalienable Palestinian right of return." And while insisting on the Palestinians' right to return to Kuwait, the UN would allow its schools to be used to teach children that Palestinians have a historical right to rule Kuwait, and to claim it by jihad.

In January 2000, Israel's government, under severe pressure from President Clinton, accepted his demands, and announced it would grant Yassir Arafat's Palestinian Authority a state of its own in the West Bank and Gaza. Faced with the granting of so many demands, Arafat was able to find a pretext for continued war only by insisting that neither he nor anyone else would ever make peace unless Israel also granted the "right to return"—thereby destroying any hope for peace. UNRWA's mission—as perverted by the Arab bloc— had succeeded.

The best step the United Nations could take towards creating peace in the Middle East would be to abolish UNRWA, which has long been an obstacle to a just resolution of the problems of the Palestinian people.

THE UN NEEDS ANOTHER MEMBER

It's time to change the name of the "United Nations." Originally used to identify the anti-Axis coalition of nations in World War II, today's "United Nations" members are rarely united on anything. As the UN's actions against Taiwan's membership application demonstrate, the UN does not even live up to its own definition of "nations." The mechanics of that rejection reveal a growing internal danger at the UN for the United States.

Article 4 of the United Nations Charter states that "Membership in the United Nations is open to all other [non-founding] peace-loving states which accept the obligations contained in the present Charter and, in the judgment of the Organization, are able and willing to carry out these obligations."

In July 2007, Taiwan applied for membership in the United Nations, as it has many times before. By the Charter's standards, Taiwan should have been speedily admitted.

First of all, Taiwan is "peace-loving." It engages in no form of international aggression. And the UN hasn't exactly been strict about the "peace-loving" requirement for membership, since North Korea was admitted in 1991—even though North Korea is still legally in a state of war dating back to its invasion of South Korea. (An armistice was signed in 1953, but there has been no treaty or other act to legally end the war; in 2009 North Korea repudiated the armistice.)

No one seriously claims that Taiwan is unwilling to carry out the obligations of a UN member state; its track record of adhering to international law is strong, and far better than that of many current UN members.

And, obviously, Taiwan is a "nation." The standard international law definition of a "nation" is contained in the Montevideo Convention on the Rights and Duties of States:

> "The state as a person of international law should possess the following qualifications: (a) a permanent population; (b) a defined territory; (c) government; and (d) capacity to enter into relations with the other states."

Taiwan plainly has all of these, including formal diplomatic relations with about two dozen other states, and the "capacity" to have relations with every state.

So what's the problem?

Secretary-General Ban Ki-moon claims that Taiwanese membership is "legally impossible." He points to the 1971 General Assembly resolution which took the China seat away from the Chiang Kai-Shek dictatorship, and awarded it to the Mao Tse-tung dictatorship.

Moon would have a point if Taiwan were seeking to take over the seat currently held by the Chinese Communists, and thus to occupy the permanent Chinese membership in the Security Council.

But General Assembly resolution 2758 says nothing regarding Taiwan's status or its membership in the UN. Instead, it simply declares that "the representatives of the Government of the People's Republic of China are the only lawful representatives of China to the United Nations." Further, the resolution declares the General Assembly's decision "to expel forthwith the representatives of Chiang Kai-shek from the place which they unlawfully occupy at the United Nations and in all the organizations related to it."

The "representatives of Chiang Kai-Shek" claimed to be the legal rulers not only of Taiwan, but of China, and asserted that Taiwan and China were part of the same nation.

The resolution settles the question of who holds the China seat, but it says nothing about defining the territorial scope of "China." The resolution is silent about whether Taiwan is part of China. (In over three thousand recorded years of Chinese history before Mao started the revolution, you can find only a single period, 17 years in the late 19th century, when a Chinese government even claimed sovereignty over all of Taiwan.)

Likewise, General Assembly resolution 2758 is silent about Tibet, a nation with a long record of independence, which was invaded and conquered by Mao in 1951.

As the delegations of several nations pointed out to the General Assembly in September, Ban Ki-moon violated the UN's own rules by personally rejecting Taiwan's application, rather than by forwarding it to the Security Council. According to Article 4 of the UN Charter, the Security Council is the body which is supposed to make membership recommendations for a final decision by the General Assembly.

Ki-moon's power-grab sets a terrible precedent of the Secretary-General arrogating to himself and the Secretariat the authority which belongs to the Security Council. Protecting the powers of the Security Council (where the US has a permanent seat and a veto) from infringements by UN staff is essential in preventing the UN from becoming even more aggressively anti-American than it already is.

In June 2007, a US State Department spokesman told reporters that while the US supports Taiwan's democratic development, "Consistent with our one China policy, we do not support Taiwan's membership in international organizations that require statehood, including the United Nations."

Like Rip Van Winkle, the State Department appears to have missed what's happened in the last couple decades. The "one China policy" dates from the 1971 Shanghai Communiqué, issued by President Richard Nixon and genocidal tyrant Mao Tse-Tung. It states: "The United States acknowledges that all Chinese on either side of the Taiwan Strait maintain there is but one China and that Taiwan is a part of China. The United States Government does not challenge that position."

The document was a diplomatic lie, for in 1971 there were many people in Taiwan who considered Taiwan to be separate from China. They were, however, prevented from voicing their opinions, because the Chiang Kai-Shek police state silenced them, in order to maintain its ridiculous claim to be the legal ruler of China. The Communiqué might have more accurately stated "Both governments on either side of the Taiwan strait claim to hold sovereignty over the territory of the other, and both will ruthlessly persecute any person in their respective countries who says otherwise."

The latter statement is still accurate for China, but in Taiwan, everything has changed. The Chiang regime is long gone, replaced by a vibrant democracy. In 1973, Freedom House rated Taiwan a 6 (with 7 being the worst possible score) for Political Rights, and 5 for Civil Liberties. Now, Taiwan scores a 2 and 1. (Japan, by comparison, gets a 1 and 2.)

China, meanwhile, progressed from 7/7 to 7/6. Mao's genocides are over, and these days the Chinese government outsources mass murder to client states such as Sudan, Zimbabwe, Burma, and North Korea.

The Heritage Foundation's 2007 *Index of Economic Freedom* ranks Taiwan as the 26th freest economy in the world, while China is 119th.

In Taiwan, only a minuscule band of Chiang die-hards claim that the Taipei government is legally sovereign over China. (Although China would be a lot better off if it were governed by Taipei democracy rather than Beijing kleptocracy.)

These days, just 6 percent of Taiwan's people consider themselves "Chinese." There is a rough balance between the large percentage who consider themselves Taiwanese only, and those who consider themselves both Taiwanese and Chinese. By about 8:1, the people of Taiwan reject China's claim of sovereignty over Taiwan, and China's efforts to interfere with Taiwan's self-determination.

The Chinese government, meanwhile, continues to push its campaign to smother Taiwan. In the 1960's, Taiwan had formal relations with more than 60 nations, including the United States, but with the loss of formal relations with Costa Rica in 2007 (which Beijing demanded as a condition of expansion of foreign aid and trade), the number of countries recognizing Taiwan has been reduced to 23.

Also in 2007, Beijing pressured the World Organization for Animal Health to downgrade Taiwan's membership to "non-sovereign member" and to start referring to Taiwan as "Taipei, China." Sort of like referring to Poland as "Warsaw, Russia," since Russia ruled part of Poland for a while.

The American Declaration of Independence affirms the inherent right of all people to self-determination, and, unlike the Shanghai Communiqué, the Declaration will never be obsolete. It is shameful that the United States does not formally recognize Taiwan diplomatically but instead relegates Taiwan to the same non-recognized status as the rogue tyrannies of Iran, Cuba and North Korea.

Yet the United States does have strong unofficial relations with Taiwan through the Taipei Economic and Cultural Representative Office in Washington, and the American Institute in Taiwan, both of which pretend not to be diplomatic offices. As former Colorado Congressman Tom Tancredo noted, the Taiwanese "maintain more than 100 quasi-embassies or 'Trade Offices' in nearly every country in the world. And most of these countries (including the United States) maintain a reciprocal mission in Taiwan's Capital City, Taipei. Why? The reason is obvious: Because they all realize that the totalitarian government of China doesn't really speak for the people of democratic Taiwan."

The bipartisan Congressional Taiwan Caucus has more than 150 members. Like Israel, Taiwan is a lot more popular with Congress and the American people than it is with the State Department.

President Bush in his second inaugural address told the nations of the world, "When you stand for your liberty, we will stand with you." It is well past time for the US to put those words into action and support Taiwan's bid for UN membership.

In the short run, China would use its Security Council veto to defeat the application, but China should at least start paying a diplomatic price for its hostility to Taiwan's right of self-determination. The more countries that support Taiwan's membership, the more that the Chinese government will fear that an invasion of Taiwan would be devastating to China's economic relationship to the rest of the world.

Deterring dictatorships from attacking democracies, and preserving the peace, are, after all, the reason the UN was founded in the first place.

LAW ENFORCEMENT ABUSE AND SOLUTIONS

OFFICER POLITICS: POLICE DEPARTMENT SCANDALS ARE A RESULT OF INCREASED FEDERAL INVOLVEMENT AND RACIAL HIRING PRACTICES

In September 2000, the Los Angeles Police Department (LAPD) became the largest police department in US history to submit to federal government control, through a voluntary consent decree with the US Department of Justice (DOJ). This sort of court-ordered supervision of local police departments has become a frequent solution to corruption and brutality scandals. But as the Los Angeles scandal illustrates, over-federalization is one of the major causes of the problem in the first place.

The Los Angeles scandal, the worst in the long-troubled LAPD's history, began in the Rampart Division, which covers one of the most dangerous neighborhoods in America. Rampart's territory is eight square crime-ridden miles west of downtown Los Angeles. With 375,000 residents and 350 police officers, the barrios of Rampart are home to the highest concentration of gang members in Los Angeles: sixty gangs, comprising as many as eight thousand members. The Rampart Division also routinely leads the city in homicides, drug activity, and violent-crime arrests.

In August 1998, Rampart police officer Rafael Perez was arrested on charges of stealing eight pounds of cocaine from a police evidence room. Just before his second trial, in September 1999 (the first resulted in a mistrial), Perez plea-bargained to a five-year term—in exchange for divulging information about one of the worst police corruption scandals in American history. Perez recounted that many Rampart officers planted drugs or guns on innocent suspects, knowingly made false arrests, assaulted innocent people, shot people illegally, and perjured themselves extensively. Some even robbed a bank.

The fallout from the scandal was enormous. More than a hundred criminal convictions have been overturned. Dozens of LAPD officers were relieved of duty, were suspended or fired, or quit. Officers were charged with crimes ranging from perjury to attempted murder. In September 1999, LAPD Chief Bernard Parks convened an internal Board of Inquiry, which reported that similar problems also existed in the Central 77th and Southeast stations.

The city of Los Angeles entered into a consent decree with the DOJ in September 2000, allowing federal oversight of the LAPD. The DOJ had previously sued or investigated more than a dozen cities, including Pittsburgh and Columbus, in pursuit of similar decrees, but the Los Angeles consent decree was unusual for two reasons. First, the LAPD is one of the largest metropolitan police departments in the world; and second, the department's quick capitulation to federal demands was quite different from the usual local pattern of vigorously fighting against federal takeovers.

Los Angeles was hardly alone in its troubles. In 1995, six Atlanta police officers were convicted or pled guilty to corruption charges, and five others were suspended. In New Orleans, more than eleven police officers were convicted in a 1994 cocaine distribution and murder-for-hire scandal. Between 1992 and 1996, thirty police from Manhattan's 30th Precinct were convicted of crimes, mostly narcotics-related offenses. And the list goes on, including Detroit, Chicago, Miami, and Washington, DC According to a 1998 General Accounting Office (GAO) report, of 950 FBI–led corruption cases opened against law enforcement officers between 1993 and 1997, 640 resulted in convictions.

The facts behind the Rampart scandal offer some insights into what is going wrong within some American law enforcement organizations. Many of the abuses within the Rampart Division were perpetrated by members of special anti-gang Community Resources Against Street Hoodlums (CRASH) units, of which Perez was a member. These CRASH units were created in the late 1980s to quell rising gang violence. But as the LAPD Board of Inquiry noted, "The subcommittee found a general lack of adequate supervision among CRASH units, [and] many other specialized units seem to suffer from the same problem." CRASH officers would often sign their own booking recommendations and arrest reports, even though the LAPD required that these forms be signed by sergeants or other superior officers.

Despite the express anti-gang purpose of the units, many CRASH arrests were general drug arrests not involving gangsters. "This suggests a philosophy of productivity for the sake of numbers," observed the LAPD Board of Inquiry. In practice, the CRASH units degenerated into little more than autonomous general police squads. CRASH members were no more experienced or better trained than other officers, and the Rampart corruption highlights the dangers that result from creation of special police units outside the normal command structure.

The problems are not unique to CRASH and Los Angeles. Chicago broke up its Gang Crimes Unit in the wake of a drug protection and distribution scandal that hit the news in December 1998. In Albuquerque, the city's Special Weapons and Tactics (SWAT) team was dismantled after a study by Sam Walker of the University of Nebraska found that "the rate of killings by the police was just off the charts." And again in Los Angeles in the mid-1990s, twenty-seven sheriff's deputies were convicted of skimming millions of dollars in drug money while serving on an "elite narcotics unit."

It is difficult to believe that the Rampart scandal and other such disasters would have been possible without the drug war. Planting evidence on people was one of the most frequent misdeeds of the Rampart officers. Because drug laws (like gun laws) are premised on the criminalization of mere possession of a small object, framing people is easy. At Rampart, the police lied not just when testifying against people they had framed, but routinely, in order to gather evidence. "Rampart CRASH officers frequently reported that suspects discarded contraband by tossing it on the ground within clear view of officers only a few feet away," observed the Board of Inquiry, though the scenario is obviously implausible.

Framing for possession is made even easier by the severe mandatory penalties for possessory offenses. A defendant being framed may still plead guilty if the plea bargain will result in a lesser term than the five- or fifteen-year mandatory sentence he may face if he demands a jury trial and the jury believes the police officer. Even someone as dim-witted as Inspector Clouseau can figure out that many "dropped in plain view" evidence reports are "testilying." Therefore, the police commanders who accept such reports, the district attorneys who prosecute on false evidence, and the judges who accept such false testimony are all knowingly abetting illegal police conduct. Thus the sphere of corruption widens.

It should be noted that the Rampart scandal was discovered only after Officer Perez was caught stealing cocaine from a police evidence room. The 1998 GAO report shows that "on average, over half the police officers convicted as a result of corruption investigations were convicted of drug-related offenses."

Although drug prohibition can provide a temptation for police officers to line their pockets illegally, an even greater factor is the departments' hiring practices—and the federal government policies imposed on them. The LAPD Board of Inquiry report began: "The major cause in the lack of integrity in American police officers is mediocrity." The report, however, did not identify the major causes of police mediocrity: too-rapid expansion of police forces, plus race and sex discrimination in hiring.

When Dick Riordan campaigned for mayor of Los Angeles in 1993, he promised to add three thousand new police officers. Riordan kept his promise, swelling the LAPD to nearly ten thousand officers, with the aid of federal funding. But were all these new hires as qualified as those already on the force? In a poll of LAPD employees conducted by the Board of Inquiry, "Respondents overwhelmingly pointed to the Department's lowered hiring standards as a major factor in the breakdown of integrity and ethical standards."

Federal grants included in the 1994 Clinton crime bill provided the funds for many of these new hires. The LAPD also kept hiring more rapidly than it should have, because the department was required to prevent forced attrition to avoid the loss of federal grant money. Thus President Clinton's 1994 legislation to put a hundred thousand more police officers on the street could be described as a plan to give deadly weapons and life-or-death power to a hundred thousand people who did not meet the standards to be hired as police officers in 1993.

If there were an oversupply of highly qualified applicants, federal hiring subsidies might do no harm. But during the Clinton years, the number of quality applicant for jobs with a starting salary in the low $20,000s to low $30,000s was shrinking. To make matters worse, most big-city police departments are not allowed to hire the best applicants in the pool. They must reject qualified applicants because of their race or sex in order to hire less-qualified applicants with various preferred characteristics. In Los Angeles, for example, the LAPD maintains five separate civil service hiring lists for police candidates: black, Hispanic, female, bilingual Asian/Pacific Islander, and all other. (The last category apparently includes white males, Indian males, and monolingual Asian/Pacific Islander males.)

Although many police departments voluntarily discriminate on the basis of race and sex, the LAPD's hiring practices are different in being the result of previous consent decrees intended to remedy past discrimination by the department. By the time of Rampart, the LAPD had become 14 percent black, 32 percent Hispanic, 5 percent Asian, and 18 percent female. But diversity in the LAPD did not stop the Rampart scandal from happening.

When police departments discriminate, poor and minority citizens suffer the most. A 2000 article in *Economic Inquiry* by economist John Lott quantified the problem. Looking at data from 1987, 1990, and 1993 for a wide variety of American cities, Lott examined the effect of consent decrees that impose race-conscious hiring requirements on police departments. He found that race-based hiring results in substantial increases in crime rates.

Presumably, discriminatory hiring practices lower the qualifying standards to allow the hiring of recruits who have less education, less previous employment experience, and more criminal or financial troubles in their own background, as well as recruits who are often younger than those found in departments in which race does not matter. The effects of the resulting crime increase are felt most severely in the highly urbanized neighborhoods where so many poor and minority citizens live. Aggravating the decline in police quality is the fact that the typical race-based consent decree increases the size of the police department by about one-third over time.

Consent decrees requiring race-conscious hiring may sometimes be a legitimate remedy against employers who have been proven to have discriminated. But when such remedies are imposed on police departments, more people—especially more inner-city minorities—are raped, robbed, murdered, and victimized by police corruption. Until the job pool of qualified police officers becomes much larger, increased harm to minority citizens will be the inevitable effect when courts impose racial quotas on police departments.

Naturally, as federal laws and decrees cause more chaos in local police departments, the feds' response is to take an even firmer grip on crime policies. Exercising power under section five of the Fourteenth Amendment, in 1994 Congress authorized the Department of Justice Civil Rights Division to bring lawsuits against local police abuses that form a "pattern and practice" of violating constitutional rights.

The particular standards of the federal consent decrees often ensure that the effort to deal with the problem officers will also cause trouble for the good ones. An officer committing more than a certain number of uses of force within a year—no matter how legally justified—must be "counseled" by a lieutenant. Likewise, an officer may be counseled, transferred, or sent for retraining based on a certain number of complaints against him, even if all of the complaints are anonymous and none of them are proven to be true.

So although the federal law is legitimate in principle, one should not expect too much from it. The DOJ had been investigating the LAPD since 1996 and failed to discover the Rampart abuses, let alone stop them. Nor has the DOJ always selected targets based on the "pattern and practice" standard of the statute. In Columbus, for example, the DOJ sought to put the police department under a court order based on only three alleged cases of misconduct.

Structural reforms to the LAPD (the Board of Inquiry alone made more than one hundred recommendations) and federal oversight may help, but they do not address the quality problems caused by federal subsidies for police hiring and by race and sex discrimination in hiring. Therefore, the only long-term solution will be for police departments to stop focusing on quantity and to start improving the quality of new police hires.

SMASH-UP POLICING: WHEN LAW ENFORCEMENT GOES MILITARY

The 2000 kidnapping of Elian Gonzalez by a Janet Reno goon squad earned a Pulitzer Prize for photographer Alan Diaz, who caught the federal agent waving a machine gun at the terrified boy. The picture shocked many Americans, but there's something even more shocking that's not in the picture: Similar events—in which people are assaulted in their homes by SWAT teams waving machine guns, spewing foul language, threatening to shoot people, and trashing the house as a tactical distraction—happen every day in the United States, without media attention.

Because of the war on drugs, law enforcement throughout the US has been militarized. The Founding Fathers worked hard to prevent oppression by standing armies, but the militarization of law enforcement is making more and more Americans subject to precisely the kind of violence the Founders worried about.

The Los Angeles police department started the trend in the 1960s when future police chief Daryl Gates created the first Special Weapons and Tactics (SWAT) team. Gates had originally wanted to call it a "Special Weapons Attack Team," but changed the name for public-relations purposes.

In the 1980s, violent home invasions under the pretext of drug-law enforcement became routine. In 1988, for example, LAPD officers, including members of the department's task force on gangs, broke into and destroyed four apartments on Dalton Avenue; the apartments were suspected to be crack dens, but in fact were not. The officers who participated in the raid were promoted.

Criminologist Peter Kraska notes that "perhaps as many as 20 percent" of police departments in cities with a population over 50,000 have put their paramilitary units into street police work. In many cases, money for these deployments comes from "community policing" grants from the federal government.

When law-enforcement agencies create SWAT teams, they often assure the public that the squads will be used for hostage rescue and similar activities. Fortunately, there are not enough actual hostage takings to keep the SWAT teams busy; as a result, the paramilitary units have a tendency to look for other tasks, ones in which there is no need for their special violent skills.

Today, the vast majority of SWAT deployments are to serve search warrants in cases of suspected drug sales or possession. Serving a search warrant by violently breaking into a house (as opposed to knocking first and demanding entry) is justifiable in certain situations—such as when the occupants are known to be armed and dangerous—but not in most. Former New York City police commissioner William Bratton explained: "In those instances where the suspect might be armed, we would call in a special tactics unit. Over time, though, it became common to always use the tactical unit no matter what or who the warrant was for. They used stun grenades each time and looked at it as practice."

The victims of these raids are not just people who break the drug laws. In Denver in September 1999, Ismael Mena was shot dead in his home during an invasion by a SWAT team. The officers were acting on the basis of a search warrant claiming that $20 worth of crack had once been sold in Mena's home. In fact, the "confidential informant" had given the wrong address.

The desire of smaller law-enforcement agencies to emulate their big brothers is one cause of police militarization; Washington's encouragement is another. A federal statute requires that surplus military equipment (such as M-16 automatic rifles, night-vision scopes, and even combat vehicles) be donated to domestic law enforcement. Another federal law subsidizes local police hiring of ex-military personnel, and it is ex-military who account for almost all SWAT-team members. The Navy SEALs, the Army's Delta Force, and other elite military attack forces provide extensive free training to police tactical teams, and the training is funded by congressional drug-war dollars. But military training—which stresses absolute obedience and swift annihilation of the target—is not appropriate for good police behavior, which, after all, requires capturing suspected criminals (not killing them), minimizing the use of force, and acting with a scrupulous regard for the Constitution.

In contrast to ordinary police officers, who usually dress in blue, "tactical officers" are garbed in black to maximize their intimidating effect. Michael Solomon, a Rutgers University professor who studies the psychology of clothing, explains that black uniforms tap "into associations between the color black and authority, invincibility, the power to violate laws with impunity."

The weapon of choice for SWAT teams is often the Heckler & Koch MP5 submachine gun—the kind that the immigration agent waved at Elian Gonzalez. Heckler & Koch's advertising to civilian law enforcement has conveyed the message that by owning the weapon, the civilian officer will be the equivalent of a member of an élite military strike force, such as the Navy SEALs. One ad linked civilian law enforcement to military combat, with lines like "From the Gulf War to the Drug War."

The most dangerous aspect of police militarization is not the machine guns: It is the change in police attitudes. In a constitutional republic, policemen are supposed to be "peace officers." Police militarization promotes maximal use of force, even when no force at all is required. If the Bureau of Alcohol, Tobacco and Firearms had not had so many "Special Response Teams," BATF might have reacted differently at Waco—taking up David Koresh's telephone offer to let them come and investigate his guns. What they did instead was "serve" a search warrant through a 76-man helicopter, grenade, and machine-gun attack on a home containing dozens of children.

Janet Reno's initial justification for using a SWAT team (instead of normal immigration agents) to snatch Elian Gonzalez was that somebody in the house or in the crowd outside might have been armed. Her theory offers a rationale for SWAT-team invasion of any home in the US, any time there is a search warrant to be served; about half of all households contain firearms, and the police do not know which ones.

In the 1995 decision in *Wilson v. Arkansas*, a unanimous Supreme Court rejected the idea that mere invocation of the words "guns" or "drugs" could justify no-knock "dynamic entries." But even after *Wilson*, no-knock operations carried out by tactical teams are routine in drug cases.

New York University law professor Paul Chevigny points out that in the long run, the police are the biggest losers from police militarization and its accompanying mentality: "The police think of themselves as an occupying army, and the public comes to think the same. The police lose the connection with the public which is a principal advantage to local policing, and their job becomes progressively more difficult, while they become more unpopular."

An erosion of public confidence in the police has to be a matter of grave concern for anyone who cares about the future of law and order.

RESTORE FLEXIBILITY TO US SENTENCES

Harsh laws and severe punishments, observed Confucius, are a sign that something is wrong with the state. But you don't need to be a brilliant philosopher to recognize that America's prisons are in a state of crisis.

Federal mandatory minimums have made a bad situation worse. In large part because the rigid minimums make almost no distinction among the circumstances of cases, today's sentences for non-violent crimes lack any semblance of balance. If a man helps unload a boat of hashish just once to pay for his wife's cancer treatments (an actual case), he is subject to the same minimum sentence as the mastermind of the whole scheme.

As a result of present policy, more than 20 percent of federal prisoners are low-level, non-violent drug offenders. Every year there are more congressional bills proposing increases in the mandatory minimum penalties. The late Chief Justice William H. Rehnquist noted that mandatory minimums "frustrate the careful calibration of sentences from one end of the spectrum to the other that the [federal Sentencing] guidelines were intended to accomplish."

Expensive as prison is, it can be a bargain when it keeps violent criminals from preying on the innocent. But loading our prisons with non-violent drug offenders means that there is less room for the more dangerous criminals. The end result is that we have a higher percentage of people in prisons than almost any other nation on earth.

Criminal justice professionals agree that reform is needed. A survey of America's prison wardens found that they strongly oppose mandatory minimum sentences for drug offenders and that 65 percent of them believe we should reduce sentences for non-violent offenders, and increase them for violent criminals.

Like the wardens, almost all federal judges—including Reagan and Bush appointees—oppose inflexible mandatory sentences. The reason that we have highly-paid, experienced federal judges is to judge.

No sensible judge would send a young person to prison for five years without parole for a first offense involving possession of a small quantity of drugs. Judges can make the distinction between a person who makes a solitary mistake, and a person who directs a major criminal enterprise.

Yet, because of the congressionally imposed mandatory minimums, judges are prevented from taking the facts of a case into account during sentencing. Long ago, Plato wrote, "We should exhibit to the judges...the outline and form of the punishment to be inflicted...But when a state has good courts, and the judges are well trained and scrupulously tested, the determination of the penalties or punishments which shall be inflicted on the guilty may fairly and with advantage be left to them." That wisdom still stands.

Crime rates have fallen, but there is no sign that the demagoguery associated with crime issues is waning. In their eagerness to pander to the mass media, politicians often sanction quick fixes. Long-term solutions, such as alternative sentencing for drug offenders, are needed in order to reintroduce balance into our sadly misguided sentencing policies—among which, mandatory minimums may well be the least constructive.

JURORS' RIGHTS TO VOTE THEIR CONSCIENCE

In a criminal trial, may the jury consider whether it is fair that the particular defendant be punished? Or are juries required only to decide whether the defendant broke the law, and to avoid questions of whether the law is just or the defendant's actions were justified by circumstances?

According to a poll by the *National Law Journal,* 76 percent of Americans believe juries have the right to bring their conscience into the jury room—and to acquit a defendant who is technically guilty but morally innocent. Writers like Joan Biskupic strike back at this idea by claiming that a juror's right to vote his conscience is tantamount to "vigilantism" or "anarchy."

Given all the confusion about juror rights, Clay S. Conrad's superb book *Jury Nullification*: *The Evolution of a Doctrine* is especially helpful. Tracing the jury-rights controversy from medieval England to modern America, Conrad shows that independence of the jury has always been one of the most important safeguards of civil liberty.

Many famous early cases of jury independence involved freedom of the press, and arose when the British government, either in England or in the colonies, prosecuted newspaper publishers such as John Peter Zenger or religious dissidents such as William Penn. Although Zenger and Penn were in fact guilty of the crimes they were accused of (Zenger had criticized the New York governor in print, and Penn had published illegal religious tracts), juries voted to acquit them.

In the early American Republic, the jury's right to acquit a technically guilty defendant was widely acknowledged by the Founders, including Supreme Court Chief Justice John Jay. Thomas Jefferson and John Adams, though at opposite poles on many issues, were of one mind on the need for jury independence.

The most important exercises of jury independence in the eighteenth century focused on free speech. The middle of the nineteenth century witnessed frequent acquittals of individuals who had helped runaway slaves, in violation of the Fugitive Slave Act. In the 1920s, juries helped speed the repeal of Prohibition by refusing to convict those whose crime was selling beer or fermenting wine.

But while early American courts were receptive to jury independence, later courts grew hostile. In the 1895 case *Sparf v. Hanson*, a divided Supreme Court held that although jurors possess absolute power to acquit whenever they want, federal judges are not required to inform them of that right. In Maryland, Indiana, and Texas, where state constitutions explicitly guarantee the jurors' right to judge the law, judicial constructions have, in effect, nullified this right—or at least nullified the right of juries to be informed about such rights.

Conrad refutes various criticisms of jury independence. He argues that jurors who vote their conscience are not "nullifying" the law. Rather, they are exercising their discretion, ruling that it would not be fair to apply a particular law in a particular case. District attorneys constantly exercise similar discretion—not bringing charges in the first place—and no one accuses them of "nullification" or "anarchy."

The claim that racist juries in the South used to acquit criminals who attacked blacks has some basis in fact, but acquittals in cases where the district attorney really tried to win a conviction were rare. In some places today there appears to be a pattern of black juries refusing to convict black defendants. The proper remedy for such cases, Conrad suggests, is ensuring that people are not excluded from jury service on the basis of race.

Although most judges today do not tell juries their rights, more and more jurors appear to be following their personal judgment. Nationally, about 20 percent of criminal prosecutions result in a hung jury, compared to only about 5 percent in earlier decades. In response, some opponents are calling for allowing more non-unanimous jury verdicts. Advocates of jury independence rejoin that laws which inspire jury revolts should be repealed.

Jury independence has become more relevant today than in any other period since the 1920s. And not since Lysander Spooner's 1852 classic *Trial by Jury* has such a substantive book about jury independence appeared as Clay Conrad's. It is a definitive guide for citizens who want to bring their consciences to jury service.

CULTURE

TUNE OUT, LIGHT UP: IN TERMS OF DESTROYING YEARS OF LIFE, TELEVISION IS FAR WORSE THAN TOBACCO

American teenagers—and adults too—would enjoy the fuller complement of life if they turned off the television, and lit up a cigarette. You see, in terms of destroying years of life, television is far worse than tobacco.

According to figures from the Centers for Disease Control and Prevention, the average smoking-related death cuts about 12 years off a person's life. Between a quarter and a half of all smokers eventually die of a smoking-related disease. (Citations are in Jacob Sullum's excellent book about the anti-smoking movement: *For Your Own Good*, pages 67-68.) So, on the average, smokers lose 3-6 years of their life, due to their habit. (These figures are based on mortality statistics from 1990, and reflect smokers who began smoking in the early 1960s and in previous decades, when tar levels in cigarettes were much higher. The smoking risks from today's cigarettes would be considerably lower.)

Of course these lost years of life tend to come during old age; a person who would have lived until age 80 dies at 75, due to smoking.

According to a 1998 survey by the A.C. Nielsen Company, the average American watches television for three hours and 46 minutes every day. By the age of 75, this average American will have spent over ten years watching television.

So if you give up cigarettes, you'll have three to six extra years to do things. If you give up television, you'll have ten extra years. Moreover, the extra time you gain by not smoking adds years only to the end of your life, by which time you may have other health problems, and not be fully able to enjoy all the different activities you would like. But if you give up television, you gain ten extra years spread through your life, and at a time when you are younger and more vigorous—or at least middle-aged and not arthritic.

It's true that years lost as a result of television are not precisely comparable to years lost due to tobacco: the tobacco years lost amount to total unconsciousness (death), while the years lost to television amount to only partial unconsciousness ("zoning out" hour after hour of television, in a semi-daze).

On the other hand, outside of your health, tobacco has no ill effects. In contrast, television even impairs the enjoyment of the time when television addicts are not watching television. Heavy television watchers are considerably more fearful of crime; television watchers are heavier, as a dozen studies show that television promotes obesity (tobacco promotes weight control); television sharply reduces meaningful conversation between parents and children.

As for tobacco, the harms to non-smokers are limited to offensive odors. As Jacob Sullum details, the alleged health dangers of second-hand smoke are junk science. Tobacco use does not harm society, except to the extent that it provides extortion revenue for tort lawyers and their government allies.

In short, if your eighteen-year-old starts smoking a pack of cigarettes every day, and announces that she plans to continue the habit for the rest of her life, you can be thankful that she is not following the bad example of your neighbor's kid, who watches four hours of television every day. Your daughter will have a longer, fuller, more active life than will your neighbor's kid.

Of course, it would be better still if your daughter cut down to five cigarettes per day; then, there would be hardly any health risks, Sullum explains. And likewise, if your neighbor's kid cut back to just an hour of television a day, he could still enjoy his favorite shows, while having lots more time to enjoy real life.

Perhaps one day, American adults will develop enough common sense to teach their children that moderation is the best policy for almost everything, including tobacco and television.

THE FOUNDERS' READING OF ROMAN HISTORY

Why is the Second Amendment, like much of the rest of the constitutional limitations on abuse of government power, under such consistent attack? One of the most important reasons is the depressing historical ignorance of most Americans, even those with a college education.

When the new semester begins at your local liberal arts college, count the number of classes where the ultra-p.c. autobiography *I Rigoberta Menchu* will be required; compare this with the number of classes where Tacitus, Livy, Plutarch, or any other classical historian, will be required reading.

The Menchu book has been proven to be a hoax; for example, she claims that she became a Communist because the Guatemalan army stole her father's land. It turns out that her father just lost a boundary dispute with one of his relatives. She claims that she was a dirt-poor illiterate peasant. Actually, her family was far from poor, and she learned how to read at the private school her family sent her to. Yet American professors continue to insist that students, in order to acquire a well-rounded understanding of the human condition, must read lies from a Communist rather than true accounts of the story of Western Civilization.

But suppose that modern education was turned upside-down, and students were required to read Tacitus and Livy and other classical historians, rather than modern prevaricators. The Founders of the American Republic had all learned the sad story of the Roman Republic. What the Founders knew, and what very few current college students will ever learn, are lessons that illustrate the importance of a virtuous armed populace, as an essential check on the inevitable depredations of a central government and its standing army.

Although the fact that almost all the Founders had a classical education is well known, Carl Richard's excellent book *The Founders and the Classics: Greece, Rome, and the American Enlightenment* is the first book to examine exactly what the Founders learned from ancient history. Let's look at some of the lessons which illuminate the Second Amendment.

The Founders understood that events of many years past could provide useful guidance for the present. John Adams wrote that whenever he read Thucydides and Tacitus, "I seem to be only reading the History of my own Times and my own Life."

While virtuous Romans and Greeks were models to the Founders, the anti-models were no less important.

And no one was worse than Julius Caesar, the murderer of the Roman Republic.

While the Founders believed that tyranny should be actively resisted, modern gun prohibition groups claim that anyone who believes that illegitimate government can be resisted by force under the Second Amendment is an "insurrectionist."

Actually, the Founders carefully distinguished between legitimate resistance to tyranny, and illegitimate insurrection against lawful authority. In the Founders' eyes, the former was clearly appropriate.

For example, after the imposition of the Stamp Act in 1765, John Adams praised "the same great spirit which once gave Caesar so warm a reception" and "which first seated the great grandfather" of King George III on the throne of England. Ceasar's assassin Brutus was venerated, as was the much earlier Lucius Brutus, who was credited with leading the overthrow of the Rome's Tarquin monarchy in 510 B.C.

Thomas Jefferson lamented that so many good Romans chose suicide rather than life under an Emperor, when "the better remedy" would be "a poignard [a small dagger] in the breast of the tyrant."

Caesar's use of the standing army to subdue Rome, after Caesar had subdued Gaul, was used by anti-federalists to show that even an army drawn from the best and most faithful and most honorable parts of society could still be used to enslave their country.

Even Founders, such as James Madison, who felt at least a small standing army to be necessary, were aware of the dangers. As Madison wrote in *Federalist* 41, "the liberties of Rome proved the final victim to her military triumphs."

Denunciations of the perils of standing armies frequently pointed to the many coups perpetrated by Imperial Rome's standing armies. During the final months of Watergate, many citizens worried that President Nixon would mobilize the 82d Airborne Division in order to retain power.

This was precisely the fear of the imperial presidency articulated by George Mason: "When he is arraigned for treason, he has the command of the army and navy, and may surround the Senate with thirty thousand troops. It brings to recollection the remarkable trial of Milo at Rome."

Here, Mason was referring to the famous trial of T. Annius Milo in 52 B.C. Milo and Clodius were rival demagogues and gang leaders in the decaying Roman Republic. When Milo and his gang ran into Clodius and his gang on the Appian Way (the main intercity road), Clodius ended up dead.

Milo was put on trial, with the great orator Cicero serving as his defense attorney. But while Cicero wrote a brilliant argument in Milo's defense, he was intimidated into not delivering it as written, after Milo's enemy Pompey surrounded the courtroom with troops.

Although Milo was deprived of the benefits of Cicero's eloquence, history was not. The written version of the speech survived, and was studied by the many high school and grammar school students in colonial America who were expected to read Cicero in the original in order to master the Latin language:

> "There exists a law, not written down anywhere, but inborn in our hearts; a law which comes to us not by training or custom or reading but by derivation and absorption and adoption from nature itself; a law which has come to us not from theory but from practice, not by instruction but by natural intuition. I refer to the law which lays it down that, if our lives are endangered by plots or violence or armed robbers or enemies, any and every method of protecting ourselves is morally right. When weapons reduce them to silence, the laws no longer expect one to wait their pronouncements. For people who decide to wait for these will have to wait for justice, too—and meanwhile they must suffer injustice first. Indeed, even the wisdom of a law itself, by sort of tacit implication, permits self-defense, because

it is not actually forbidden to kill; what it does, instead, is to forbid the bearing of a weapon with the intention to kill. When, therefore, inquiry passes on the mere question of the weapon and starts to consider the motive, a man who has used arms in self-defense is regarded as having carried with a homicidal aim."

Thus, natural law and common sense make it "morally right" to use deadly force to defend against a deadly attack.

James Wilson quoted the above words of Cicero, in full, in a lecture series he gave to the law students at the College of Philadelphia (later named the University of Pennsylvania) in 1790. The lectures were attended by President Washington, Vice-President Adams, Secretary of State Jefferson, and other leaders.

Today, most American states allow an adult with a clean record to obtain a permit to carry a firearm for lawful protection. The Brady Campaign, which opposes armed self-defense, naturally opposes these laws, and claims that they will lead to murder. But Cicero points out the logical distinction in Roman law: carrying a weapon for lawful defense was perfectly lawful; only carrying with malign intent was a crime.

Later in the written speech, Cicero declared, "Civilized people are taught by logic, barbarians by necessity, communities by tradition; and the lesson is inculcated even in wild beasts by nature itself. They learn that they have to defend their own bodies and persons and lives from violence of any and every kind by all the means within their power."

This lesson, unfortunately, has been unlearned by too many modern Americans who live in what attorney Jeffrey Snyder, in his brilliant *Public Interest* essay, terms "A Nation of Cowards."

The Founders greatly feared the vicious cycle of corruption of the citizenry fostered by Rome's ever-expanding government. For example, the Roman free bread program produced a vast body of citizens too lazy to work to earn their daily bread.

Similarly, modern American police chiefs who warn citizens not to use force to protect themselves from force "have created a population of millions of people without the courage or character to protect themselves or their families from deadly assault," Snyder writes.

The Roman historian Livy wrote a 142 volume history of Rome; 35 of the volumes survived to be available to the American Founders. Despite pressure from the Emperor Augustus Caesar, Livy refused to revise his history, which strongly supported Rome's honorable past aa a Republic, rather than its degraded present as an Empire.

Livy tells us that in the days before the Republic was established, under the Roman King Servius Tullius (578-35 B.C.) "the right to bear arms had belonged solely to the patricians." But then "plebians were given a place in the army, which was to be re-classified according to every man's property, i.e., his ability to provide himself a more less complete equipment for the field..." Thus, all citizens "capable of bearing arms were required to provide" their own weapons.

This was obviously a militia.

But when Rome moved away from a militia system, toward a mercenary standing army, the character of the citizenry began to decay, so that they eventually became unfit for self-government. Edward Gibbon's *The Decline and Fall of the Roman Empire* explains: "In the purer ages of the [Roman] commonwealth, the use of arms was reserved for those ranks of citizens who had a country to love, a property to defend, and some share in enacting those laws which it was their interest, as well as duty to maintain. But in proportion as the public freedom was lost in extent of conquest, war was gradually improved into an art, and degraded into a trade."

As the Roman standing army secured the vast Roman Empire against barbarian incursions, the people of the Empire, having lost their martial valor, lost their capacity for self-government. "They received laws and governors from the will of their sovereign, and trusted for their defense to a mercenary army," Gibbon lamented. The once-great Romans became, morally speaking, "a race of pigmies," and an easy target for the German tribes whose conquest of decrepit Rome finally "restored a manly spirit of freedom."

From the destruction of the Roman Republic by Julius and Augustus Caesar, to the later conquest of the degenerate Roman people by the barbarians, what was the lesson drawn by Gibbon? "A martial nobility and stubborn commons, possessed of arms, tenacious of property, and collected into constitutional assemblies, form the only balance capable of preserving a free constitution against the enterprises of an aspiring prince."

To the American Founders, private ownership of the tools of liberty (such as firearms and printing presses) was important, but even more important than owning tools of liberty was understanding liberty's importance. In the 1772 annual oration in memory of the Boston Massacre, Joseph Warren recalled Roman history: "It was this noble attachment to a free constitution which raised ancient Rome from the smallest beginnings to the bright summit of happiness and glory to which she arrived; it was the loss of this which plunged her from that summit into the black gulph of infamy and slavery."

As Carl Richard summarizes, the Founders studied the destruction of Rome's liberty and learned "to fear conspiracies against that liberty. Steeped in a literature whose perpetual theme was the steady encroachment of tyranny on liberty, the founders became virtually obsessed with spotting its approach, so they might avoid the fate of their classical heroes." They knew that "George III was hardly Caligula or Nero; however illegitimate, the moderate British taxes were hardly equivalent to the mass executions of the emperors.

But since the founders believed that the central lesson of the classics was that every illegitimate power, however small, ended in slavery, they were determined to resist such power."

The Second Amendment, besides its practical effect in ensuring that physical power will not be a government monopoly, helps to preserve a "noble attachment to a free constitution" by teaching the people that resistance to tyranny is not "insurrection," but is the command of the Constitution.

The ownership of firearms by modern Americans is important not just for practical reasons (such as protecting homes from criminal invaders) but for moral ones. A homeowner who never has to use his gun for self-defense still possesses something that his unarmed next-door neighbor does not: he has made the decision that he, personally, will take responsibility for defending his family. The armed homeowner's self-reliance has powerful moral consequences, as does the disarmed neighbor's decision that his family's safety will depend exclusively on the government, and not on himself.

The moral, character-building aspect of defensive firearms ownership is one of the most important reasons why tyrants—as well as more benign people who believe in the supremacy of the state—are so determined to disarm as many people as possible.

Not only does firearms ownership interfere (as a practical matter) with totalitarian government domination of society, firearms ownership creates a population which is independent and self-reliant, and which does not see itself as dependent on the state.

Uncertain Uncertainty: Postmodernism unravels

When Michael Frayn's award-winning play, *Copenhagen*, came out, it seemed too good to be true. Werner Heisenberg, the German physicist who identified the "Uncertainty Principle" in quantum physics (in which full knowledge is under some circumstances impossible to attain) might or might not have tried to subvert Nazi Germany's nuclear-weapons program. Heisenberg's Uncertainty Principle, the most famous idea of modern physics, had become a cornerstone of postmodern thinking, in which the possibility of objective truth is denied; so it was very fitting to see a postmodern play in which even the moral principles of the Uncertainty Principle's creator are themselves uncertain.

Truth, however, turns out to be more stubborn than the postmodernists wish. New evidence has emerged that Heisenberg was not opposed to the Nazis. Moreover, new research suggests that much of what Heisenberg taught about physics may be wrong, and that reality is not so indefinite as the postmodernists want to believe.

Along with Heisenberg, the great founder of quantum mechanics was the Danish physicist Niels Bohr, also a leading character in the play *Copenhagen*;

Bohr died in 1962, Heisenberg in 1976. Recently-revealed letters from Bohr's archive show that Heisenberg did not sabotage the German nuclear effort at all, despite his post-war claims to have done so. According to one letter, which Bohr wrote after the war, but never sent to Heisenberg: "you…expressed your definite conviction that Germany would win and that it was therefore quite foolish for us to maintain the hope of a different outcome of the war and to be reticent as regards all German offers of cooperation…you spoke in a manner that could only give me the firm impression that, under your leadership, everything was being done in Germany to develop atomic weapons…." According to Bohr, Heisenberg had a "certain conviction of a German victory and confidence in what it would bring."

Heisenberg's accommodating relationship with Nazism is hardly unique among the great thinkers of postmodernism. Martin Heidegger, the most influential philosopher of the 20th century and the founder of postmodernism, adored National Socialism. Heidegger's inaugural speech as Rektorat at the University of Frieburg lavishly praised *der Führer* for offering Germany the opportunity to reject modern industrial capitalism, and to recover its true, authentic culture.

Heidegger called human existence *Dasein* ("being-there"), meaning that existence was controlled by one's culture. Since an individual had no control over "thrown-ness" (*geworfen*—what culture he was born into), there is nothing fundamentally unique about an individual, nor is there anything which all humans have in common. The theory turned out to be a powerful philosophical foundation for Nazism: Individual Germans had no existence outside their German culture and, having no common traits with humanity, Germans should have no qualms about subjugating other people. National Socialism, Heidegger explained, was true Being.

Likewise reinforcing Nazism was Heidegger's insistence that authentic living was impossible unless one had rejected the hope of an immortal soul (and thus rejected the possibility of facing a Final Judgment), and instead grappled with inevitability of "Being-toward-Death."

Among Heidegger's admirers was literary critic Paul de Man, who collaborated with the Nazis during the occupation of Belgium, penning literary essays for a pro-Nazi newspaper in which he condemned Jews for their supposed vulgarity, and proposing deportation as a solution to the "Jewish problem." After the war, de Man moved to Yale, where he founded the "Yale School" of deconstructionist literary criticism; beginning at Yale, de Man's theories spread throughout American universities, thereby politicizing humanities and literature departments with radical anti-Westernism and anti-rationalism.

A litany of the stars of post-modernism is mostly a litany for admirers of totalitarianism. Although the Marxist Jean-Paul Sartre participated in the French Underground during World War II, he defended Stalinism and Maoism, even the Cultural Revolution. Sartre wrote the introduction to Marxist psychiatrist Frantz Fanon's book *The Wretched of the Earth* (published in 1961, but still very influential on campuses today). The book describes the Algerian anti-colonial war against France, and extols the purifying force of violence, especially racial terrorism of natives against the distinct "species" of whites and their native allies. Fanon inspired murderous racists and hatemongers around the world, including the Black Panthers.

The intellectual founder of the 1979 Iranian revolution was Ali Shariat, who studied at the Sorbonne, and liked Fanon and Sartre so much that he translated them into Farsi. Another deconstructionist disciple of Heidegger's, Michel Foucault, swooned that Ayatollah Khomeini was "a kind of mystic saint." Foucault welcomed the Ayatollah's "political spirituality" which would take Iran back to its natural roots, overthrowing the modernizing forces of global capitalism. In this regard, the Ayatollah's program for Iran was similar to Hitler's program for Germany.

Indeed, postmodernism has been the intellectual Axis of Evil of many mass killers. As Walter Newell wrote in *The Weekly Standard*: "Just as Heidegger wanted the German people to return to a foggy, medieval, blood and soil collectivism purged of the corruptions of modernity, and just as Pol Pot [who, like Shariat, studied at the Sorbonne] wanted Cambodia to return to the Year Zero, so does Osama dream of returning his world to the imagined purity" of the seventh century. For Franz Fanon and Osama bin Laden, terror is "good in itself, a therapeutic act," Newell notes.

If you don't believe *The Weekly Standard*, try *The Hindustan Times*, which explained that "Osama bin Laden is not a medieval but a post-modern phenomenon."

The enmity between postmodernism and capitalism is not accidental. Capitalism believes that individuals are unique, and should be able to act in a free market to fulfill their unique desires. Rather than being prisoners of their culture, individuals are free to pursue their own dreams. Rather than seeking a reversion to the primitive, supposedly authentic past, capitalism looks forward to a dynamic, ever-changing future, in which authenticity is created by the individual, rather than imposed by an omnipotent Hitler or Khomeini.

What does all this have to do with Werner Heisenberg? The answer is that Heisenberg provided what was seen as the scientific foundation for postmodernism.

Post modern architect Philip Johnson notes that a core value of postmodernism is "a loathing for 'bourgeois values' (a.k.a. truth, beauty, and goodness)." Yet, preferring Rigoberta Menchu (communist author of a fraudulent autobiography about her nonexistent "peasant" childhood in Guatemala) to Jane Austen (an advocate of truth, beauty, and goodness) is itself nothing more than a literary taste. Why should students be taught that a taste for totalitarian untruths is *superior* to a taste for literature founded on eternal values?

The dominant approach has been to attack language itself. Great emphasis is placed on the contingency of language, the difficulties of being sure what another person really means, the inseparability of any text from its cultural context, barriers to genuine communication, and so on. This has been the project of, most famously, Heidegger's disciple Jacques Derrida and, in a very different way, another disciple, German Marxist Jürgen Habermas.

For some people, though, undermining language is insufficient. A person can understand the contingency of knowledge and communication, and still come away believing in Western democracy, in rational science, and in eternal values. This is precisely what the great Protestant philosopher Reinhold Neibuhr did in the middle of the 20th century. Political thinkers who were influenced by Neibuhr, such as Arthur M. Schlesinger, Jr., confidently proclaimed that American democracy was morally superior to Stalinism. Similarly, James Madison's *Federalist* 37 explained how the limitations of human language created "unavoidable inaccuracy" in the communication of ideas. Yet Madison did not view the problem as proving that truth did not exist, or that preferring freedom to tyranny was merely an arbitrary taste.

Heisenberg's contribution was to provide a scientific foundation for the attack on the very existence of truth, and hence on the existence of moral values. The Heisenberg Uncertainty Principle began with Heisenberg's experiments in subatomic physics. He found that you could know an electron's position, or you could know an electron's momentum, but you couldn't know both at the same time; by measuring one, you would change the other. Taken to a much broader level, because one is always part of the system one is observing, it is impossible to know anything about the system with certainty.

Some extensions of the Uncertainty Principle can be thought-provoking and benign. For example, in 1979, Gary Zukav and David Finkelstein authored *The Dancing Wu Li Masters: An Overview of the New Physics*, which used the Uncertainty Principle, as well as many other elements of quantum mechanics, relativity theory, and other (then) cutting-edge physics to introduce the reader to Eastern mysticism.

But as Marxist sociology professor Stanley Aronowitz (City University of New York) has argued in his book *Science as Power: Discourse and Ideology in Modern Society*, Heisenberg's work also seems to legitimize the whole postmodern project. Because of physics' reputation as the most rigorous and neutral of all the sciences, the work of Heisenberg and his colleague Niels Bohr seem to supply the definitive proof for postmodernism's skepticism about truth and universal values. If, as Aronowitz and other postmodernists argue, Heisenberg showed that even science does not have objective truth, then literature and the humanities certainly cannot.

The modern academy's use of physics in the service of postmodernism was criticized in several books: *The Flight from Science and Reason*; *A House Built on Sand: Exposing Postmodernist Myths About Science;* and *Higher Superstition: The Academic Left and its Quarrels with Science*. The latter book so enraged the postmodern academy that an entire 1996 issue of the journal *Social Text* was devoted to attacking it. That special issue of *Social Text*, long a cutting-edge pomo journal, included counter-essays by the journal's co-founder Stanley Aronowitz and other postmodernists. The concluding article was "Transgressing Boundaries: Toward a Transformative Hermeneutics of Quantum Gravity" by New York University physicist Alan D. Sokal.

Sokal began by affirming postmodern principles: "it has become increasingly apparent that physical 'reality,' no less than social 'reality,' is at bottom a social and linguistic construct." Thus, "scientific 'knowledge,' far from being objective, reflects and encodes the dominant ideologies and power relations of the culture that produced it." Sokal went on to link various scientific or mathematical subjects (such as Paul Joseph Cohen's work on the mathematical Axiom of Choice) with social concepts with which they had no relation (such as radical feminism).

In most cases, Sokal simply asserted that the scientific theory supported the (always-leftist) social result. The meat of the article was an argument that quantum gravity (a genuine field of study, involving attempts to reconcile quantum mechanics with the theory of relativity) proved the case for "progressive" politics. Sokal concluded by urging that science, especially mathematics and physics, be conducted with the intent of supporting radical feminist and other "progressive" causes. He even argued that the value of *pi* was socially constructed.

A short while later, Sokal announced in the magazine *Lingua Franca* that the whole thing was a hoax. Although Sokal is a Marxist who had worked with the Sandinistas in Nicaragua, he objected to postmodernism's misuse of hard science. He wrote that his essay was a parody of how postmodernism had combined 1930s physics, linguistics theory, and political correctness to produce an academic literature that meant absolutely nothing. The Bohr/Heisenberg denial of reality had reached its culmination; one could write articles using Bohr and Heisenberg to describe things having nothing to do with physics. And, like the subatomic world described by Bohr and Heisenberg, the article could be incomprehensible, lacking any fixed reality. Later, Sokal coedited a follow-up book, *Fashionable Nonsense: Postmodern Intellectuals' Abuse of Science*.

Aronowitz and the rest of the postmodernists were not acting contrary to the intentions of Heisenberg, who hoped that his theories of physics "will exert their influence upon the wider fields of the world of ideas [just as] the changes at the end of the Renaissance transformed the cultural life of the succeeding epochs." Max Born, another founder of quantum physics, wrote that "epistemological lessons" from physics could answer questions such as the relationship between capitalism and socialism. Niels Bohr was even more aggressive in promoting the Uncertainty Principle into a general statement of the nature of reality, and insisting that principles from quantum mechanics were not just interesting metaphors with which to discuss society, but scientific facts about human culture.

Yet it turns out that Heisenberg's principle (and hence, the scientific basis of postmodernism) may be losing its "privileged position" of indisputable scientific truth.

The physicist Carver Mead, of the California Institute of Technology, is the author of *Collective Electrodynamics: Quantum Foundations of Electromagnetism* (MIT Press, 2000) which suggests that much of what Bohr and Heisenberg claimed was wrong. (Bohr, by the way, was always anti-Nazi, was spirited out of Denmark in 1943 by the Danish resistance, and went on to collaborate with Einstein in the Manhattan Project.)

At a debate series in Copenhagen, Albert Einstein uttered his famous line "God doesn't play dice with the universe"—as Einstein objected to Heisenberg's Uncertainty Principle, and to Bohr's vision of the randomness and incomprehensibility of reality.

Carver is attempting to topple Bohr/Heisenberg from their current roles as the ultimate geniuses of physics, just as previous intellectuals debated the auras of authority and infallibility which once, wrongly, surrounded Karl Marx and Sigmund Freud.

According to Carver, Bohr beat Einstein in the Copenhagen debates, held in 1927 and 1930, simply through the force of Bohr's intimidating, dictatorial personality. What Bohr and Heisenberg pronounced as true for all time turns out simply to be the product of their limited understanding, Carver argues.

The conflicts that Bohr/Heisenberg claimed between their own quantum mechanics and Einstein's theories of relativity turn out to be resolvable into a single unified theory, says Carver. Carver argues that Bohr and Heisenberg were wrong in claiming that the laws of logic do not apply at the subatomic level, and also wrong in claiming that the subatomic world is fundamentally random.

Another blow to the Heisenberg Uncertainty Principle came in 2008. The core of the principle is that measuring a quantum particle (e.g., an electron) will change the particle's state; the reality cannot be separated from the observer. For example, an electron (under current theory) does not exist in a single place; rather, the electron is like a wave, and has the potential to exist in a variety of different places. But once you measure the electron, Bohr showed, the quantum state collapses; instead of being potentially in many places at once, the electron is only in a single place.

But Andrew Jordan (University of Rochester) and Alexander Korotkov (University of California, Riverside) have found a way to perform a "weak" measurement that only partially collapses the quantum state. After the measurement is completed, they can undo the measurement's effect, so that the electron reverts to its original quantum state—as if the measurement had never taken place at all.

So it now appears that scientists *can* measure subatomic particles without changing the reality of what they are measuring.

Only time will tell if the work of Jordan, Korotkov, and Mead to recon-ceptualize quantum physics will gain wide acceptance. But the very existence of that work suggests that Heisenberg and Bohr are just as subject to "con-testation" as any other idea; the Bohr/Heisenberg view is not an unarguable scientific fact upon which to found a philosophy of human existence.

If Heisenberg and Bohr were wrong that quantum events (e.g., where an electron is) are fundamentally random, and cannot be observed without changing their state, then the use of their theory to label traditional literature as politically incorrect may also be wrong.

Postmoderism's hostility to big narratives is not just a function of par-ticle physics, however. The underlying rationale is ideological, as explained by the newsletter of the Association of Muslim Social Scientists: The core of post-modern is suspicion of meta-narratives, and this suspicion should lead to "de-centering of the West, since the most powerful narrative of the last 200 years has been the one that told the tale of the West's destiny." So Muslims should "understand post-modernism as the de-centring of the West." The author goes on to describe the demonization of "Bin Laden's 'terrrorism'" and the rejec-tion of postmodernism as two forms of false consciousness impeding Muslim political action.

Destroy-America-first does pretty well in university bookstores. September 15, 2001, was the paperback publication date for *Empire*, a 500-page combination of postmodernism, Marxism, and antiglobalism. It was writ-ten by Duke literature professor Michael Hardt and Antonio Negri, an Italian terrorist and poet then in prison for his role as a leader of the murderous Red Brigades. Negri was good friends with Michel Foucault and Jacques Derrida. *Empire* became one of the hottest university bestsellers of the new century.

But many more Americans of the 21st century have been reading *Lord of the Rings*, which retells "the tale of the West's destiny" to vindicate freedom and destroy evil.

The meta-narrative of the times has been the Harry Potter series. Neither *LOTR* nor *Potter* is a direct Christian allegory, but both narratives are infused with The Greatest Story Ever Told. They promote the brotherhood of man, the capacity of an individual to change the world, the possibilities of hope rather than the limits of our current condition—and they pronounce that our actions are to be judged according to eternal moral standards. The heroes in *LOTR* and in *Harry Potter* are offered ultimate power, and they refuse it, be-cause the power would be in the service of evil.

At the end of Harry Potter's book one, Harry confronts the Hitlerian Lord Voldemort and the Quislingish Professor Quirrel. Voldemort orders Harry to cooperate with him, and Quirrel claims: "There is no good and evil, only power." Harry refuses, risking his life.

Heisenberg was offered the same choice by Hitler. The newly revealed Bohr letters explain that Heisenberg's justification for building the A-bomb for the Nazis was that Heisenberg was certain they would win. Heisenberg obviously did not believe that it would be morally better to be killed by the SS than to help the Nazis build a weapon of mass destruction which would be used to murder millions of innocents. Heisenberg's collaborationist rationale fit precisely with the Hitler/Voldemort philosophy that power is the only reality. Indeed, "there is no truth, only power," summarizes Heisenberg's theory of physics and its application to moral philosophy

We did not really need J. K. Rowling or new discoveries in subatomic physics to remember that freedom is good and tyranny is evil. But we do need to recover our nation's moral compass.

A few years ago Americans listened to a president discuss the meaning of "is" as if he were at a Modern Language Association meeting. September 11 showed us the face of pure evil. It is no coincidence that the places in America which have been the most reluctant to call al Qaeda evil have been the places where postmodernism is strongest.

We will continue to debate the nature of language and of the subatomic, and we will continue to tolerate and celebrate diverse cultures. We can do all of these things without teaching college students (including foreign students who may one day rule their homelands) that living as a serf under the tyranny of Wahhabis, Nazis, or Stalinists is more authentically human than living as a free American.

George W. Bush was our first post-postmodern president. He can't tell Heisenberg from Heidegger but, unlike them, he can tell right from wrong:

> "It is always and everywhere wrong to target and kill the innocent. It is always and everywhere wrong to be cruel and hateful, to enslave and oppress. It is always and everywhere right to be kind and just, to protect the lives of others, and to lay down your life for a friend."

May postmodernism soon lie on the ash heap of discarded lies.

GUNS OF OUR FREEDOM

Shortly after the Constitution was sent to the people for ratification, anti-federalists warned that the Constitution would make the federal government too strong in relation to the people. Not so, replied the Federalists. Tench Coxe—an ally of James Madison and Alexander Hamilton who would later serve in the Washington, Adams, Jefferson, and Madison administrations—explained:

> "The power of the sword, say the minority of Pennsylvania, is in the hands of Congress. My friends and countrymen, it is not so, for the powers of the sword are in the hands of the yeomanry from sixteen to sixty. The militia of these

free commonwealths, entitled and accustomed to their arms, when compared with any possible army, must be tremendous and irresistible.

"Who are the militia? are they not ourselves. Is it feared, then, that we shall turn our arms each man against his own bosom. Congress have no power to disarm the militia. Their swords, and every other terrible implement of the soldier, are the birthright of an American. What clause in the state or [federal] constitution hath given away that important right....[T]he unlimited power of the sword is not in the hands of either the foederal or state governments, but where I trust in God it will ever remain, in the hands of the people." [A Pennsylvanian, "To The People of the United States," *Philadelphia Gazette*, Feb. 20, 1788.]

What were those weapons, so recently used in the American Revolution, which Coxe and rest considered "the birthright of an American"?

At the start of the war, the most common musket, in both Patriot and Redcoat hands, was the Brown Bess, an iron-barreled musket which fired a .75 caliber ball. The "Brown" part of the name may have come from the walnut stock, or from the barrel's color, once it had been rust-proofed. "Bess" was probably chosen because it sounded good with "Brown," and because fighting men have often given their weapons female nicknames.

When the French intervened on America's side in 1778, they brought their Charleville Muskets—named for the town near Belgium which hosted the Royal Manufactory of Arms. The French model fired a slightly smaller ball, .70. It was distributed copiously to the Americans, and later became the pattern for the federal army's Springfield Musket of 1795.

Muskets took a while to reload, so army formations typically deployed musket-men in two or three lines. The first line would fire in unison, then drop to their knees to reload, while the lines behind them fired.

Muskets were not accurate, and musketmen were not even expected to aim at particular targets. Rather, the objective was to deliver a mass of musketballs into the enemy line. The muskets were an ideal weapon for the kind of fighting man that the British used.

Life in any European standing army was brutal. Soldiers were drilled and disciplined until they could no longer think. They were expected to obey unquestioningly, and to move in precise lock-step formations. Only people who had no other choice joined the army as enlisted men, and the army was composed of "the dregs of society" rounded up from gin mills and gaols. The British troops were drilled and drilled until they could perform coolly and automatically in the heat of combat, and did not question whether orders made sense. Several volleys of disciplined musket fire, followed by a screaming bayonet charge (the Brown Bess had a 17-inch bayonet), were often sufficient to carry the day for the British—as at Lexington, Manhattan or Camden.

Muskets (like today's shotguns) have smooth barrels. In contrast, rifles have twisting grooves in the barrel, which give the bullet its spin. This stabilizing spin helps the rifle bullet travel much further, and more accurately, than does the musket ball. It was the rifle—utilizing the American virtue of individual initiative, that became the quintessentially American weapon of the Revolution. America's first great rifle-makers were Germans who settled in Pennsylvania (the "Pennsylvania Dutch"). Around 1720, the Germans began adapting their German rifle designs to American conditions, by lengthening the barrel to 40-45 inches (producing longer-range accuracy), and using Maplewood stocks. The typical caliber was .60.

Like the muskets, all these rifles were flintlocks, meaning that the gunpowder was ignited by a spark from metal striking flint. All of the guns used loose gunpowder made from salt-peter ("blackpowder"); modern smokeless powder did not come until the latter part of the nineteenth century.

During the Revolution, there was neither the time nor the inclination to decorate the rifles with the kind of engraving often seen on later versions, including today's replicas.

The Pennsylvania Rifle had a shattering effect against British Redcoats. The British musketeers could fire and reload three times as fast as the American rifleman, and knew how to march in disciplined linear formations in open terrain. Although there were many open-terrain battles during the war, there were also plenty of guerilla actions, in which Patriots hid behind rocks and trees and sniped at small enemy patrols.

While muskets were easy to use, the Kentucky rifle was effective only in the hands of a skilled marksman, who could hit a target the size of a man's head from 200 yards away. A lucky shot could travel 400 yards. Whether in open combat or in a guerilla context, the American riflemen specialized in sniping at the British officers, causing them considerable apprehension, and distracting them from command.

Some of the gunmakers of the Pennsylvania Rifles eventually moved to Ohio, Tennessee, and other parts. After the rifles figured prominently in the great American victory at the 1815 Battle of New Orleans, at the end of the War of 1812, the rifles became universally known as "Kentucky Rifles," since the popular song celebrating the great battle was "The Hunters of Kentucky." As the song exulted: "For Jackson he was wide awake, and not afraid of trifles; for well he knew what aim we'd take with our Kentucky Rifles."

The superior range of the Pennsylvania Rifle had allowed the Americans to engage the Redcoats beyond musket range during the first part of the Revolutionary War. But at the battle of Brandywine on September 11, 1777, the British deployed a special 100-man company firing a new rifle invented by Scotsman Andrew Ferguson. The innovative breech-loading design (as opposed to muzzle-loading, in which the gun is loaded by ramming the bullet down the muzzle, and through the full length of the barrel) allowed the Ferguson rifles to fire 4-5 shots per minute, and the gun could even be reloaded while a soldier marched towards the enemy.

Although the British won at Brandywine, and captured Philadelphia as a result, Ferguson was wounded, and the British Army foolishly lost interest in rifles for the rest of the war. Not until 1819 would a nation adopt a breechloader as its standard military weapon, when the United States chose the Hall Carbine.

While some people believe that handguns did not exist when the Patriots were fighting for their right to arms, handguns were actually hundreds of years old by then. Handguns had grown common enough in the early sixteenth century that legislation was proposed as early as 1518 (by the Holy Roman Emperor Maximilian) to address them; and by the latter part of the 1500s, handguns were standard cavalry weapons. When the Second Amendment was ratified in 1791, state militia laws, requiring most men to supply their own firearms, ordered officers to supply their own pistols.

The Revolutionary War handguns were mostly very large .50-caliber single-shot pistols, often built by the same gunsmiths who made the Pennsylvania Rifles. Colonel Samuel Colt's multiple-shot revolver lay decades in the future— although there were predecessors available, such as "pepperbox," which used revolving barrels, each containing its own bullet.

Today, only two of Ferguson's breechloading rifles are still in existence, and the pepperbox proto-revolvers are found only in museums or the homes of wealthy collectors. But the kinds of muskets and rifles with which the American Revolution was fought are still in common use. Many hobbyists build old-fashioned rifles or muskets from kits, and many others buy manufactured blackpowder arms, to take advantage of the special blackpowder-only hunting seasons in many states. Some of these guns incorporate new technology (such as in-line loading), while others are remarkably faithful to the old designs.

Whether you are shooting an old-fashioned replica of a Brown Bess, or a high-tech polymer pistol from Glock, you are exercising the freedoms that great Patriots such as "the Swamp Fox," Francis Marion, helped win for us two centuries ago. To celebrate Independence Day, why not exercise the right you still have (and which the Redcoats' descendants do not) by taking a niece or a neighbor to a target range, or by buying your first gun, or by sending an extra contribution to one of the groups who are continuing humanity's long-running battle against tyranny and disarmament?

Participating responsibly in that battle also means understanding when the proper way to fight is through the political process, and the very limited circumstances under with other approaches can be appropriate. The Declaration of Independence continues to provide indispensable guidance, particularly in a political period where some disgusting extremists compare our President to Hitler, as some other extremists did with our previous President.

First of all, as the Declaration explains, King George's actions left no doubt of his intention to reduce the Americans "under absolute Despotism." The same was true of the Mexican tyrant Santa Ana, against whom the Texans rebelled. Significantly, neither the thirteen American colonies or nor the Texans had any means of seeking redress within the system. They had no representation in Britain's Parliament or the Mexican government. King George and Santa Ana had contemptuously rebuffed their humble petitions. These circumstances are entirely different from the present, when no-one but the willfully self-deluded could believe that Obama or Bush is or was seeking absolute despotism. Our political system of elections provides us what the colonists and the Texans lacked: a non-violent means of changing their rulers.

As Supreme Court Justice Joseph Story explained in Commentaries on the Constitution and Familiar Exposition of the Constitution of the United States, the proper use of the Second Amendment against a tyrannical federal government would not be for revolution or insurrection, but only for the restoration of lawful constitutional government against usurpation. The same point was made by Thomas Cooley and many other great constitutional scholars of the nineteenth century.

The decision about what dire circumstances could authorize violent resistance is not in the hands of self-said revolutionaries—such as Charles Manson, the Oklahoma City bombers, the Columbine murders, or the people who have attempted to assassinate Presidents.

Constitutionally, that decision belongs solely to the state governments. It is they, and only they, who could authorize taking up arms pursuant to the Second Amendment. That is the scenario that Madison explicated in Federalist 46. As Jefferson elaborated, the only exception would be if the state legislatures themselves were prevented from meeting, in which case the decision would be made by special state conventions.

The late David Caplan, one of the Founding Fathers of modern Second Amendment scholarship, traces the principle back to article 61 of Magna Carta, which authorized a majority of the barons to seize but not harm the king and his family if the king violated the great charter. The principle is supported by the medieval, renaissance, and enlightenment Catholic and Protestant political philosophers who wrote that forcible resistance should be led by "intermediate magistrates." John Locke and Algernon Sidney adopted their ideas, and Jefferson said that he based the Declaration of Independence on Locke, Sidney, Cicero, and Aristotle.

Today, not a single state has invoked the right of armed resistance under the Second Amendment; thus, the conditions for constitutionally legitimate armed resistance do not exist.

A crucial purpose of the Constitution in general and the Second Amendment in particular is to prevent insurrection, which is illegitimate violent resistance to lawful government. The first clause of the Second Amendment recognizes the importance of the all the People in maintaining law and order.

In the last decade, we have reduced the number of school shootings because, post-Columbine, students no longer dismiss talk of school violence as idle chatter; students have informed the authorities about potential plots, and many lives have been saved.

Similarly, any good American, and especially an American who is faithful to the Second Amendment, has a moral and constitutional duty to inform law enforcement of credible information that a person may commit unlawful armed violence. American history shows that nothing has been more disastrous for Second Amendment rights than the murder of our elected officials. Anyone who could have acted to prevent such a murder, and failed to do so, would and should forever be regarded by most Americans as morally worthless, and by Second Amendment patriots as a coward and traitor.

AMERICAN HEROES

CHAPTER 11

THOMAS JEFFERSON

The greatest writer of the early American republic, and the greatest exponent of natural rights and the dangers of government power was Thomas Jefferson. It is no wonder then, that Jefferson has been so aggressively vilified by the partisans of political correctness. Jefferson was likewise disdained by many in the 19th and early 20th century who, quite correctly, saw his ideas as an obstacle to the large national regime they wished to build.

How sad it is that Bill Clinton bears the middle name "Jefferson"—even though the real Jefferson taught his nephew Peter Carr: "Nothing is so mistaken as the supposition that a person is to extricate himself from a difficulty, by intrigue, by chicanery, by dissimulation, by trimming an untruth, by an injustice...It is of great importance to set a resolution, not to be shaken, never to tell an untruth."

William Jefferson Clinton exemplifies a lesson taught by Thomas Jefferson: "There is no vice so mean, so pitiful, so contemptible and he who permits himself to tell a lie once, finds it much easier to do it a second and third time, till at length it becomes habitual, he tells lies without attending to it...This falsehood of tongue leads to that of the heart, and in time depraves all its good dispositions."

Let's look at another Jeffersonian virtue which William Jefferson Clinton attempted to destroy: the virtue of arms, and all that it entails about the relationship between the people and their government.

In the same 1785 letter to nephew Peter Carr (who was also Jefferson's ward), Jefferson advised the fifteen-year-old about building character through the shooting sports: "A strong body makes the mind strong. As to the species exercise, I advise the gun. While this gives a moderate exercise to the body, it gives boldness, enterprize, and independence to the mind. Games played with the ball and others of that nature, are too violent for the body and stamp no character on the mind. Let your gun therefore be the constant companion of your walks."

Jefferson's views on the importance of arms for youth remained strong two decades later, as expressed in his 1818 *Report of the Commissioners of the University of Virginia*: "the manual exercise, military maneuvers, and tactics generally, should be the frequent exercise of the students, in their hours of recreation."

It might not have surprised Jefferson to learn that a people who never learned to use sporting arms while growing up, and whose main connection with sports was watching them as passive spectators through a passive medium (television), might not develop the boldness and independence of mind to want real independence and responsibility in their own lives. Instead, they would prefer the comfortable servitude of a nanny state.

Of course the benefits of early training in arms extended to more than good character. As Jefferson pointed out to Giovanni Fabbroni in 1778, the Americans had a lower casualty rate than the Redcoats. "This difference is ascribed to our superiority in taking aim when we fire; every soldier in our army having been intimate with his gun from his infancy."

Even so, Americans were not as well-armed as Jefferson wished. The only book Jefferson wrote was *Notes on the State of Virginia* (1782), in which he explained the arms shortage that had developed during the Revolutionary War:

> "The law requires every militia-man to provide himself with arms usual in the regular service. But this injunction was always indifferently complied with, and the arms they had have been so frequently called to arm the regulars, that in the lower parts of the country they are entirely disarmed."

So as President, Jefferson successfully urged Congress to appropriate federal funds to provide firearms to state militiamen who did not have their own guns. Congress complied, and during Jefferson's second term and Madison's first, "public arms" were supplied at federal expense to state militias all over the nation.

The militia was intended to prevent the conquest of America by a foreign power, but it was also intended to prevent the conquest of America by a central national government and its standing army. Jefferson's first inaugural explained that "a well-disciplined militia" is "our best reliance in peace and for the first moments of war, till regulars may relieve them" and also a guarantee of "the supremacy of the civil over the military authority; [and] economy in the public expense."

As Jefferson understood, there was an intimate connection between sovereignty and the possession of arms. As long the people were armed, the people would rule.

In an 1811 letter to Destutt de Tracy, Jefferson acknowledged that demagogues could arise. But while the force of a demagogue "may paralyze the single State in which it happens to be encamped, sixteen other, spread over a country of two thousand miles diameter, rise up on every side, ready organized for deliberation by a constitutional legislature, and for action by their governor, constitutionally, the commander of the militia of the State, that is to say, of every man in it able to bear arms; and that militia, too, regularly formed into regiments and battalions, into infantry, cavalry and artillery, trained under officers general and subordinate, legally appointed, always in readiness, and to whom they are already in habits of obedience."

In France, thought Jefferson, the republicans fell because there were no local centers to resist national control. "But with us, sixteen out of seventeen States rising in mass, under regular organization, and legal commanders, united in object and action by their Congress, or, if that be in *duresse*, by a special convention, presents such obstacles to an usurper as forever to stifle ambition the first conception of that object."

Without arms, the weak were the prey to the strong, as in the feudal system of Europe, where the largest and the strongest made quasi-slaves of the rest of society. But as Jefferson explained in his famous October 1813 letter to John Adams, the proliferation of firearms had allowed an aristocracy of virtue and talent to supplant the aristocracy of brute force:

> "For I agree with you that there is a natural aristocracy among men. The grounds of this are virtue and talent. Formerly, bodily powers gave place among the aristoi. But since the invention of gunpowder has armed the weak as well as the strong with missile death, bodily strength, like beauty, good humor, the politeness and other accomplishments, has become but an auxiliary ground for distinction."

Because arms and sovereignty were so bound together, Jefferson argued that property ownership should not be the sole basis for voting rights. Anyone who served in the militia deserved the vote: "Let every man who fights or pays, exercise his just and equal right in their election." (Letter to Samuel Kercheval. July 12, 1816.)

Indeed, as Chilton Williamson detailed in his 1960 book *American Suffrage from Property to Democracy 1760-1860*, arguments like Jefferson's were used throughout the United States to broaden suffrage; property-owner or not, a man who bore the burden of militia service ought to belong to the polity.

And what of those excluded from the polity? Jefferson recognized that if the slaves were ever armed, then slavery would end. In 1814 he wrote to Edward Coles, "Yet the hour of emancipation is advancing, in the march of time. It will come; and whether brought on by the generous energy of our own minds; or by the bloody process of St Domingo, excited and conducted by the power of our present enemy [England], if once stationed permanently within our Country, and offering asylum and arms to the oppressed, is a leaf which our history not yet turned over."

Modern gun prohibition advocates sometimes assert that while guns might have been alright in Jefferson's time, there is too much gun misuse today for people to be allowed to have weapons. The most sophisticated version of this theory is developed by Indiana University law professor David Williams in articles in the Yale, Cornell, and New York University law reviews. Since Americans today are no longer virtuous and united, they are no longer "the people" envisioned by the Second Amendment, Williams writes; accordingly, the Second Amendment right to arms has disappeared.

Jefferson would not have agreed, for he was familiar with misuse of guns. Writing to his grandson Thomas Jefferson Randolph, he emphasized the necessity "of never entering into dispute or argument with another. I never saw an instance of one of two disputants convincing the other by argument. I have seen many, on their getting warm, becoming rude, & shooting one another."

If the widespread presence of guns in Jefferson's Virginia led to need-less deaths over petty arguments (just as it would on the 19th century American frontier, or in the 21st century inner city), how could Jefferson still champion a right to arms?

Because he recognized that a disarmed people would not, in the long run, remain an independent, responsible, and free people. The price of trying to save fools from their folly would be the liberty of all.

Back in June 1776, three weeks before the Declaration of Independence, Jefferson's draft constitution for Virginia set forth the first constitutional pro-posal in history to provide for a right to arms. (The 1689 English Bill of Rights included an arms right, but that measure was only a statute.) Jefferson's pro-posal "No freeman shall be debarred the use of arms within his own lands or tenements" was not adopted that year by Virginia.

The Jeffersonian intellectual revolution, however, was only beginning. When writing in 1824 to the great English Whig John Cartwright, Jefferson could observe: "The constitutions of most of our States assert, that all power is inherent in the people;... that it is their right and duty to be at all times armed..."

A few days before Jefferson died on July 4, 1826—the fiftieth anniver-sary of the Declaration of Independence—he could see that the revolution he had helped to spark was burning throughout the world: "All eyes are opened, or opening, to the rights of man. The general spread of the light of science has already laid open to every view the palpable truth, that the mass of mankind has not been born with saddles on their backs, nor a favored few booted and spurred, ready to ride them legitimately, by the grace of God. These are the grounds of hope for others. For ourselves, let the annual return of this day forever refresh our recollections of these rights, and an undiminished devotion to them..."

This Fourth of July, take some time out from the baseball, hot dogs, apple pie, and Chevrolet, and ponder what the holiday really commemorates: The American Passover, the beginning of a long national journey toward freedom, founded on the truth that God created man to be free. What will you do to nurture the legacy of freedom and responsibility bequeathed to you by the great Thomas Jefferson?

ANDREW JACKSON AND THE BATTLE OF NEW ORLEANS

"There was a time when the United States had heroes and reveled in them. There was a time when Andrew Jackson was one of those heroes, along with the men who stood with him at New Orleans and drove an invading British army back to the sea." So begins Robert Remini's excellent book *The Battle of New Orleans*, which aims to recover America's history and one of its greatest heroes.

Before the War Between the States, the Battle of New Orleans was celebrated nearly on a par with Independence Day—each anniversary commemorating the triumph of American liberty and virtue over the British monarchy.

Andrew Jackson's victory at New Orleans capped his campaigns against the British and the Indians in the southeast, ensuring American control over the region. Without the new cotton-producing states such as Mississippi and Louisiana, slavery might have withered in the 1830s and 1840s, rather than expanding. So it is understandable that postbellum America lost interest in the events of 1815.

Today, however, slavery is long gone from the United States (although slave labor products pour into the United States from China). The time has come for Andrew Jackson and his brave army to reclaim their place in the American pantheon.

To the extent that junior high school history textbooks mention the Battle of New Orleans, they insist that the Battle was irrelevant, since the battle was fought on January 8, 1815, and the Treaty of Ghent, ending the war, was signed on December 24, 1814. But this isn't so.

Had the British captured New Orleans—the key to the economy of almost all the Louisiana Territory—it is doubtful that they would have relinquished it, despite what the Treaty of Ghent required. Indeed, the British had violated the Treaty of Paris, which ended the American Revolution, by refusing to evacuate their forts east of the Mississippi.

Before conveying the Louisiana Territory to the United States in 1803, France had acquired the Territory from Spain in the 1800 Treaty of San Idelfonso. Under that Treaty, Spain had the right of first refusal before France could sell the Territory to any third party. The Louisiana Purchase was a plain violation of Spain's rights under the Treaty of San Idelfonso, and Britain would have had a strong legal case for conveying Louisiana back to Spain—if Britain had been in control of Louisiana.

There would have been more immediate consequences too. As noted in the song "The Hunters of Kentucky" (celebrating the Battle of New Orleans, the song became the Jackson presidential campaigns' theme song), New Orleans is "famed for wealth and beauty." British General Packenham had promised his soldiers "beauty and booty"—meaning that they could rape the women and pillage the city.

The British Army was fresh from its triumph over Napoleon, and the forces invading New Orleans were the best in the world—victors of the Peninsular Campaign in Spain. Against the best-trained, best-equipped army in the world, the Americans did not even have enough weapons for their forces. Remini quotes a contemporary observer: "From all the parishes the inhabitants could be seen coming with their hunting guns" because "there were not enough guns in the magazines of the United States to arm the citizens."

The Tennessee militia hardly looked like a professional army, with their rough clothes, unshaven faces, and raccoon caps. The Kentucky militia was even worse, arriving in rags, and disappointed to find out that there was no blankets in the city for them. The Redcoats called them "dirty shirts." Yet, as Remini explains, "most of these men could bring down a squirrel from the highest tree with a single rifle shot. Their many years living in the Tennessee wilderness had made them expert marksmen..."

The ladies of New Orleans, meanwhile, armed themselves with daggers, in case the men lost and the British rapists entered the city. When Andrew Jackson had been a child, his mother had admonished him not to cry; she told him that crying was for girls. When he asked what boys were for, she replied, "fighting." But at New Orleans, the women too were prepared to fight; not a single lady fled the city. They busied themselves with sewing, making new field blankets, shoes, shirts, and pants for the men.

If "diversity" were really highly valued in our schools, then the Battle of New Orleans would be known by every student in the nation. The men who fought on January 8, 1815, were a magnificent combination of professional soldiers, militia, irregulars, free Blacks, Creoles, Cajuns, Spanish, French, Portuguese, Germans, Italians, Indians, Anglos, lawyers, privateers, farmers, and shop-keepers.

When objections were raised to arming the free Blacks of Louisiana, Jackson replied: "place confidence in them, and...engage them by every dear and honorable tie to the interest of the country who extends to them equal rights and privileges with white men."

There were many heroes at New Orleans. When the British army captured Gabriel Villeré's plantation, he made a sudden break, fleeing with British soldiers close behind, yelling "Catch him or kill him." Hiding in an oak tree, he was forced to kill a favorite dog which had followed him, and which would reveal his location. Villeré eventually got to a neighboring plantation, hastily rowed upriver, and conveyed the news that the British army had arrived.

After the British landing, Jackson spent four nights without sleep, as he rode about the American fortifications—ordering improvements in the defenses, receiving reports about British movements, and inspiring his men. He never even dismounted to eat. As "The Hunters of Kentucky," later put it: "For Jackson he was wide awake, he was not scared of trifles. "

While the British maneuvered outside the city, nightly raids by the "dirty shirts" killed British sentries, took their equipment, and kept the whole army off balance.

During an engagement by the Cypress Swamp on December 28 (eleven days before the main battle), the Tennesseans waded though the muck, and leapt from log to log like cats, driving off the British beefeaters. "The Hunters of Kentucky" would later boast that "He led us down to Cypress Swamp, The ground was low and mucky." There, "every man was half a horse, and half an alligator."

In one encounter on the day of the main battle, a dirty shirt took aim at a wounded British officer, who was walking back to his camp. "Halt Mr. Red Coat," yelled the American, "One more step and I'll drill a hole through your leather."

The officer complied, sighing, "What a disgrace for a British officer to have to surrender to a chimney-sweep."

Although the British greatly outnumbered the Americans, January 8, 1815, turned into one of the worst days in British military history. Over two thousand British soldiers were killed, captured, or wounded. The Americans lost only seven killed, and six wounded, although their total casualties from skirmishes on other days amounted to 333.

As news of the battle spread throughout the United States, the American inferiority complex to the British began to recede. The Americans had smashed the best that Britain could throw at them. Newspapers quoted Joan of Arc's words from Shakespeare's *Henry VI, Part 1*: "Advance our waving colours on the walls; Rescued is Orleans from the English." Jackson's upset victory was as important for America's future as Joan of Arc's was for France.

Next January 8, tell your children about Andrew Jackson and the Battle of New Orleans, and teach them how Americans of both sexes, and all races, creeds, and colors united to fight for freedom, and defeated the best soldiers of the greatest empire in the world.

Don't mess with (armed) Texans: The real lesson of the Alamo

On February 24, in the year 1836, in San Antonio, Texas, a brave man wrote a letter. It was the last letter ever sent from a missionary fort named the Alamo.

> "To the People of Texas & all Americans in the World—Fellow Citizens and Compatriots—
>
> I am besieged by a thousand or more of the Mexicans under Santa Anna—I have sustained a continual Bombardment & cannonade for 24 hours & have not lost a man—The enemy has demanded a surrender at discretion, otherwise the garrison are to be put to the sword, if the fort is taken—I have answered the demand with a cannon shot, & our flag still waves proudly from the walls—I shall never surrender or retreat. Then, I call on you in the name of Liberty, of patriotism & everything dear to the American character, to come to our aid with all dispatch—The enemy is receiving reinforcements daily & will no doubt increase to three or four thousand in four or five days. If this call is neglected, I am determined to sustain myself as long as possible & die like a soldier who never forgets what is due to his own honor & that of his country—Victory or Death."

William Barret Travis Lt. Col.

The Texans were besieged at the Alamo because they were fighting a revolution against the Mexican military dictatorship of General Antonio de Padua María Severino López de Santa Anna y Pérez de Lebrón. Santa Anna had been systematically obliterating the right of self-government that the Mexican government had guaranteed to Texan settlers, and the rights guaranteed to all Mexicans by the 1824 Mexican Constitution. All the Texans' peaceful petitions for redress of grievances had been met with contempt.

The war began at Gonzales, Texas, when the Mexicans tried to seize a small cannon that the settlers had used to scare away Indians. The Texans were armed only with Bowie knives, a few pistols, and flintlock rifles, many of which dated back to the American Revolution. The Texans raised a flag that dared, "Come and Take It." The Mexicans tried, and then retreated.

The rationale for the war was articulated in the Texas Declaration of Rights, which set forth fundamental principles of liberty that are still at issue around the globe. These included the notions that:

> "All political power is inherent in the people, and all free governments are founded on their authority and instituted for their benefit; and they have at all times an inalienable

right to alter their government in such manner as they may think proper.

....

14th. Every citizen shall have the right to bear arms in defence of himself and the republic. The military shall at all times and in all cases be subordinate to the civil power.

15th. The sure and certain defence of a free people is a well-regulated militia; and it shall be the duty of the legislature to enact such laws as may be necessary to the organizing of the militia of this republic."

At the Alamo, 136 Texans withstood a siege by the main Mexican standing army from February 23 to March 6, 1836, before finally being destroyed. The defenders of the Alamo did not sacrifice their lives in vain; they gained Sam Houston crucial time to rally the Texan people. The moral example of the Alamo inspired men all over Texas to put their own lives on the line for freedom.

On April 21, 1836, Sam Houston's volunteers met what historian William Jackman called "the flower of the Mexican army"—the best of Santa Anna's 1,500 professional soldiers. The Texans numbered only about half that. But the Texans launched a surprise evening attack on Santa Anna's fortified positions. When the Texans rushed into battle, they yelled "Remember the Alamo!" and "Remember Goliad!" (Goliad was where Santa Anna had murdered 280 American prisoners.)

As the Texans advanced with their rifles and Bowie knives, a single fife and a single drum played the love song "Will You Come to the Bower?"

> *Will you come to the bower I have shaded for you?*
> *Your bed shall be of roses, be spangled with dew.*
> *Will you, will you, will you come to the bower?*
> *Will you, will you, will you come to the bower?*
> *There under the bower on soft roses you'll lie,*
> *With a blush on your cheek, but a smile in your eye.*
> *Will you, will you, will you smile my beloved?*
> *Will you, will you, will you smile my beloved?*
> *But the roses we press shall not rival your lips,*
> *nor the dew be so sweet as the kisses we'll sip.*
> *Will you, will you, will you kiss me my beloved?*
> *Will you, will you, will you kiss me my beloved?*

An odd song for combat? Not to the Texans, who were fighting to protect their wives and families.

In the first hour of battle, the Texans killed 600 Mexicans and captured 200 more. Within a day, the rest of the Mexican army, including Santa Anna himself, had been captured. Texan casualties were 6 dead and 30 wounded.

The Mexican standing army was crushed, and although Mexico refused to formally recognize Texan independence, the dictatorship gave up trying to conquer Texas. Sam Houston was elected the first president of the Republic of Texas, whose people were now free to pursue their own destiny of liberty and greatness.

The "Texan War Cry"—sung to the same tune as the "Star Spangled Banner"—celebrated the victory of a self-armed people over the professional army of a tyrant:

> *Oh Texans rouse hill and dale with your cry.*
> *No longer delay, for the bold foe advances.*
> *The banners of Mexico tauntingly fly,*
> *And the valleys are lit with the gleam of their lances.*
> *With justice our shield, rush forth to the field.*
> *And stand with your posts, till our foes fly or yield.*
> *For the bright star of Texas shall never grow dim,*
> *While her soil boasts a son to raise rifle or limb.*
>
> *Rush forth to the lines, these hirelings to meet.*
> *Our lives and our homes, we will yield unto no man.*
> *But death on our free soil we'll willingly meet,*
> *Ere our free Temple soiled, by the feet of the foe men.*
> *Grasp rifle and blade with hearts undismayed,*
> *And swear by the Temple brave Houston has made,*
> *That the bright star of Texas shall never be dim*
> *While her soil boasts a son to raise rifle or limb.*

The attitudes expressed in the "Texan War Cry" profoundly shaped American culture, and, even in the early 21st century, these ideas are at the core of the American gun culture: A true man will use a firearm to protect women from predators. The free people of a nation must defend it personally, with their own arms. Mercenary soldiers—"hirelings" in the pay of unfree governments—are morally and militarily inferior to American freedom fighters. Dying in defense of freedom is better than living under tyranny. And the quintessence of freedom—the precise reason why the stars of liberty shine—is the patriot's rifle.

These attitudes did not start with the Alamo; their roots precede the American Revolution. Yet it would be a serious mistake to underestimate the influence of Alamo imagery on almost every generation of American youth. The Texan War of Independence helped ensure that the moral lessons of the American Revolution were not seen as one-time events, but the recurring facts of the eternal struggle between freedom and tyranny.

The Battle of San Jacinto deserves a place of high honor among the greatest victories of freedom over tyranny, including Normandy, Inchon, and Saratoga. The Alamo deserves its own place of honor among great battles such as Thermopylae, where freedom warriors fought to the last man, and where, by their ultimate sacrifice, saved their people's liberty.

"Remember the Alamo" is a cry of bravery and freedom that rings true not just at one particular time, but for all time.

THE HERO OF GETTYSBURG: WINFIELD SCOTT HANCOCK SHOT STRAIGHT

When we remember Gettysburg, the turning point of the American Civil War, we should take care to remember the man who was dubbed "The Hero of Gettysburg." After proving himself one of the greatest American generals of all time, he later became the Democratic nominee for president of the United States. Throughout his life, he offered a model of honesty and patriotism which should forever be emulated by Americans.

When he was a child, he befriended and defended the victims of bullies. At a time when even abolitionists looked down on black people, his son said of him, "My father has always impressed on my mind that all men are born free and equal."

He was a great warrior. When he was the Democratic nominee for president, he refused to accept campaign contributions. He was a superb American, admired by people of all political persuasions for his unimpeachable integrity and devotion to public service.

He was Winfield Scott Hancock, born on February 14, 1824, near Philadelphia, Pennsylvania. And in 1881, he was elected the sixth president of the National Rifle Association.

Named after the military hero Winfield Scott, Winfield Scott Hancock served ably as an infantry lieutenant in Indian Territory, and then as an officer in the Mexican War. As a child, he learned from his lawyer father a deep respect for common law. When Winfield departed for the United States Military Academy at West Point in 1840, his father placed in his luggage the Constitution of the United States, and Blackstone's *Commentaries*, with the instruction to read each at least once a year. Blackstone, of course, was the author of the most influential legal treatise ever written, the analysis of common law and civil liberty which declared the right "of having arms for their defence, suitable to their condition" to be one of "the natural rights of resistance and self-preservation, when the sanctions of society and laws are found insufficient to restrain the violence of oppression."

In 1856-58, Hancock and his wife Almira were stationed in Florida, where the Seminole Indians still carried out raids. While in Florida, Almira Hancock learned how to shoot.

When the Civil War began, the Hancocks were serving in Los Angeles. There was very little pro-Union sentiment in the city; most people wanted California to join the Confederacy, or to create an independent Western republic. As historian Glenn Tucker explains, "Probably all that saved the far-away section of Southern California for the Union at this critical moment was Hancock's care in seeing that his precious guns, ammunition, and supplies were adequately protected."

Hancock "recruited every Union sympathizer in the neighborhood to be ready on a moment's notice. He armed Mrs. Hancock..." He set up a barricade around a federal arms depot, and prepared to fight. Later, federal cavalry made the hundred mile journey from Fort Tehone, and their arrival ended the prospect of an anti-Union uprising. Hancock was credited with saving southern California for the Union.

Hancock then headed east to join the fighting. His first major engagement was the battle of Williamsburg (May 4-5, 1862) in the Peninsula campaign; there he forced the Confederates to retreat by breaking their left flank. General George McClellan said "Hancock was superb today." Thereafter, he was known as "Hancock the Superb."

At Antietam (Sept. 17, 1862), Hancock took command of the Second Corps after Israel B. Richardson was killed in action. Hancock's division fought at Fredericksburg (Dec. 13, 1862), in the grueling assault on Marye's Heights. After the Confederate victory at Chancellorsville (May 3, 1863), Hancock led the rear guard which protected the Union withdrawal.

On the first day of the Battle of Gettysburg (July 1, 1863), Hancock formed the Union defensive positions at Little Round Top and Cemetery Ridge—the key positions which held the Union center. As McClellan had observed, Hancock "had a wonderfully quick and correct eye for ground."

On the third day of Gettysburg, Hancock commanded the First, Second, and Third Corps—three-fifths of the Union army. That day, Robert E. Lee flung the Virginia militia and Confederate Lt. General James Longstreet into "Pickett's Charge," a bold offensive gamble to win the battle, and perhaps the war, in a single day.

The charge began, and Hancock was everywhere, ordering the regiments and brigades. The steady advance of Pickett's men was the high water mark of the Confederacy. A bullet ripped through Hancock's saddle, opened an inch-wide hole in his body, and lodged eight inches inside his groin—along with a nail and a piece of wood as big as the bullet. Hancock looked as if he had been cut with a butcher's knife.

Hancock refused to be carried to safety, and continued to direct the combat from his stretcher. Pickett's Charge was repulsed, and the Union dubbed Hancock "the hero of Gettysburg." The Confederates called him the "Thunderbolt of the Army of the Potomac."

President Lincoln explained, "When I go down in the morning to open my mail, I declare that I do it in fear and trembling lest I may hear that Hancock has been killed or wounded." Lincoln also wrote "Some of the older generals have said to me that he is rash, and I have said to them that I have watched General Hancock's conduct very carefully, and I have found that when he goes into action he achieves his purpose and comes out with a smaller list of casualties than any of them."

Fittingly, the Uberti "Gettysburg Tribute" historic rifle includes an engraving of Hancock.

Although the wound caused him pain for the rest of life, Hancock recuperated sufficiently to return to fight in the Wilderness Campaign, where, in the Battle of Spotsylvania (May 12, 1864) he earned the rank of Major General for breaking through a Confederate salient in less than an hour and capturing almost 3,000 prisoners.

He was not always victorious in battle, and his Second Corps suffered terrible losses at Cold Harbor (June 3, 1864). But as General Grant recalled, "his name was never mentioned as having committed in battle a blunder for which he was responsible." McClellan called him "brilliant in the extreme." William Tecumsah Sherman declared him "one of the greatest soldiers in history."

During Reconstruction, Hancock was appointed Governor of the 5th Military District, which encompassed Texas and Louisiana. Hancock refused to bully the defeated and vulnerable citizenry of Texas and Louisiana. His General Orders No. 40 of November 29, 1867, announced how he intended to govern. Predicting "they will crucify me," Hancock wrote:

> "[T]he great principles of American liberty are still the lawful inheritance of this people, and ever should be. The right of trial by jury, the habeas corpus, the liberty of the press, the freedom of speech, the natural rights of persons and the rights of property must be preserved. Free institutions, while they are essential to the prosperity and happiness of the people, always furnish the strongest inducements to peace and order."

General Orders No. 40 was published all over the country. Hancock's policy was joyfully received by the South as a sign that the war was finally over, and by Northerners who looked forward to reconciliation and the restoration of constitutional government.

But for the radical majority in Congress who believed that the southern states were conquered areas deserving punishment, Hancock's words were anathema. In a famous letter to the civil governor of Texas, William Pease—one of those who found fault with General Orders No. 40—Hancock defended the right of critics of the national government to express their opinions, no matter how vehement:

> "[I]t is the privilege and duty of any and every citizen, wherever residing, to publish his opinion freely and fearlessly on this and every question which he thinks concerns his interest....It is time now, at the end of almost two years from the close of the war, we should begin to recollect what manner of people we are; to tolerate again free, popular discussion, and extend some forbearance and consideration to opposing views. The maxims, that in all intellectual contests truth is mighty and must prevail, and that error is harmless when reason is left free to combat it, are not only sound, but salutary. It is a poor compliment, to the merit of such a cause, that its advocates would silence opposition by force; and generally those only who are in the wrong will resort to this ungenerous means."

Hancock recognized that there was a great deal of intimidation by carpetbaggers who had employed the threat of federal retaliation in order to prevent their political enemies from voting. Hancock refused to allow the military to be part of the problem. In Special Orders No. 213 of December 18, 1867, Section IX, he declared:

> "Military interference with elections, 'unless it shall be necessary to keep the peace at the polls,' is prohibited by law; and no soldiers will be allowed to appear at any polling place, unless, as citizens of the State, they are registered as voters, and then only for the purpose of voting...."

He likewise refused to use military force to interfere with the operation of the courts, unless the civil authorities asked him for aid.

Hancock's generous policy toward the conquered South was unique among the military governors of the time. His supporters thought he provided a model for national reconciliation. Congress and the military hierarchy disagreed. General Grant repeatedly countermanded Hancock's orders. In response, Hancock wrote to a congressional ally: "I may expect one humiliation after another until I am forced to resign...[But n]othing can intimidate me from doing what I believe to be honest and right."

The conflict came to a head when Hancock, a Democrat, appointed fellow Democrats to the New Orleans City Council. On February 27, 1868, only six months after his appointment, he requested and received reassignment to the West.

Although Hancock was considered as a possible Democratic presidential nominee in 1876, the party nominated New York Governor Samuel J. Tilden, who ran against Republican Rutherford B. Hayes. The election of 1876 was one of the dirtiest in American history. There were disputes in Oregon, Florida, South Carolina, and Louisiana about who had won the state's electoral votes. Hayes was eventually declared the winner by a single electoral vote, after a special commission voted 8-7 along partisan lines to award all the contested votes to Hayes.

But in some of the contested states, the reason the vote had been so close was that Democrats had illegally prevented many black people from voting. So although the Republicans had perpetrated numerous dirty tricks in ballot counting, Hancock the Democrat defended the legitimacy of Republican President Hayes. As Hayes recorded in his diary,

> "one of the ablest and most influential Democrats in the country [Hancock], who was perfectly familiar with the inner history of the whole affair on the Democratic side, told me that no intelligent or candid man of his party could claim the election for the Democratic party if he conceded the validity of the Fifteenth Amendment. Said he, 'If the negro vote is entitled to be considered, you should have had more States than were counted for you.'"

If Hancock had not written General Orders No. 40, he might have quietly achieved more of the goals expressed in Orders No. 40. However, it was those forthright written words that placed him on the path to a presidential nomination. In a letter to Hancock, former Pennsylvania Supreme Court Chief Justice Jeremiah S. Black, who had also served as Attorney General under President Buchanan, wrote that General Orders No. 40 would give him "a place in history which your children will be proud of."

In 1880, the Democrats nominated Winfield Scott Hancock for president. Hancock's running mate was William H. English, a banker from Indiana. Neither Hancock nor English would accept personal donations. Although local Democratic organizations (like local Republican organizations) spent their own money, the Republican candidate James A. Garfield also accepted huge personal donations. As Hancock's biographer notes, "Undoubtedly, his extreme punctiliousness about money at a time when the opposition party was spending lavishly impaired his prospects."

There were no personal charges that could be used against Hancock, so Republicans focused on the presumed political naïveté of military figures (a hypocritical charge for a party that had twice nominated Ulysses Grant—who, like Hancock, had not previously held elective office).

The popular vote was the closest in American history, as Garfield edged Hancock by only 9,464 votes. Garfield won the Electoral College 214 to 155. Democratic disunity in the swing state of New York, with 35 electoral votes, cost Hancock the presidency of the United States.

But Hancock did not retire from public life. Instead, he set to work to fix one of the problems which had been revealed by the Civil War. During the Civil War, it was widely known that Confederate soldiers, many of whom had grown up on farms, were superior to the more urbanized Union army with regard to firearm proficiency.

The Union soldiers' training was inadequate. Many of them fired only a single round in all of their training, and some fired none at all. In 1864, Hancock had taken an informal survey of his own men and found that a third of them had never shot their guns. It was also suspected that Custer's 1876 disaster at the Little Big Horn was partly due to the army's lack of skill with firearms.

Former Union officers founded the National Rifle Association in 1871 in New York State to promote marksmanship. Unfortunately for the NRA, Alonzo B. Cornell was elected governor of New York in 1880. Cornell was openly hostile to the nascent National Guard. Cornell naïvely predicted: "There will be no war in my time or in the time of my children." He added, "The only need for a National Guard is to show itself in parades and ceremonies. I see no reason for them to learn to shoot if their only function will be to march a little through the streets. Rifle practice...is a waste of money...."

When Gen. George W. Wingate, an attorney and then vice president of the NRA, attempted to convince Governor Cornell that American soldiers should be skilled in the use of arms, Cornell bellowed back: "Then we should take their rifles away from them and sell them to benefit the Treasury. It would be more practical and far less expensive to arm them with clubs which require no instruction in their use."

Cornell had won office as a fiscal conservative, and his cuts to the New York National Guard budget financially destabilized the fledgling National Rifle Association.

Hancock was elected NRA President in 1881, based on hopes that his prestige as a nationally recognized and beloved figure would bolster the organization. In this regard, Hancock was a forerunner of NRA President Charlton Heston, whose prestige also boosted the NRA. (And of Ulysses Grant, who after having twice been elected President of the United States, was elected President of the National Rifle Association in 1883.)

As President, Hancock explained, "The object of the NRA is to increase the military strength of the country by making skill in the use of arms as prevalent as it was in the days of the Revolution."

By aiming to revive the Revolutionary tradition of the American marksman, Hancock and the NRA were taking sides in one of the cultural battles of the era. As the Industrial Revolution matured, more and more American workers were performing simple, repetitive tasks in huge factories. The view that individuals were mere cogs in the industrial machine had its parallel in warfare—in the view that the ordinary soldier should just follow orders blindly and shoot in the general direction of the enemy's mass. A random hail of bullets was all that infantry was supposed to produce.

The contrary view—of Hancock and other NRA leaders—was that Americans were more than brutes in service of the military-industrial complex. They were individuals who should be the masters of their arms, and whose personal skills should be encouraged and celebrated with competitions and prizes. The Americans of 1881 could, in Hancock's view, be every bit as competent and personally excellent as the Americans of 1781.

The same cultural conflict which led to the founding of the NRA continues today. On one side are pessimists who insist that modern Americans are too clumsy and hot-tempered to be trusted with guns. On the NRA side are people who believe that the virtues and skills of the Founding generation can and must be emulated by Americans of every generation.

The best biographies acknowledge a subject's foibles. Hancock's biographers, however, did not tell us what his faults were. His wife of 36 years, Almira, did not reveal his faults, and she destroyed many of his personal letters. His political rivals could find little more to complain about than his stubborn honesty and integrity.

General William T. Sherman told an interviewer, "if you will sit down and write the best that can be put in the English language of General Hancock as a soldier and as a gentleman, I will sign it without hesitation." When Winfield Scott Hancock passed away in 1886, former President Hayes said succinctly, "he was through and through pure gold."

HER OWN BODYGUARD: GUN-PACKING FIRST LADY

She was the most famous spokesperson for civil rights, at a time when the idea of equal rights for people of color was very politically incorrect. "We can't afford to have two kinds of citizens," she insisted. "We must have equal citizenship for anybody in our country."

And though she was a well-known talker, she also walked the walk. In 1958, at age 74, she made plans to go down to the little town of Monteagle, Tennessee, to speak at a civil-rights workshop at the Highlander Folk School.

The Ku Klux Klan learned about her plans. The day before her trip, the elderly, gray-haired woman was contacted by the FBI. "We can't guarantee your safety," they told her. "The Klan's put a bounty on your head, a $25,000 bounty on your head. We can't protect you. You can't go." But the little old lady answered, "I didn't ask for your protection...I have a commitment. I'm going."

And she did. She flew down to the Nashville airport, where she was joined by a friend, an elderly white woman aged 71. The pair got into the car, laid a loaded revolver on the front seat between them, and drove into the night. No Secret Service or police escort. Just the two little old ladies with a handgun to keep them safe. They set out for their destination, a "tiny labor school[,] to conduct a workshop on how to break the law, how to conduct non-violent civil disobedience." They drove through the heart of Klan territory to teach people how to fight for freedom.

If she were alive, and if Rosie O'Donnell's dreams were to come true, that gray-haired grandmother today would be thrown in jail. "I don't care if you think it's your right...You are not allowed to own a gun, and if you do own a gun I think you should go to prison," O'Donnell proclaimed. But the old lady probably wouldn't listen to Rosie, any more than she listened to all the other people who told her what she wasn't supposed to do.

That determined grandmother was Eleanor Roosevelt. And it was Eleanor's handgun, not some hired bodyguard, that helped her stay alive in the face of real danger.

What a perfect example of how the Second Amendment is the cornerstone of our Bill of Rights, the guarantor of all others. It was the exercise of her Second Amendment rights that empowered Eleanor Roosevelt to use her First Amendment rights to crusade for the Fourteenth Amendment rights of blacks.

Many of the people she empowered also used Second Amendment rights to secure their freedoms. Professor John Salter, who later became director of the Indian Studies program at the University of North Dakota, recounts his earlier experiences: "I worked for years in the Deep South as a full-time civil rights organizer...I, too, was on many Klan death lists and I, too, traveled armed: a .38 special Smith and Wesson revolver and a 44/40 Winchester carbine. The knowledge that I had these weapons and was willing to use them kept enemies at bay. Years later...this was confirmed by a former prominent leader of the White Knights of the KKK..."

Mrs. Roosevelt broke many traditions. She was the first First Lady to give a press conference, the first to testify before Congress, the first to write a newspaper column, the first to become a political figure in her own right. But when it came to firearms, Eleanor Roosevelt was following a family tradition.

In *The Roosevelts of Hyde Park: An Untold Story*, Eleanor and Franklin's son Elliott described the early days of his parents' marriage: "The young bridegroom [FDR]... retained a boyish delight, consistently encouraged by Granny, in collecting stamps, ship prints and wild bird specimens. The birds were shot in the woods and fields around Hyde Park with the gun [of] his father, James Roosevelt..."

In *Before the Trumpet*, Geoffrey Ward detailed how the young Franklin's interest in natural science turned him into a hunter: "Soon eggs and nests no longer satisfied; he wanted to collect the birds themselves, and at ten he began asking for a shotgun"—a shotgun which was presented on his eleventh birthday. "With it came a set of rules: There was to be no shooting during the mating season; nesting birds were off-limits; only one member of each species was to be collected." By the age of 14, Franklin Roosevelt had shot and identified more than 300 species of birds native to Dutchess County, New York.

Eleanor's father, Elliott Roosevelt, also liked to shoot. Her autobiography explained: "As a boy of about fifteen he left St. Paul's School after one year, because of illness, and went out to Texas. He made friends with the officers at Fort McKavit, a frontier fort, and stayed with them, hunting game and scouting in search of hostile Indians. He loved the life and was a natural sportsman, a good shot and a good rider."

Eleanor's uncle Theodore, who walked her down the aisle at her wedding, was perhaps the best-known gun enthusiast in American history. An avid hunter (and, therefore, a strong conservationist), Theodore Roosevelt owned and used a dizzying array of firearms, eventually coming to like semi-automatic rifles best. While living in the Badlands of North Dakota, Roosevelt and his companions used their rifles for a daring capture of some men who had stolen a boat; the event was immortalized in a Frederic Remington painting. When President McKinley was assassinated by an anarchist in 1901, Theodore Roosevelt succeeded to the presidency. The new president was justifiably concerned about his personal security, so he began carrying a concealed handgun.

When Theodore Roosevelt visited Harvard University, then-president Charles W. Eliot was chagrined to discover Roosevelt strapping on a holster in his room, ignoring the Massachusetts law restricting concealed handguns.

President Roosevelt concluded his Sixth Annual Message to Congress, on Dec. 6, 1906, with a call for the government to help citizens develop firearms proficiency:

> "We should establish shooting galleries in all the large public and military schools, should maintain national target ranges in different parts of the country, and should in every way encourage the formation of rifle clubs throughout all parts of the land. The little Republic of Switzerland offers us an excellent example in all matters connected with building up an efficient citizen soldiery."

Roosevelt would repeat this call with greater urgency in his Seventh Annual Message, on Dec. 3, 1907, demanding that the government do its utmost to encourage children to use guns:

"While teams representing the United States won the rifle and revolver championships of the world against all comers in England this year, it is unfortunately true that the great body of our citizens shoot less and less as time goes on. To meet this we should encourage rifle practice among schoolboys, and indeed among all classes, as well as in the military services, by every means in our power. Thus, and not otherwise, may we be able to assist in preserving the peace of the world. Fit to hold our own against the strong nations of the earth, our voice for peace will carry to the ends of the earth. Unprepared, and therefore unfit, we must sit dumb and helpless to defend ourselves, protect others, or preserve peace. The first step—in the direction of preparation to avert war if possible, and to be fit for war if it should come—is to teach our men to shoot."

Thus, it should not be surprising that TR's niece—the woman who later would accurately be described as the personification of 20th-century liberalism—was not afraid to use a gun, or to teach disobedience to unjust laws.

The 1958 trip to Tennessee was hardly the first occasion when a revolver was Eleanor Roosevelt's chosen companion. For 25 years, packing heat had been habitual. As she recalled in her autobiography, she first carried a handgun shortly after she moved into the White House, in 1933:

"Driving my own car was one of the issues the Secret Service people and I had a battle about at the very start. The Secret Service prefers to have an agent go with the President's wife, but I did not want either a chauffeur or a Secret Service agent always with me; I never did consent to having a Secret Service agent. After the head of the Secret Service found I was not going to allow an agent to accompany me everywhere, he went one day to Louis Howe [FDR's secretary], plunked a revolver down on the table and said 'Well, all right, if Mrs. Roosevelt is going to drive around the country alone, at least ask her to carry this in the car.' I carried it religiously and during the summer I asked a friend, a man who had been one of Franklin's bodyguards in New York State, to give me some practice in target shooting so that if the need arose I would know how to use the gun."

After leaving the White House upon the death of her husband, Mrs. Roosevelt moved to New York City, where she obtained a permit to carry a handgun. She was the subject of a constant stream of death threats from nuts who were offended by her newspaper column and her humanitarian political activities.

From nearly the first day that Eleanor Roosevelt became First Lady, she refused to be a victim, and she exercised her choice to carry a handgun for protection. She could have shut up and avoided controversy—or she could have spoken out while hiding herself in the White House or in her family's estates in rural New York. But she refused to let hatemongers and criminals dictate how she would live.

In her 1960 book, *You Learn by Living*, Mrs. Roosevelt urged her readers not to cower before the world's dangers, but to stare them down: "You gain strength, courage and confidence by every experience in which you really stop to look fear in the face...*You must do the thing which you think you cannot do.*" (Emphasis in original.)

That was the spirit of the young girl who took responsibility for her little brother Hall, after the divorce and death of their parents. That was the spirit of the young wife who stood up to her domineering mother-in-law, Sara Delano Roosevelt, and refused to let Sara push Franklin into seclusion after he was stricken with polio in 1921. Eleanor then had to overcome her terror of public speaking, and to begin giving political speeches on behalf of her crippled husband. When Louis Howe would listen to a speech and tell her what she had done wrong, Eleanor Roosevelt did not quit; she resolved to do better the next time. She could have enjoyed a comfortable retirement in New York, but instead looked fear in the face—and drove straight into the dark heart of Klan country, ready to chase away the nightriders with her handgun.

Although some of Eleanor Roosevelt's views—such as her hopes for the United Nations—were mistaken, her courage and perseverance deserve the respect of people of all political backgrounds. May she continue to inspire people for many generations to come.